**IRE AND**  **ORGE**

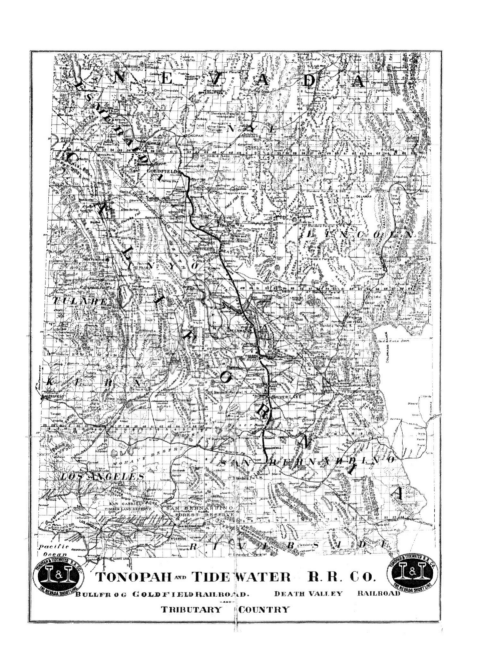

TONOPAH AND TIDEWATER R. R. CO.

BULLFROG GOLDFIELD RAILROAD.   DEATH VALLEY   RAILROAD
AND
TRIBUTARY COUNTRY

FIRE AND FORGE

A DESERT RAILROAD, A WONDER METAL, AND THE MAKING OF AN AEROSPACE BLACKSMITH

KATHLEEN L. HOUSLEY
WITH HARRY ROSENBERG

iUniverse LLC
Bloomington

FIRE AND FORGE
A DESERT RAILROAD, A WONDER METAL,
AND THE MAKING OF AN AEROSPACE BLACKSMITH

iUniverse books may be ordered through booksellers or by contacting:

iUniverse
1663 Liberty Drive
Bloomington, IN 47403
www.iuniverse.com
1-800-Authors (1-800-288-4677)

Because of the dynamic nature of the Internet, any web addresses or links contained in this book may have changed since publication and may no longer be valid. The views expressed in this work are solely those of the author and do not necessarily reflect the views of the publisher, and the publisher hereby disclaims any responsibility for them.

Any people depicted in stock imagery provided by Thinkstock are models, and such images are being used for illustrative purposes only.

Certain stock imagery © Thinkstock.

ISBN: 978-1-4917-0790-6 (sc)
ISBN: 978-1-4917-0789-0 (hc)
ISBN: 978-1-4917-0791-3 (e)

Library of Congress Control Number: 2013916538

Printed in the United States of America.

iUniverse rev. date: 10/29/2013

CONTENTS

INTRODUCTION

I first met Harry Rosenberg when I was researching my book *Black Sand: The History of Titanium*. He was one of twenty-three metallurgists and engineers I interviewed who had played key roles in the establishment of the titanium industry beginning in the 1950s. The story of titanium is unusual because the metal came about as a direct result of the arms race between the United States and the Soviet Union. It took both a massive effort and massive amounts of money to transform titanium from a reactive laboratory curiosity into aircraft. The task was so daunting it required scientists and engineers who were of a higher order of magnitude intellectually. Harry's expertise was the development of titanium alloys about which his knowledge is encyclopedic.

Over and above our discussions about titanium, Harry occasionally recounted to me stories of his remarkable upbringing in one of the most extreme environments in the world—the Mojave Desert near Death Valley—in one of the most unusual dwellings—a red caboose. Harry's father was responsible for the maintenance of bridges and the railbed for the Tonopah and Tidewater Railroad, so the Rosenberg family traveled from washout to washout across a fiery land prone, paradoxically, to devastating floods of the Amargosa and Mojave Rivers. If there was any place on Earth where a perpetually curious child could be forged into a metallurgist, this was it.

Besides stories about the railroad, Harry told me about sidewinders beneath his bed, crusty prospectors, and deadly mine collapses. It all sounded like Western folklore, except that it was true. But Harry is not nostalgic about his past. On the contrary, to him, the Mojave Desert is both austerely beautiful and extremely hostile. By a stroke of luck amplified by monumental personal effort, Harry managed to leave the Mojave to attend San Jose State College and then Stanford University where he earned his doctorate in materials science.

In the course of his life, Harry was awarded numerous important patents for aerospace alloys, electronic-grade titanium, and tantalum. He was one of the founders of the Alta Group (now a Honeywell company), which manufactures the highest-purity titanium in the world, essential to the manufacture of computer chips. However, he is just as proud of the fact that he created a workplace environment that encouraged mentoring and decision-making by all employees. In recognition of his groundbreaking work in materials science, he received the Titanium Achievement Award in 2011 from the International Titanium Association.

But no matter how far he has traveled, no matter the number of his successes, Harry has never really left the Mojave Desert and the Amargosa River along which the railroad ran. *Amargosa* means "bitter" in Spanish, referring to its mineral-rich water. For most of its 185 miles, it is invisible. North of the Amargosa Canyon, it emerges from the sand on its way to Death Valley where it ends at Badwater. The Amargosa River is both life-sustaining and life-taking, both sweet and bitter—and it flows through Harry's veins. It lies behind his search to understand the nature of human violence and his efforts to increase the chances for peace.

I had the opportunity to travel the route of the T & T with Harry and his wife Joselyne in December 2011. The light was oblique, far from the direct glare of summer, and yet it was strong enough to make me squint. The weather was cool, not at all the blast-furnace conditions for which the region is famous. The desert silence was so profound it was disconcerting. In the enormity, only a trained eye could find what little remained of the railroad, which was torn up in 1942. Fortunately for me, Harry has the best of all trained eyes because he grew up on the line, from Ludlow in the south to Beatty in the north. On our trip, he didn't need coordinates to locate where the water tank once stood at the Rasor siding, he knew it by the lay of the land and the position of the old athel trees. So also he had no trouble finding the siding at Evelyn where not even a rusty nail remains. All he needed was a dry wash and the presence of Eagle Mountain rising abruptly nearby.

Harry took us to see the talc and lead mines where he worked as a young man and the hot springs near where his father built a motel after his railroad career came to an end. Oddly, it was our last night in Las Vegas before flying home that stands out in my memory. Harry, Joselyne, and I were having dinner together, and I began to talk about the Nobel Prize–winning physicist Richard Feynman and his ability to visualize an answer in its totality before he fully discerned the problem. Harry is nearly deaf, a disability that came from working as a miner, so he struggled to hear me. But when I mentioned Feynman's gift of insight, Harry understood what I was saying, and his eyes lit up because he is gifted in a similar way. He calls these moments when everything instantly becomes clear his *aha moments*.

We also talked about Feynman's ability to make a complex subject understandable; for example, when he dropped an O-ring into a glass of ice water to demonstrate to the members of a government commission what caused the *Challenger* disaster. Harry has the same ability, and I have been the beneficiary many times. For example, in an e-mail, he explained titanium's hexagonal crystal structure, beginning as if he were telling me a fairy tale: "It is little known to lay folk, but nearly all metals exhibit different properties in different directions. Strength and modulus are prominent in that regard. So is ductility in titanium. Think of a cylinder with six sides. Think of that cylinder as made up of layer upon layer of marbles packed such that each marble has six neighboring marbles in its own row along with three more from each of the next rows above and below in a closely packed arrangement." In another e-mail, he included a photo of a sidewinder and the pattern it makes in the desert sand as a way to explain deformation, a metallurgical term, writing that "the sidewinder metaphor may seem whimsical but by his nature the sidewinder gets from here to there one hump in his back (kink) at a time. Like edge-kinks humping along the screw dislocation over one barrier after another in a titanium-aluminum alloy, the sidewinder moves toward his destiny."

Harry's patient efforts on my behalf did not make me a metallurgist just as exploring the route of the T & T Railroad with him did not make me a desert rat. What I can say is that the glimpse I was given into Harry's life is like the glimpse I was given at a remote siding called Riggs, looking westward toward Telescope Peak, which climbs to a height of 11,043 feet on the far side of Death Valley. The immensity was beyond my comprehension, but it was not beyond my appreciation.

Kathleen L. Housley

ACKNOWLEDGMENTS

Harry Rosenberg's story is part of three larger stories: the first is life in the Death Valley region during the Great Depression and World War II; the second is the development of titanium and the huge role the new metal played in the Cold War and commercial aerospace; and the third is the change in the field of metallurgy that, beginning midcentury, shifted from an emphasis on getting ore out of the earth to what it is today—materials science. Harry's life cannot be understood separate from these stories.

Much has been written on the history of the Death Valley region, but not all of it is reliable. Among the best sources of information is the book *Death Valley and the Amargosa: A Land of Illusion* by Richard E. Lingenfelter. A research physicist at the University of California, Lingenfelter is also a meticulous historian who separates fact from fiction, truth from tall tale.

For information on the Tonopah and Tidewater Railroad, David Myrick's two-volume work *Railroads of Nevada and Eastern California* is essential. There is an excellent website dedicated to the Tonopah and Tidewater Railroad that is maintained by John A. McCulloch, with records, recollections, newspaper articles, and photographs. David T. Sprau's articles and presentations on the T & T are carefully researched and reveal many fascinating details.

There are also the guidebooks of Dennis Casebier, an expert on Mojave Desert history. I found his *East Mojave Heritage Trail: Rocky Ridge to Fenner* to be particularly helpful because it oriented me geographically before I visited the area. Casebier incorporates history into his guidebooks. He was instrumental in establishing the Goffs Schoolhouse Museum and Cultural Center, which houses an extensive archive and library.

Two books by Ken Lengner and George Ross are important: *Remembering the Early Shoshone and Tecopa Area* and *Tecopa Mines*. They are filled with photos, stories, and technical detail; for example, how drilling and blasting were done in the mines. George Ross has spent his entire life in the Death Valley region, is a friend of Harry Rosenberg's going back to the 1930s, and appears several times in *Fire and Forge*, probably the most memorable moment occurring in the baseball game against the tough Darwin mine team when both he and Harry hit home runs as players, making the team the stuff of legend.

Ethel Proctor Talbot, Harry's last remaining aunt, recounted the history of the Proctor family up through 1935, with close attention to the years when the family lived in Crucero and Cronese. She was especially helpful in describing the catch-as-catch-can nature of education in that remote region. She read the manuscript for accuracy in reference to family details.

For the story about the development of titanium, I relied on my own research for my book *Black Sand: The History of Titanium*. I first met Harry in writing that book, which is available through the International Titanium Association. I am one of the editors, along with M. Ashraf Imam (Naval Research Laboratory, Washington, DC) and F. H. (Sam) Froes (Institute for Materials and Advanced Processes, University of Idaho), of "Titanium and Titanium Alloys," *Kirk-Othmer Encyclopedia of Chemical Technology*, published online by John Wiley & Sons Inc. In addition, I am the editor of *Titanium News*, a newsletter published by Sims Metal Management Aerospace (now ELG Utica Alloys), in Hartford, Connecticut.

For the third story on the changes in metallurgy, I received help from William D. Nix, Lee Otterson Professor of Engineering (Emeritus), Department of Materials Science and Engineering, Stanford University. Dr. Nix served as chairman of the department from 1991 to 1996. He was at Stanford when Harry returned for his PhD in materials science in the late 1960s, so he knew personally about Harry's struggle to master new material and how it was indicative of a sea change in the field.

David B. Snow, PhD, Senior Research Scientist (retired) at United Technologies Research Center, East Hartford, Connecticut, was helpful in making arcane metallurgical terminology more understandable. He attempted to prevent the types of errors that can come from oversimplification. He did so by lending me textbooks and patiently explaining the intricacies of metal deformation and alloy development.

I interviewed Harry Rosenberg at length several times; visited with him and his wife Joselyne at their home in Pittsburgh; and traveled with them to the Death Valley region. He has in his possession letters of his parents, his mother's diary for 1935, photographs, and memorabilia. Quoted material also comes from lengthy e-mails between us as well as Harry's written recollections of his childhood and career. *Fire and Forge* would not have been possible were it not for Harry's prodigious memory and his scientific attention to detail.

I also would like to thank the people I interviewed and with whom I corresponded, including: Roger Broadwell, Edward Cawley, Donald Cooper, Joseph Green, Harold Kessler, Brother Rene David Roy, Ethel Proctor Talbot, and Lauren Wright. They shared their knowledge generously and, when necessary, reviewed the text for accuracy.

A special thanks goes to Joselyne Mivumbi Rosenberg, Harry's wife, whose story about growing up in Rwanda and the 1994 genocide is told in the last chapter. Josy was not only forthcoming with information but also served as a most gracious hostess, welcoming me into the Rosenberg home. She was a wonderful traveling companion in the Mojave, navigating dry washes and spinning wheels in deep sand. She even attempted to drive through a dust storm so that Harry could locate yet one more siding on the T & T Railroad. Finally, the storm forced us to retreat to the motel in Shoshone, California, to hunker down as the wind roared all night long and sand sifted through the air vent in the ceiling. I count Josy among my friends, and I would travel with her anywhere.

Finally, I would like to thank the four people who read the entire manuscript: William Nix, Stanley Seagle, Judy Palmer, and Dennis Casebier. Stan spent his career in the titanium industry as an executive for Reactive Metals Inc. in Niles, Ohio, now RTI International Metals. He has taught highly regarded courses on titanium around the world for the International Titanium Association. One of the men I interviewed for *Black Sand*, Stan has an excellent memory and is generous in sharing what he knows. I met Judy Palmer on my trip to Shoshone in 2011, having dinner with her, the Rosenbergs, and Susan Sorrells at the Crowbar Restaurant, which Susan owns. (Susan is the granddaughter of Charlie Brown, who helped establish Shoshone and who played a major role in the Death Valley region. She is steadfastly committed to maintaining its history, the Shoshone Museum being the most obvious example of her dedication.) Judy is a pediatrician who was a faculty member at Stanford University until her retirement. She lives part of the year in Palo Alto and the other part in Shoshone where she has become an expert on the local history, in particular the life of the mine owner, Louise Grantham, about whom she has written.

A biography, as opposed to a memoir, has the benefit of third-person objectivity instead of first-person subjectivity. Interviewing people with differing views is valuable as is reading as broadly as possible. The use of endnotes and a bibliography in *Fire and Forge* add to that objectivity by enabling readers to go further. However, no matter how hard a biographer tries, objectivity is more a goal pursued than a goal obtained. There are always areas in which records no longer exist, data is fragmentary, and memories don't line up. What I have attempted to do in those cases is to point out the absence or discrepancy. Only in retrospect does Harry Rosenberg's life appear to be a seamless whole. What connects the disparate parts are his boundless curiosity and equally boundless energy. Those two characteristics are rock-solid facts; it is how they play out over eighty-five years that requires interpretation.

PART I
DEATH VALLEY, INVISIBLE RIVERS, AND A RUN-DOWN RAILROAD

Now, the Devil said, "This is all I have needed
To make a Hell" and at once he proceeded,
He piled the sands in queer ridges and drifts
Shattered the rocks into ragged sharp rifts,
Scattered in places a sparse growth of brush
Caused winds hot to dance with a staggering rush …
One can't describe here the fear that prevails
Snakes walk on their bellies and talk with their tails.

From *Rhymes of The Mighty Mohave* by Elmo Proctor, grandfather of Harry Rosenberg

CHAPTER 1:
THE MIDDLE OF NOWHERE

Until he was six years old, Harry Rosenberg lived in a red caboose on the run-down T & T Railroad, which crossed the Mojave Desert to the east of Death Valley—a hard, elemental landscape across which the hot wind blew with abrasive force, funneling down the barren mountains and over the salt wastes. It was during the Great Depression, but life had always been so tough in the desert that it was difficult for things to get worse. T & T stood for the Tonopah and Tidewater Railroad that ran from Beatty, Nevada, through the arid Amargosa Valley south to Ludlow, California, where it connected with the Atchison, Topeka, and Santa Fe Railroad. It also intersected with the Union Pacific Railroad in a desolate spot called Crucero, meaning in Spanish a "crossing."

The T & T rail line, built by the Pacific Coast Borax Company, began operations in 1907 primarily to carry borax from the mines in the Death Valley region. The famous twenty-mule teams, capable of pulling thirty tons fully loaded, had stopped hauling ore eighteen years earlier in 1889; since then, no effective means of transportation had been found to take their place. No matter how valuable the ore, whether it was borax, talc, or lead (the only exception being gold), without a railroad, it was prohibitively expensive to ship it out of such a remote area, and many a man had gone bankrupt trying. Even *with* a railroad, the desert exacted a high toll in human life, particularly during the construction phase when workers quit faster than they could be hired. One journalist for the *Goldfield News* likened the summer working conditions to a "death pit."[1] It was far better when the daytime temperature was 50 degrees Fahrenheit in January instead of 120 degrees in July. However, a train must run year-round, so its crews must work year-round, regardless of the weather.

The T & T came into existence in a boom time when gold strikes drew hordes of men into the Mojave Desert with the promise of easy fortunes. Industry moguls, such as Francis Marion Smith, known as the "Borax King," and William Andrews Clark, known as the "Copper King," built their own rail lines to reap even greater rewards. But just as the T & T was named after two areas it never reached—the gold fields in Nevada and the Pacific Coast—so also it never turned the huge profits Smith expected. The T & T showed a profit for only four years out of its thirty-three years of service (1907–40). Clark's rail line, running from Las Vegas to Goldfield, did even worse, ending operations in 1918.

In the preface to his book *Death Valley and the Amargosa: A Land of Illusion*, Richard E. Lingenfelter writes that "it is a land of the deluded and the self-deluding, of dreamers and con men. Even its hardest facts are tinged with aberrations."[2] That statement is certainly true of the prospectors, the mine owners, the railroad magnates, and the thousands upon thousands of investors who ended up with worthless stock, but it was not true of the railroad workers who kept the T & T operating under grueling conditions. Nor was it true of the miners. They knew what to expect, what they were supposed to be paid, and what the risks they had to face were. They were hopeful that their jobs would continue but were ready to move on if they did not. Some of them loved the desert; most endured it. They were not romantics about the land and its history. They were not aware of how wars on other continents were affecting mineral prices in the United States or how skullduggery on Wall Street was affecting the value of gold. There were trains to be kept on schedule, leaving Crucero in the predawn glow at 4:45 a.m., arriving at Beatty in the glaring noonday light exactly at 12:05 p.m. There was borax as well as talc and lead that had to be blasted out of the earth, shoveled into ore cars, and brought down spurs to the railroad stations at Acme and Gerstley. Let others dream. There was work to be done.

At the time Harry's father (after whom he was named) began working for the T & T in 1916, the 168 miles of roadbed were so bad, derailments were a common hazard. One of the reasons was that most of the cars and engines had seen hard service elsewhere and some had no brakes. Harry describes the conditions as follows:

> *Imagine a barren desert of mountains, sand dunes, deep valleys—one far below sea level—and searing heat with*

relentless windstorms that pick up gritty dust that literally sand-blasts paint off one's car. Imagine too a secondhand railroad slicing across the salty badlands of the Mojave Desert. Secondhand meant already in gross disrepair, a state of affairs never cured, because it was simply incurable.

Another reason for the poor condition of the roadbed was sudden destructive floods. Like many desert waterways, the Amargosa River and the Mojave River flow underground and are usually bone-dry on the surface, except through canyons. But a cloudburst can summon them forth, turning them into dangerous torrents with the power to wash out tracks, sweep away bridges, and take lives. So also places with cool picturesque names, such as Silver Lake and Soda Lake, are playas that are so hard and desiccated, they can be used as airfields—that is, until there is a storm. Any rail line that dared to cross such unpredictable places in those early days was inherently unstable and in constant danger of collapse.

It doesn't rain often in the desert, but when it does, it can be a gully washer. If a bridge went out, the line had to be shut down. The great flood in 1916 put the track that crossed Silver Lake—which was normally parched—under water and grossly weakened the bed, requiring miles of track to be moved eastward. The damage from the flood in 1938 was so extensive it brought the T & T to its knees. When track was out or a trestle damaged, it meant that no trains passed and no minerals got to the railhead until the line was restored.

In the 1930s, the T & T's headquarters, main terminal, and shops were to the east of the Funeral Mountains at Death Valley Junction, which served as the Rosenbergs' legal address, but home was wherever the outfit—as the repair crew and railcars were called—was working, such as Rasor, Zabriskie, or Sperry Wash. Most of those places are gone now. Once the mines in Death Valley and the Amargosa region became unprofitable to work, there was no reason to maintain either the T & T or the little waterless sidings along the line. Beatty, Death Valley Junction, Shoshone, Tecopa, Baker, and Ludlow still exist, but other places, including Riggs, Leeland, and Val Jean have disappeared.

Val Jean was one of the loneliest spots on earth. The outfit parked there just once in my memory in 1934 when I was six. It was in deepest wilderness. There was no road to Val Jean, although our Model A Ford, being a forerunner of the Jeep in its ability to manage rough country with reliability, gave us access. There was no section crew, no water, only a siding. About eight years later, in 1942, when I was fourteen, my father and I went there on the motorcar that ran on the rails. He was taking an inventory of the rails just before they were pulled up and sent to Egypt for the war effort, the line having been abandoned. That day, we stopped for lunch at Val Jean. Aside from the railroad itself, there was virtually no evidence of human habitation. I looked around, and along with a long-lost toy, I found a bird's nest, complete with two sparrow chicks with their beaks opened wide for lunch. No telling how long they had been waiting. They were completely mummified by the infernal heat and dry air.

Until the final rail was taken up in 1942, the T & T was the center of young Harry Rosenberg's life. After the death of his mother in 1935 when he was only seven years old, he and his brother, Lloyd, went to live with their grandparents in Cronese, about five miles away from the railroad junction at Crucero, but every summer, they went back on the line to live with their father and the men of the outfit. To this day, Harry can hear in his dreams the sound of the engines blowing out steam and the heavy clank of metal on metal as sledgehammers drive in iron spikes. And he can also recall, particularly at night, a desert silence so profound that as a little child he would hear the beating of his own heart and mistake it for the sound of footfall beyond the walls of the caboose.

The family's geographical origin on his father's side was Hesse, which is now part of Germany. Peter Rosenberg was a Hessian soldier who came to America to fight for the British in the Revolutionary War. Hessian troops were hired out to other nations not as individuals but by military units under the command of their own officers. They were not actually mercenaries because in most cases they were conscripted and did not have a choice about military service. Britain hired approximately thirty thousand Hessians to augment their troops in the Colonies, thereby enriching substantially the coffers of Hesse's ruler. In the Battle of Trenton, December 26, 1776, only eight months after the Battles of Lexington and Concord in Massachusetts that started the war, approximately a thousand Hessian soldiers under the command of Colonel Johann Rall were captured by the Continental Army under the command of General George Washington, Rosenberg among them. Under perilous conditions caused by severe winter weather, Washington and his troops had crossed the ice-clogged Delaware River on Christmas night, catching the British and the Hessian troops off guard. The prisoners were transported back across the Delaware River to Pennsylvania under equally perilous conditions and were sent to internment camps first in Charlottesville, Virginia, and then in York, Pennsylvania. Family lore has it that Peter escaped. In fact, there is evidence that the Americans looked the other way, allowing Hessians to escape so that the strapped Continental Congress, then located in York, did not have to pay for their upkeep. Furthermore, it was common practice for Hessian prisoners to be paroled to German farmers in Pennsylvania because there was very little danger of their crossing back to the British side, nor were they considered a physical threat to their captors. After the war ended, many chose to remain in the United States, Peter Rosenberg among them.

Peter's descendants (some of whom were silversmiths) eventually moved from York, Pennsylvania, to the small town of Robins, Iowa, near Cedar Rapids, where they were farmers. There, Harry Sr. was born on August 8, 1895, to David and Margaret Stamy Rosenberg. He had a sister, Beulah, and a brother, Solomon, nicknamed Solly. Spurred by the same desire to improve their lot that had goaded preceding generations to head west, the Rosenbergs moved to Long Beach, California, in the early 1900s where David entered the booming real estate business.[3] At that time, Long Beach was the fastest growing city in the United States with large tracts of farmland being divided into neighborhoods and multistoried buildings being constructed in the downtown business district. Its most famous attraction was the amusement area known as the Pike, which glittered along the shore with a carousel, Ferris wheel, and roller coaster. To Midwesterners, the Pike was as much a wonder as the Pacific itself.

When Harry Sr. was old enough to work, having dropped out of school in tenth grade, he held various odd jobs, including carpenter and machinist, but he didn't like living in Long Beach, which was too crowded and confining for him. He needed more space. Unfortunately, he was a generation too late. The edge of the continent had been reached, and there was no frontier left. Only the desert offered the chance of empty land for a restless young man to explore. Harry took the chance, arriving in the Mojave on May 20, 1916, at the age of twenty looking for employment. He found it with the T & T Railroad as a carpenter on a bridge and building gang.

> *My father was something of a nomad who found the regimen of the city a bit hard to take. He was a crack shot with his sharp blue-gray eyes and wanted to be able to go hunting, and he could fix anything. He was of medium build, about five-eight in height, with large bones and powerful hands— very strong. He also had feet so wide he could not get shoes to fit, so he always had to cut slits in the sides to be able to wear the widest ones available. I think that the rootless life of living on the railroad doing rugged physical work suited him. He didn't really settle down in one place and call it home until after World War II when he bought land in Tecopa. By then, he was in his fifties and the T & T was history.*

The gang's primary function was replacing washed-out bridges and railbed. The average rainfall in the desert is only about four to six inches, but following a cloudburst, the water cannot sink in rapidly, causing flooding. The gang had their hands full that spring and summer of 1916 because in January, an intense series of storms had swept in from the Pacific Ocean, lasting several days. To the south, Lake Arrowhead in the San Bernardino Mountains received torrential rains. The unusual storms flooded the normally dry Mojave River, which surged out of Afton Canyon, filling the playa lakes, including Silver Lake, and submerging the railroad track that had been laid unwisely across its heretofore dry bed.[4] It took many months for the water to go down during which time the T & T trains had to be detoured via a giant loop: traveling north from Ludlow to Crucero on its own rails, east to Las Vegas on the Salt Lake rails, northwest to Beatty on the rails of its rival Las Vegas and Tonopah Railroad, and then south to Tecopa on its own rails again. When Harry Sr. arrived, the crews were still in the process of permanently rerouting miles of track, along with moving the remaining buildings (the depot and warehouse having collapsed) to the east of Silver Lake.[5]

The next year, Harry Sr.'s budding railroad career was interrupted by the entry of the United States into the First World War. He went to Camp Lewis in American Lake, Washington, for basic training and then after further training was sent to Scotland as a member of the US Army Signal Corps, which at that time had responsibility for aviation.

> *My father was selected to fly a Jenny biplane on which a*
> *machine gun was synchronized to shoot bullets between the*
> *two propeller blades powered by a big Liberty engine. Flying*
> *out of Scotland, all went well until he made his first kill—a*
> *German observation balloon. When he circled to verify*
> *the kill, he noticed the observer simply step over the side*
> *several hundred feet up. No parachute. Imagine yourself in*
> *his shoes. Yeah, he got sick. In another incident, he shot off*
> *his propeller in practice, probably because the synchronizer*
> *had failed, which severely undercut his confidence. Although*
> *he saw service in Belgium and France, these events ended*
> *his flying days; he never flew again, not even by commercial*
> *airline. One of the other stories he told me was that while in*
> *Scotland, the soldiers never had enough to eat. Right next to*
> *the aerodrome was a turnip patch, and he and some other*
> *men would sneak out at night and eat them raw. It must*
> *have been awful, but when he told me the story, he laughed*
> *about it.*

During the war, the T & T came under the control of the United States Railroad Administration, as did all railroads in the nation because they were vital to national defense, carrying troops, supplies, munitions, and ordnance to eastern ports to be shipped to Europe. The T & T played a part because it was carrying not only borax but also lead (the price of which had soared threefold during the war) from the mines in Tecopa as well as from the carbonate lead mines in Death Valley. It also carried some shipments of manganese that was hauled over the sands from Owl Hole Springs in Death Valley to the remote Riggs siding. The change in control did not make a difference to the T & T's operations other than that the US Railroad Administration decided that the Las Vegas and Tonopah (William Andrew Clark's rival line) was an unnecessary duplication, and it was abandoned. The T & T returned to normal operations in March 1920 with the end of the US Railroad Administration.

At the time his unit was demobilized after the war, Harry Sr. held the rank of corporal. He returned to civilian life, working for a while as a cabdriver and a machinist in Long Beach. But the immensity of the desert drew him back, and on April 16, 1922, he once again found himself a railroad man in the middle of nowhere in the dual positions of foreman of the bridge and building gang as well as section foreman stationed at Leeland, Nevada, twenty-four miles south of Beatty, the railroad's northern terminus. At that time, Leeland was nothing but a station and a water tank with no inhabitants other than the section crew that was responsible for maintaining approximately twenty-five miles of track. It was named after the Lee family who lived in Tecopa at Resting Spring Ranch, so called because it had good water that could support crops and was a welcome stopping point on the trail. In 1882, Philander Lee and two companions made a borax strike in Monte Blanco near Furnace Creek Wash that they sold for $4,000. Lee used his profits to buy the ranch, thereby becoming one of the few prospectors in the region who actually made money on a strike and used it wisely instead of drinking and gambling it away. His sons also made a gold strike and had a mining camp in the Funeral Mountains to the west of the T & T station at Leeland. However, Leeland never turned into a revenue-producing stop, its sole distinction being that it was the first station in Nevada, the railroad having crossed the California border several miles south.[6]

> *In 1922, the railbed was so bad that the average speed was limited to something like fifteen miles per hour in many places. All that could be done was to start at one end and rework it all the way to the other end. So my father and his crew started work at Beatty, Nevada, and progressed southward, one mile at a time. Slowly, the entire road of 168 miles became traversable by train at thirty miles per hour or so.*

As for female company, it was a male world, although for a while, a city girl named Maud lived with Harry Sr. in the T & T caboose, which had been converted into living quarters. When that relationship fizzled, he began to court a local desert woman—one of the few—named Nona Proctor. Tall and pretty, she was also thin and frail, so much so it seemed as if she could easily be carried away by a gust of wind. She had brown eyes like her mother's and light-brown hair like her father's that was cut in the flapper style of the Roaring 1920s with bangs swept to one side of her forehead. She had a high, nervous laugh that could be both ingratiating and endearing. They met at a picnic in 1925 in Crucero where three or four railroad families lived and where she and her family had first settled after moving from Southern California. But they didn't start dating until a year or two later. Harry Jr. recalls that one of the things that attracted Nona to Harry Sr. was that he owned an unusual car, a four-cylinder Durant Star coupe. The main drawback was her mother's opposition.

> *My grandmother Ella May, who was always called May, didn't like my father at all because he had had a girlfriend living with him on the T & T. She told my mother, "You'll have to live with him, not me." But my father wasn't hard to live with. I never saw him pick a fight. Of course, he got into disagreements, but he was pretty congenial, more intelligent than average, and he had few peers in building things, although sometimes he did things by brute strength that he could have done more easily by using his head a little.*

Nona Proctor's family had moved to Crucero from Coachella in 1917 when she was twelve years old. Her ancestors were of pioneer stock, albeit with an unusual twist. Her great-grandparents, Neils Johnson and Ann Willden Johnson, had settled in Chatsworth, California, in 1874 where they had a farm, having left the Utah territory and the Mormons ten years earlier in 1864 under less than friendly circumstances. Born in Sheffield, England, in 1845, Ann Willden had sailed to the United States in 1849 at the age of four following the conversion of her parents to Mormonism. The family arrived in New Orleans, eventually making their way north to Council Bluffs, Iowa, then west to Brigham Young's new Zion in the Territory of Utah, settling in Cedar Creek.

Ann and Neils were married in 1860 when she was fifteen. In 1864, they decided to go to Nevada, but they were stymied by her father and brothers who were adamantly opposed to the move for religious reasons. In a memoir written by one of her daughters, Ann recalled: "The Mormons believed that any Mormon who left Utah would lose her soul, and when I was to be married, my father talked very seriously to Neils and to me about not leaving Utah—that he would rather see me dead than to leave the valley. His thought was, 'Better to be killed than to have a lost soul.'" When the young couple went ahead with their plans to go to Nevada, her father and brothers had Neils arrested on the false charge that he had stolen horses. But that setback only made them more determined to leave. Neils went first, and Ann followed after, traveling with a small wagon train. The first few days on the trail were very tense with the expectation that Ann's father and brothers would overtake the train and kill her. "My father did start after me and got as far as Wildcat Canyon, but the canyon was filled with so much snow, he could not get through, so returned home." A second attempt also met with failure, and Ann made it safely to Nevada where she met Neils. Before their departure, Ann's brother had queried her as to whether she was being forced against her will to leave Utah: "I told him that I very much wished to go, that I wanted to get far away from Utah and the 'religion of polygamy.'"

Also driving Ann's rejection of Mormonism was her personal knowledge of the infamous Mountain Meadows Massacre in which her older brothers John Alexander Willden and Ellott Willden, eighteen and twenty-four years old respectively, had taken part as privates in the Mormon Militia Company F in Cedar City. The Mountain Meadows Massacre took place in 1857 when the Mormon militia slaughtered 120 members—men, women, and older children—of a wagon train that had set out from Arkansas heading for California by means of the southern route across the Utah Territory. The animosity between Mormons and non-Mormons had been running high ever since the killing of Joseph Smith, the religion's founder, by a mob when he was in jail in Carthage, Illinois. That animosity was heightened further by pernicious rumors that the pioneers on the wagon train had taken part in Smith's murder and, in fact, were plotting to kill Brigham Young. It was a lethal mix of threat and false information. For his part in the massacre, Ellott Willden was indicted but never charged. John Alexander Willden was not indicted. Only one man, John D. Lee, was tried, found guilty, and executed. The catastrophe left a scar on Ann, who was only twelve years old at the time. She wrote that after the massacre, everyone knew what had happened but no one was allowed to talk about it: "Once, a dirty, ragged, sad-looking boy came to our door and asked for food. I began asking him questions about it, but mother quickly stopped me. Telling me that it would be my death knell were any of the officers to hear me, for all people were forbidden to speak of the massacre."[7]

After a few years in Nevada, Ann and Neils moved to Chatsworth, California, where they settled down for the rest of their lives, raising ten children. Their daughter Mary "Nellie" Johnson married Elon Proctor, and they became the parents of three children, the eldest being Elmo. He married Ella May Wright in 1904, and on June 12, 1905, their first child Nona (called Nonie by her family) was born in Downey. Eventually, they had six daughters and one son: Nona, Mildred (called Millie), James Alfred (called Al), Stella, Alma, Mary, and Ethel. Mildred was born in Coachella, after which the family settled in Carmenita where Elmo was a professional well driller in business with his father.[8]

Why Elmo would choose to uproot his family from Carmenita and move to such a forbidding a place as Crucero is unknown, but by 1913, the decision had been made and he filed on a piece of land under the Desert Entry Act. Although he drilled two wells and cleared twenty acres, it was not until November 1917 that the family made the move.

On October 3, 1922, when Nona was living with her aunt in San Fernando so that she could attend high school, she wrote an essay for class titled "From Desert to Desert" about the experience of traveling by wagon to Crucero. She wrote it in the slightly rapturous, hyperbolic language of a teenager, with the "merry family" leaving the "perpetual paradise" of the Coachella Valley, on the sixth day reaching "the high San Bernardino mountains," which they crossed in two days, each one being "a joy." On the twelfth day, they came to the end of the road and started on the hardest part of the trip.

> *The sand was deep and we children ran ahead to test the ground to see if we could get through. Once we came to some falls and had to go back quite a way. Another time we were caught in quick sand and we had to tramp the river bed full of grass and stones to get the wagon out. Then we came to our journey's end. Four miles from the sink of the Mojave River. Someone described the river as ending "at the end of nowhere." But the "end of nowhere" looked good to we tired travelers. It was a little after sunset and out in the sand dunes a coyote sang his welcome. That night around the campfire we sang and talked as merrily as a band of gypsies, which we must have resembled.*

The truth was less idyllic: there was nothing at Crucero except the junction of the Los Angeles and Salt Lake Railroad (which later became part of the Union Pacific) and the T & T Railroad, as well as a tiny cluster of buildings housing poor railroad workers. Crucero is located east of Afton Canyon in the Mojave floodplain, an area across which the winds whip sand eastward over the Devil's Playground, depositing it eventually in the great Kelso Dunes that rise over six hundred feet above the surrounding land. Crucero's unique geography helps to turn it into either an inferno or freezer depending on the season and the weather. Nevertheless, the Proctors tried to make it their home, living for a while in a makeshift tent-house, the canvas extending out from the sides of the covered wagon that had carried their possessions across the mountains, rivers, and shifting sands that Nona had described in her essay. Elmo attempted to raise vegetables and wheat as well as date palms, which were one of the principal crops back in the Palm Springs area. He was encouraged by the fact that date palms were being raised successfully at Furnace Creek in Death Valley. However, it turned out that although the water table at Crucero was fairly high owing to the underground flow of the Mojave River, overall growing conditions were not favorable. The only things that were found in abundance in Crucero were wind, sand, mesquite, and railroad track. In his journal entry dated January 10, 1918, Elmo wrote: "About 2 weeks ago I planted some garbanzos and some wheat. 3 days ago planted some lettuce, carrots & radishes. Also, in hotbed, some tomatoes, peppers & egg plant. Last night and today have had a very hard wind which shifted from N.W. to N.E. and became very cold; it filled up the furrows in garden and undermined sleeping room on east end." Ultimately, the challenges to farming were too great and Elmo's farming endeavor was a dismal failure.[9]

To make matters worse, there was no doctor, the closest one being in Yermo thirty-five miles away on the far side of Afton Canyon. There is a family story that Elmo's and May's sixth child, Mary, was born on April 23, 1920, without a doctor. However, Ethel (the youngest member of the family) remembers being told by her mother that they telegraphed the doctor in Yermo, who borrowed a railroad handcar from the Union Pacific and proceeded to pump his way eastward along the track through Afton Canyon. It was nighttime when he arrived in Crucero, and the Proctors lived about a mile west of the rail crossing. Because the directions he had been given were sketchy, he started yelling as loud as he could into the darkness. Finally, Elmo heard him and yelled back. Mary was born prematurely but survived. When Elmo asked the doctor how much he owed him, the doctor replied, "Just pay me what you can," and then returned to Yermo the same way he had come.[10]

As for education, there was only a single elementary school teacher (who also served as school district superintendent) assigned by the State of California. Beginning in 1918, she commuted by train every Sunday from Barstow to Crucero to teach Nona, Millie, Al, and Stella, ages thirteen, ten, eight, and five, respectively. There was no library or any way to get books other than by mail. In 1922, when she was seventeen years old and attending school in San Fernando, Nona wrote to her sister Mildred about a vivid dream she had experienced in which she was a librarian in Crucero. "Imagine that. I think when Crucero gets a library I will be far too old to work in it. However, I wish some dreams would come true."

Despite the challenges of getting books, Nona was considered by her family to be literary and poetic like her father, although physically she resembled her willowy mother. Her sister Mary recalls that when she was very small, she would often see Nona, then an older teenager, climb to the top of a sand dune they called Lookout near the homestead in Crucero. It was surrounded by large mesquite bushes that cast shade on the sand and provided some protection from the wind. "She spent much time there, sitting in the sand under the ancient mesquite branches reading, dreaming and watching activity at the [train] station. We were all familiar with the sight of her climbing, with a book under her arm, to the top of Lookout, not to reappear for an hour or two."[11]

Trying to improve the family's precarious situation, in 1925, Elmo decided to open a gas station on the new Route 91, then known as the Arrowhead Trail, tenuously connecting Los Angeles and Salt Lake City. As an inveterate desert rover, Elmo had often come across drivers with their automobiles stuck in the sand or, worse, with a broken axle or blown engine, so he realized that there was a need for gas, repair, and towing services. His first effort was constructed of tin with an awning that was raised each morning and lowered each evening. It was located about five miles from Crucero on the floor of Cronese Valley near Cat Mountain, so named for the sand and gravel deposit on its steep side in the shape of a sitting feline.

Living quarters were in a nearby three-room abandoned house with a leaky tarpaper roof that kept being blown off by the desert winds. There were also wide gaps between the floor planks. In fact, the word *house* was a euphemism for a decaying structure that barely provided shelter. Ethel, who had turned four years old in 1925, recalls being able to see through the gaps to the ground below. Once when she was sick, she had to take medicine that tasted horrible; the temptation was strong to pour it down through the gaps when her parents weren't watching.

The station itself was at most fifteen feet square. A few years later, Elmo doubled its size so that customers did not have to stand outside the awning to pay for gas but could come inside perchance to buy a bottle of cold soda or a candy bar, to pick up a copy of a poem about the Mojave Desert that he had written as a souvenir, or to take a look at his extensive rock collection on display. On top of the station was a large sign for Union Oil. Out front beneath one of the windows was a red-and-white Coca-Cola sign with the image of a bottle. On the side was an advertisement for Kelly tires. From the family's standpoint, the expanded station was a big improvement because there were two unattached rooms out back for sleeping and there was space inside the station for cooking and eating, which meant they no longer had to live in the ramshackle house.

Harry Jr.'s recollections of that station and his grandfather are so sharp it is as if only a day has gone by, not eighty years.

Cronese was a lonesome place and at that time the Arrowhead Trail wasn't much of a road. One pass by a grader and an oil truck produced it. But because it was the only road through the region, there was enough traffic to make my grandfather's gas station survive. I think that one of the reasons my grandfather chose Cronese, besides its proximity to the new road, was that it was out-of-the-way. My grandfather was a great storyteller and tall-tale spinner; he could keep people on the edges of their seats waiting to find out what happened next, though, as in all tall-tales, truth often got lost in the telling. He loved being the center of attention, craved it, but he didn't really like the people who paid him that attention. I really think he wanted to be away from people, prospecting in the mountains every chance he got but never finding anything. He even wrote poetry. I think that aspect of his character is one of the reasons he came to the Mojave Desert in the first place. After Lloyd and I moved in with him and my grandmother, I never remember them leaving together, not even to go shopping in one of the more populated towns, such as Barstow. One or the other always stayed at the station, unless it was a medical emergency, and

those were few. But that was it. Until the end of their lives
when illness forced them to move to San Fernando where
some family members lived, their home was in Cronese.

Despite her mother's initial negativity, Nona Proctor married Harry Rosenberg in June 1927 when she was twenty-two and he was thirty-two. There was no possibility of holding the wedding service in Cronese or for that matter anywhere in the desert. Instead, the wedding was at the San Fernando home of June Proctor Boardman, Nona's aunt. Under the headline "June Bride," the local society page reported that her gown was made of white canton crepe "simply made" and that orange blossoms fastened her tulle veil to her head and bordered the length of the veil. She carried a bouquet of pink roses. For their honeymoon, they drove the Star coupe north to Yosemite National Park and San Francisco. Then it was back to the outfit and the beginning of a difficult life. When she arrived, she found that the men of the outfit had nailed a sign to the door of the red caboose on which was written, "The boss is boss no more." Inside was a new gasoline lamp the men had purchased as a wedding present.

Apparently, Nona had a civilizing effect on the men who had thrown off many of the finer points of civilized behavior that were not of much value on the outfit. Nona wrote to June Boardman that "the cook says I am good for them. They all wear their shirts to supper now." On looking back, Harry believes that his mother knew exactly what she was getting into. "The desert had been her home since she was twelve; she'd lived at the junction in Crucero, never out of earshot of the train whistle. She'd lived in a very small gas station with six sisters and a brother. How much harder could life in a caboose be?" That Nona did not find it onerous is indicated by another letter she wrote to June from Evelyn less than a month after the wedding. "The car is an old caboose, so there are plenty of windows, six in the big room, four in the little ones. Just the right height and big enough."

Nona immediately set about cleaning off the grime and painting the inside of the caboose cream and ivory. Then she made a small rag rug from a pile of old blue shirts and worn-out BVDs (one-piece underwear) she found heaped in the caboose. Before long, the caboose felt like home, perhaps more so than the tent-house in Crucero and the gas station in Cronese in which she had spent much of her life. At least it provided the one element that was needful in the desert: shelter. Few dwellings anywhere along the T & T line were any better, and many were much worse.

Frequent letters to her extended family in San Fernando and Harry's family in Long Beach often contained requests for fresh fruit, especially oranges, which Nona's grandparents raised. Other requests were for cloth, medicine, and basic necessities that were not available in the Mojave. She included the following mailing information that the senders should write on the packages to help ensure delivery to the proper location along the T & T Railroad: "Please put off at the bridge crew."

A favorite pastime at some stations and sidings was hunting for arrowheads and other artifacts. Once when the outfit was parked at Scranton between Death Valley Junction and Leeland, Nona, Harry, and the men found several arrowheads, a stone knife, an awl, and two pestles used for grinding. Scranton was so rich in arrowheads, they speculated that it had been the site of a fierce battle between tribes. However, it is more likely that its proximity to the mountains, which were prime habitat for bighorn sheep, made it an ideal hunting camp or staging area for the Shoshones or Paiutes. Whatever the reason for the bounty, Nona was having such a good time she regretted that the repair work at Scranton was coming to an end and the outfit was about to move north to Beatty. She wanted to be able to search for a petrified tree Harry had found in the area years before, a clear indicator that the weather in the Amargosa Desert had once been more temperate. Nona never got the chance to find the tree, but eventually, she mounted the arrowhead collection on black velvet, framed it under glass, and displayed it in the caboose where it became one of the family's prized possessions.

Depending on where the outfit was parked, Nona visited with her family at Cronese and attempted to make friends with other women along the rail line, although they were few. One of her first visitors was the Danish mother of a T & T section boss. Nona wrote in a letter, "I couldn't understand much of her English and she was too deaf to understand me, but we had a good time." Both of the women enjoyed needlework and spent the visit admiring the doilies Nona had collected.[12]

Harry Weldon Rosenberg Jr. (nicknamed Bud to differentiate him from his father) was born a year later on June 14, 1928, in St. Vincent's Hospital, Los Angeles. His first outing was to the Johnson ranch where Ann Willden Johnson had lived until her death in 1920. Nona noted in Harry's baby book that they left San Fernando on August 29. "We took our baby 200 miles in our car to the Mojave desert." An early photo in that book is of Harry at the age of three months lying in the sun wearing only a diaper when the outfit was parked in Rasor. Nona wrote above the photo in a neat hand, "The weather was very hot, often above 100 degrees, so this is the way baby lived outside."

Harry's lifelong fascination with tools revealed itself very early, at least if a letter Nona wrote to June is any indication. It is dated January 20, 1930, when Harry was nineteen months old. "Harry left his tool box open and Bud is having the greasyest time of his life. He just gave me something or other in my lap and guess I'll have to wash my dress. Am going to lock up the tools and give him a bath when I get this done." At the time of the letter, Nona was pregnant again. She gave birth to Lloyd David Rosenberg on June 21, 1930. One of Harry's earliest memories is seeing his baby brother for the first time. "I remember being lifted up so I could see him through a window at the hospital in Van Nuys. The event is fixed in time. My earlier memory was of chewing my big toe in my crib." From then on, his memories would be of living on the railroad that traversed a silent vastness in which humans were specks.

The writer Edna Brush Perkins, who visited Silver Lake in the early 1920s, caught the essence of the world in which Harry would grow up in her book *The White Heart of the Mojave*. Perkins was hoping to travel to Death Valley with her friend Charlotte Jordon but was stymied in her first attempt by the total lack of roads and the trackless impassibility of sand, so instead, she spent her time in the immense valley at the foot of the Avawatz Mountains:

> A lonesome little railroad comes along the edge of the Devil's Playground from Ludlow on the Santa Fe, past Silver Lake to the mining camps of Nevada. All the supplies for the neighborhood are hauled in on it through a country of shifting sand where no wagon road can be maintained. Even a railroad, the symbol of civilization, cannot break the solitude. Great arteries of life like the Santa Fe and the Southern Pacific become very tiny veins when they cross the desert; the little Tonopah and Tidewater Railroad hardly seems to exist. You do not see the track until you stumble over it, the telegraph poles are lost in the sagebrush.[13]

CHAPTER 2:
THE T & T RAILROAD

By the time of Harry's birth in 1928, the T & T was no longer carrying borax—the white mineral that had been the primary purpose for its existence. However, from the moment that the last spike was hammered in place in October 1907, the T & T had filled another significant purpose. Inadequate transportation had been a major limitation on mine development in the Death Valley and Amargosa regions. It was usually not the inferior quality of the ore or the playing out of a seam that led to a mine's closing; rather, it was the prohibitive cost of shipping ore to the industries that needed it—be it for silver jewelry, gold dental fillings, lead batteries, or clay pots. Therefore, the coming of the T & T had an immediate effect on the Mojave region, bringing about the opening of several new mines and the reopening of some old ones. For example, the Noonday lead mines, which had closed down twenty-five years before in 1881, were reopened in June 1906 in anticipation of the T & T's completion. Three months later, on September 22, 1906, a reporter for the newspaper the *Beatty Bullfrog Miner* wrote that James Lester, the owner of the mines, "is working 50 men and has an enormous quantity of ore blocked out." In the hyperbolic style of mining camp journalism, he wrote that shipments to the smelter would start the following month.[14]

In reality, Lester's ore would have to wait eight more months because the construction of the T & T had gotten only as far as the southern entrance to the dreaded Amargosa Canyon through which the river flows on the surface. To the north of the canyon is the Tecopa basin, all that remains of an ancient lake as evidenced by a maze of eroded grayish-brown mud deposits towering over salt flats. The basin is filled with numerous hot springs and seeps that add to the river's flow just as it enters the canyon. The job of laying track through nearly eleven miles of gorge, with a workforce of approximately nine hundred men and two thousand mules and horses, took all winter and spring. Progress was a glacially slow two miles a month. The most difficult construction was in the slot-like narrows where major cuts and fills were required to get the railroad bed to fit along the base of the sheer cliffs known as the Palisades that towered up almost a thousand feet. Long wooden trestles had to be built across the river, and numerous culverts had to be dug to prevent washouts. A reporter for the newspaper the *Death Valley Chuck-Walla* wrote on January 15, 1907, that the construction through the canyon was costing Francis Smith, the Borax King, about $175,000 per mile: "That is not quite as much as the Panama canal is costing Teddy Roosevelt, for Culebra is a bit higher than the niter hills in the Amargosa and Smith won't employ Chinese to do his work. The Amargosa, however, is not at all reconciled to the harness of steel rails and railroad grades."[15] It took until May 1907 for the tracks to finally emerge from the canyon, at which point the pace of construction picked up considerably, crossing the remaining forty-one miles in five months, reaching the end of the line on October 30, 1907.

The completion of the T & T was the catalyst for several ancillary construction projects. These included the building of spurs and small connecting railroads, such as the standard gauge Tecopa R & R that ran down for eleven miles from the Noonday lead mines so that Lester could finally ship out his ore efficiently. Another spur line was constructed from Acme station (sometimes known as Morrison) near the entrance to the Amargosa Canyon, up the hill past China Ranch to the gypsum mines.

The existence of the T & T also encouraged the influx of miners and prospectors and the establishment of little communities for which the T & T served as a lifeline. Shoshone was one of the new "towns." Founded in 1910 by Ralph Jacobus "Dad" Fairbanks and his future son-in-law Charlie Brown, it was located in a mesquite grove to the west of the Amargosa River. The presence of mesquite was considered a propitious sign because it indicated sweet water. There was even a hot spring. Later on, athel trees were planted, turning the town into a small green oasis nestled at the foot of gravel-covered hills. It was also a social hub because Fairbanks and Brown were not only merchants who wanted to make a profit, they were compassionate men who helped anyone who needed assistance. Not surprisingly, Fairbanks was called "Dad" by everyone, and Brown was called "Charlie" even by the children.

Both Dad and Charlie were all-around good guys who first met in Greenwater where Dad ran a hotel and store and Charlie was a constable and prospector, although what really kept Charlie in the region was his love for Dad's daughter Stella, whom he married in 1910. Greenwater was another of those strikes—a prospect really—that never panned out. A few green stains from copper in the rocks here and there—that was all there ever was. No shear zone to speak of, no rich dike, no pegmatite, no hydrothermal mineralization or secondary enrichment, not even any water! By 1907, a lot of people had been swindled out of a lot of money. Both Dad and Charlie were wise enough to see that they would do better as merchants than as prospectors. Word was that Brown hauled the general store and some other buildings in Greenwater to Shoshone—a common practice because raw materials were hard to come by. Since there was no dining car service on the T & T, their restaurant in Shoshone served the crews and passengers and their boardinghouse put up guests and workers. The T & T was as important to them as they were to the T & T. And that was true of the other stops along the line. The T & T was the lifeline.

Much larger than Shoshone, Death Valley Junction was another center of activity along the T & T, although its size and significance waxed and waned depending on whether the mines were operating. What made it important, indeed vital, was that it was the only town in the region that had a huge mill to grind ore. It was located twenty-seven miles north of Shoshone in the Amargosa Desert a few miles east of the steep Funeral Mountains. If Shoshone gave the impression of being slightly protected by its geography, then Death Valley Junction gave the impression of being totally exposed to the elements. A traveler heading west toward Death Valley on the main road out of town might be forgiven for thinking that were it not for the rail lines bolting it to the earth as well as the immensely heavy ore cars weighing it down, Death Valley Junction would blow away in the wind.

The proliferation of rail lines in Death Valley Junction picked up steam in 1915 when the Pacific Coast Borax Company closed the Lila C, its perennially profitable borax mine with annual shipments totaling over

$1 million. At the same time, the company opened several promising new mines, including the Biddy McCarthy (also spelled McCarty) near Furnace Creek Wash, that needed to be connected by rail to the T & T to get the ore to market. Because the Lila C was already linked to Death Valley Junction by a seven-mile-long branch, the decision was made to build a seventeen-mile extension to the Biddy McCarthy and a nearby mine ironically called the Played Out. The entire twenty-four miles (including the seven miles of standard-gauge) were then converted into a three-foot, narrow-gauge track to save construction expense. To save tax money as well, it was renamed the Death Valley Railroad. At the end of the three-foot line, there was a two-foot gauge industrial track (privately owned by the mines) known as a "Baby Gauge," that ran to the Grand View and the Lizzie V. Oakey mines, which was eventually extended to the Widow Mine.[16] All of these mines shipped their ore over the mountain and down across the valley to the mill in Death Valley Junction from which the concentrated product was loaded onto the ore cars of the standard gauge T & T. As a result, business was booming and the mill was grinding constantly to keep up with the shipments, first of borax and later on, after the borax mines were closed, of bentonite clay. The only drawback for the inhabitants was the air was always filled with dust, so much so that when the outfit parked in Death Valley Junction, Nona wrote in a letter that "nice dusty clay" settled on everything, noting laconically that the cook "says the way he thickens the gravy is to set it outside a few minutes."[17]

Business was so good that in 1924, Pacific Coast Borax hired the architect Alexander Hamilton McCulloch to build a "Civic Center" in Death Valley Junction for its employees. Costing $300,000, the U-shaped adobe complex was constructed around a spacious two-acre plaza. The Spanish-style colonnaded exterior was painted bright yellow, the interior a tranquil blue, giving a sense of shelter and solace from the blazing sun. In the west wing, there were sleeping quarters for two hundred miners with showers, a gymnasium, and a pool. The south wing had among its amenities a kitchen, dining hall, clubroom, billiard hall, and barbershop. It even had an ice cream parlor and a tennis court. In the north wing was a hospital, a movie theater named Corkill Hall (in honor of the mill superintendent Fred Corkill), and staff apartments. By urban standards, the Civic Center was adequate, but by desert standards, it was a wonder of the world, a true oasis. Then just two years later, in 1926, Clarence Rasor, the field engineer for Pacific Coast Borax, made a game-changing discovery—a huge deposit of sodium borate on the Mojave in the Kramer District, approximately 150 miles to the southwest, not far from the Santa Fe Railroad. Pacific Coast Borax lost no time closing down its Death Valley operations, shifting everything to the new town of Boron. Death Valley Junction never recovered, and neither did the T & T.

By the time I came along, Death Valley Junction was still a company town but not in the way it had been in the glory days of the mid-1920s. The mill no longer processed borax. It processed clay instead. There was a grammar school, post office, general store, service station, motel, restaurant, butcher shop, depot, sewage processing building, tennis court, and Corkill Hall that was used for town meetings. The one thing it didn't have was a church. The population was too coarse, independent, and fluid. The only preacher I remember who tried to change that reserved Corkill Hall and attracted only one scared little kid from a population of eighty or so townsfolk. He soon gave up. But to me the big diesels used to drive generators were the real center of attention in Death Valley Junction. The operators would always run me off if they caught me, but I still managed to sneak peeks to see how they were started, though it was years before I understood the meaning of "compression ignition" in which the heat of compression is the igniter instead of a spark. The diesels also supplied electric power to the town and to the roundhouse where the T & T steam engines were repaired.

Besides the revenue loss from the close of the borax business, the T & T no longer carried ore from the northern gold fields because the Bullfrog Goldfield Railroad, which had connected to the T & T in Beatty, was abandoned in 1925. The boomtowns of Rhyolite and Skidoo had in the end been more bust than boom, and the income that had been anticipated had never materialized. The thousands of people who had flooded in with high hope had flooded back out with none. To make matters worse, in 1928, the lead mines in the Tecopa area closed because of falling lead prices. Because of these multiple revenue blows, in 1933, the T & T was forced to stop service over twenty-six miles of rail between Santa Fe tracks at Ludlow and the Union Pacific junction at Crucero, which then became the southern terminus. The T & T moved its main terminal and shops from Ludlow to Death Valley Junction. Despite the setbacks, a few mines and open pits remained in operation throughout the 1930s, including talc and bentonite clay.

The only other items the T & T carried were occasional passengers, mostly curious tourists to gawk at the scenery, mine investors to look at potential claims, and health seekers attracted to the dry air and hot springs. Death Valley was declared a National Monument in 1933 (it would not become a national park until 1994), and the hope was that hotels, such as Furnace Creek Inn and the revamped Amargosa Hotel (part of the former Civic Center and Pacific Coast Borax headquarters) in Death Valley Junction, would attract paying customers in the cooler winter months, when the daytime temperature was a pleasant 50 to 60 degrees Fahrenheit.

Both facilities had been built or refurbished by Pacific Coast Borax in a bid to expand the range of their business beyond mining, although they were more than happy to resurrect the twenty-mule team for publicity purposes, making it a national marketing symbol of strength over adversity, with radio broadcasts of *Death Valley Days* beginning in 1930. Each episode began with a long, slow bugle call, after which the announcer would say: "As the early-morning bugle-call of covered wagon trains fades away among the echoes, another true Death Valley Days story is presented for your entertainment by the Pacific Coast Borax Company, producers of that famous family of products: 20 Mule Team Borax, 20 Mule Team Borax Soap Chips, and Boraxo." Then a story would be recounted by a character known as the "Old Ranger," who spoke in a Western drawl. The broadcast was unique because it attempted to convince its listeners of the worth of two disparate things—borax cleaning products and Death Valley as a tourist destination—packaging them in the myth of the American West.

In another effort to increase tourism, Pacific Coast Borax turned the bunkhouse used for miners at Ryan into the Death Valley View Hotel, which was not the best idea, considering the fact that there was no water, so every drop had to be hauled in by rail. Furthermore, tourists had to transfer from the T & T to the little narrow-gauge Death Valley Railroad to get there, crossing several high, creaky trestles, and swaying around curves, a trip that was not for the fainthearted.

To carry passengers in style from Ludlow to Death Valley Junction to intersect with the Death Valley Railroad, the T & T had one car, nicknamed the Goose for the loud squawk of its air horn.

I was too young to know anything about the financial problems of the T & T, although they concerned my father greatly. After all, it was the Depression and there weren't many employment options out in the Mojave Desert. But I sure did know about the Goose. Most people assume that the Goose was a diesel because it looked like one, but it wasn't, even though its engine was as large as a diesel of the day. It was in fact a high-speed electric coach powered by a large gasoline engine. I heard its engine many times up close. It did not have the steady knocking sound all diesel engines have under compression ignition. Nor did it smoke like diesels of the day. Even at full speed, the engine throbbed more than it hummed. The Goose was modern-looking with silver trim, unlike the black freight cars or the outfit's red cars. And when you rode it, it had a smooth ride, rocking back and forth a little. I remember riding it from Shoshone to Baker going south. It was a big deal to get to ride the Goose. I saw the ore cars every day, but the Goose only came by once or twice a week, if that.

In her book *The White Heart of the Mojave*, Edna Brush Perkins writes of riding in the T & T's passenger car from Silver Lake north to Beatty where she and her friend Charlotte Jordon were to proceed into Death Valley proper in an old wagon pulled by a white mule named Molly and a red horse named Bill. Waiting for the train in Silver Lake, the women were dressed in knickerbockers and high boots and carried bedrolls and duffel bags. When it pulled in, they climbed onboard and found the passenger car was "full of old-timers who were all remarkable for the clearness of their eyes. They were friendly and courteous, men past middle age, dressed in overalls and flannel shirts, who got off at Zabriskie and such places, where it is hard to see that a town exists." The men regaled the women with stories of mines, abandoned towns, and "a river of money that has flowed into the desert and been drunk up by the sand." Gazing out the window, Perkins was impressed by the Dumont Dunes north of Silver Lake not far from Sperry Wash where the T & T enters the Amargosa Canyon. She and Charlotte had seen them from a distance the year before when they had attempted to travel from Silver Lake to Death Valley by automobile, but the women had been unable to gauge the size of the dunes correctly in the huge sweep of the desert, assuming them to be only little mounds. "Now we passed near enough to see their impressive size and how the wind makes their beautiful outlines. When the sand is deep and fine the wind is forever at work upon it, blowing it into dunes, changing their shapes, piling them up and tearing them down." The end of her ride on the T & T was Beatty, located at the base of a magnificent "big red mountain in front of a greater indigo mass," but she was surprised to find the town filled with many empty buildings falling into disrepair, indicative of a gold boom gone bust. Arriving at the hotel, Perkins wrote: "We had an impression of moving-day in that forlorn hour when everything is dismantled and the van has not come."[18]

Perkins's description, written in 1922, provides insight into why passenger service did not pan out for the T & T even after Death Valley became a National Monument. One of the biggest problems was that because it ran north/south, roughly parallel to the Funeral and Black Mountains that formed the formidable eastern wall of Death Valley, there were easier ways for people to get to Death Valley, either by the Southern Pacific Railroad on the western side or, as more and more roads were built in the 1930s, by automobile. Furthermore, it was the dramatic scenery of Death Valley that tourists wanted to see—from Badwater at 282 feet below sea level to Telescope Peak soaring up 11,335 feet, making its vertical rise one of the most extreme in the United States. For Perkins, Death Valley was indeed "the white heart of the Mojave" that beckoned mysteriously to everyone. Its dramatic scenery was bolstered by an equally dramatic history intentionally hyped by advertising to attract tourists: grim deaths, gunfights, gold strikes, lost mines, and crusty muleskinners driving teams of twenty ornery mules. From a marketing standpoint, what did the bleak Amargosa Desert with its brown hills speckled by stubbly greasewood and desert holly have to offer in comparison? It had its austere beauty, especially when the late-afternoon sun angled into the canyons, washes, and badlands bringing out the colors of the rock, but it was too diffuse a region, too "forbidding and stern," as Perkins wrote, to be packaged neatly into a tourist attraction.

Despite the severe drop in revenue, the T & T did not stop operating, upheld by a perpetual hopefulness that yesterday's bust would be tomorrow's boom. A bonanza was only one shovel away. It had happened numerous times before. Even the Lila C mine that had been closed in 1915 was profitably reopened in the 1920s when a new seam was discovered, although its second run at glory was brief. In his book *Railroads of Nevada and Eastern California, Vol. II*, David F. Myrick writes of the T & T:

Still it struggled on in the hope that something might develop. Almost every year the management would be on the verge of filing a petition for abandonment when someone would rush into the office with a story of a big development which would involve the movement of millions of tons of ore. As each such prospect failed to materialize and faded into oblivion, another would appear on the horizon and the process would repeat itself all over again.[19]

So throughout the Great Depression years, the T & T kept going, starting at Ludlow (until 1933) and heading north to Broadwell, Mesquite, Crucero, Rasor, Soda Lake, Baker, Silver Lake, Riggs, Val Jean, Dumont, Sperry Wash, Acme, Tecopa, Zabriskie, Shoshone, Gerstley, Evelyn, Death Valley Junction, Bradford, Scranton, Jenifer, Leeland, Ashton, Carrara, and finally reaching Beatty, which, like all the other little places along the line, was barely hanging on.[20]

Because the T & T kept going, the railbed and bridges had to be maintained with the same rigor as always. If one bridge was out, the trains stopped. So to keep them in shape, a repair outfit was needed, which was a string of boxcars, flat cars, and a caboose that could be moved by an engine to the siding nearest a washout or weakened bridge. The outfit would stay at that site until the work was completed, and then the engine would return, hook up, and picking up steam, chug away from the siding, moving the outfit to the next location in need of repair. Although the outfit was resupplied by passing trains, essentially, it had to be self-sufficient, carrying everything needed to do the work and to sustain life. At times of a major washout, such as the 1938 flood, the crew would number a dozen or more men plus a cook, but the typical crew was two to five men in which case they cooked for themselves.

Everything that had to do with the outfit was painted red to differentiate it from a distance from the Goose and the trains carrying ore.

Paint came in only three colors: red, white, and black, all lead-based. The steam engines were painted black with white lettering. I was in awe of those powerful black engines and also of Mickey Devine, the locomotive engineer. The water tanks at the various sidings were always white as were the mile-post signs with black lettering. Each mile-post started a new sequence of bridge numbers; for example, 98C would be the third bridge in the ninety-eighth mile. And that bridge would have its own identifying sign also painted white with black lettering. When the men weren't repairing bridges, they were painting or repairing buildings and houses belonging to the T & T as well as the outfit's boxcars and caboose because the gritty wind abraded paint as effectively as sandpaper. In one of the earliest photos of me taken when I was no more than two, I am standing with my father holding a paintbrush in my hand.[21]

First in line was the water car carrying eight thousand to ten thousand gallons—every drop of crucial importance because some of the sidings were bone-dry, including Riggs and Val Jean. It was followed by the cook car (also called the dining car), which was distinguished from the others by the thick-walled wooden icebox. It held one hundred pounds of ice insulated by sawdust. The cook car also had a hand pump to bring water into the sink from the water car via a detachable hose. That was it for running water. Next came the family's personal quarters, the caboose, followed by a sleeping car for the crew accommodating eight or so men. Then there was the all-important tool car, which was a combination of a workshop and storage shed on wheels.

The tool car was the wonder I explored to my heart's content. It had the usual tools for handling and shaping timber by hand. This was where saws and knives were resharpened after each day's work. It also had a workbench with a vise that came in handy when bolts had to be cut to length and threaded by hand. Linseed oil along with buckets of white and red lead and crusty brushes comprised the paint shop. And chemicals, like muriatic, sulfuric, and nitric acids, were kept at one end by themselves. I quickly learned which stung the most. Nitric acid was the worst; it "ate" wood as well as the skin off my hands. Caustic soda was their alkaline counterpart and was kept at the other end of the car. Kerosene, gasoline, and engine oil each had their separate drums. Electrical wiring (plug-and-knob style), fuses, and the like were also kept in the tool car. Rod for threading long bolts was kept as needed if standard sizes were not available to hold the timbers together. Telephone wire, insulators, pole-climbing spurs, and a safety belt rounded out the high-tech stuff. It was dirty and smelly. It was all too easy for a young lad to get into all sorts of mischief.

One unusual item kept in ample supply in the tool car was called a torpedo. It was a small explosive device, the equivalent of three or four powerful firecrackers. The torpedo could be attached to the track a mile away from an unsafe bridge or section of roadbed being repaired. When the train passed over it, it would blow up and alert the engineer that he must prepare to stop. In the days before telephone and radio communications, when safety equipment on the trains was primitive or nonexistent, the torpedoes were effective warning devices.

Each bridge was a hand-built affair. By unwritten rules, trains always proceeded slowly over a newly built bridge or portion thereof. But the outfit crew had to have a way to warn oncoming trains of danger. That was the purpose of the torpedo: to protect both the train and its crew from running into a collapsing trap instead of a stout bridge. When the train hit the torpedo, the report was loud enough that even a deaf engineer could hear it. Certainly the crew could hear it. But it didn't harm the steel wheels. Keeping accurate time on the outfit was an important issue because one had to know when a train was expected. My father kept his twenty-one-jewel Elgin pocket watch on time by checking in with Brownie, the telegraph operator, Blackie Mayher, the conductor, or by getting the time over AM radio from stations in Los Angeles, San Francisco, even Denver. But radio was only available at night when the AM radio waves bounced back and forth from their origin between the ground and the ionosphere to extend their reach, instead of going off into space as FM does.

Finally, there were two flat cars piled high with pine bridge timber. Some pieces were used as stringers—the sixteen-to-twenty-foot beams supporting the ties and track. There were three stringers below and parallel to each rail running from the load-bearing posts or piles known as bents. Other pieces were used as caps (technically part of a bent) that were fourteen-by-fourteen-inch timbers resting across and on top of the piles. Timber was also used for the triangular sway braces and for the pressure-bearing bottom pieces called mud sills. Ties, sometimes known as sleepers, were stored on the flat cars as well. During construction from 1906 to 1907, up to three thousand ties were used per mile.

Unattached to the outfit but part of it nonetheless was what was called a motorcar, which was a railcar equipped with a two-cylinder air-cooled, four-cycle gasoline engine with cylinders opposed 180 degrees apart. It provided transportation for the crew from the siding at which the outfit was parked to the site of the washout or bridge repair. The motorcar towed or pushed what was known as a push car, which carried lumber to the site. To Harry, the motorcar's drive train was a marvel. Power was transmitted from the crankshaft to the rear wheels by a flat polished flywheel that engaged a drive wheel at a right angle by friction at selectable radii that was connected directly to the rear axle by a chain. The problem was it could be, according to Harry, "a balky beast."

Retard the spark timing, open the throttle wide, and spin the crank to make it roar to life. I often saw what could happen if you forgot to retard the spark. It would kick back instead of starting. That was usually worth a laugh, but one time, my father cranked and cranked. Finally, it caught but kicked the crank up in his face. The next thing I saw was him spitting out teeth. But that event made his reputation. Without a flinch, he went on to work as if nothing had happened.

When it was cool, Lloyd and Harry slept in the cupola room of the caboose and their parents slept in the adjoining room. But when it was hot, the entire family climbed the ladder on the outside wall and slept crosswise on top of the cupola.

My parents would sleep laterally on the roof with my brother and me in between so we wouldn't fall off, a drop of about eleven feet. It could be 110 degrees at midnight in that area, and we just bore it. After a while, we fell asleep anyhow. When the moon was out, we always heard the yip-yip howls of coyotes. They were a part of the night, but we almost never saw one. In fact, in all my time on the desert, I remember

*seeing only four in the wild. However, their tracks and their
signs were abundant.*

At other times, the family set up their cots on the sand beside the
caboose, but then a different danger presented itself.

*In the morning, more than once when I woke up, there were
sidewinder tracks in the sand underneath our cots. I learned
never to drop my hand off the side of the cot so as not to get
bitten while I slept. I remember being told the story of a
prospector who dropped his hand off during the night and
got bitten. Someone found him the next morning. He lived
just long enough to tell the tale. To this day, if my hand drops
off the side of the bed, I instantly wake up. Neuron clusters
trained early never forget.*

On such mornings, the first order of the day was to find the sidewinder
and kill it with a rock. In some locations, sidewinders were common; in
others, they were rare. In an example of desert hyperbole, the railroad
telegraphers stationed in Crucero nicknamed the place Rattlesnake Flat.
As one telegrapher remembered it, the name was "in honor of the carpet
of sidewinders that covered the ground at night."[22] Scorpions were also
a hazard all along the line. To Harry, their tracks looked like pairs of
skinny tractor tracks. "Scorpions could never be found except when you
didn't expect to." On the aggravation level, there were flies, gnats, and
mosquitoes, especially at Tecopa, which, because of its hot springs, was the
most humid place on the line. Cursed with insects and humidity, Tecopa
was conversely blessed with frogs that were easy to catch and good to eat.

*There were frogs galore at Tecopa, and my family ate them
every time we parked there. Their home was a swampy
meadow easy to walk through. All Lloyd and I had to do was
blind them at night with a flashlight, then pick them up and
put them in a gunnysack until we caught all we could eat.
Another sadder memory of desert abundance is of Lloyd and
me visiting Donny Devine, the son of T & T's engineer Danny
Devine. I was about twelve and Lloyd ten. His house was
full of flies; never had I seen so many. We made a game out*

of killing them, keeping score. Each of us killed more than a hundred. Donny's mother was very ill, and she died not long after. I think in our own boyish way, we were trying to help.

Occasionally, the outfit would be parked on a siding, such as Leeland, that was not too far from cooler foothills. Although it was a rough drive to get to them, sometimes fifteen miles or so up a canyon with no roads, the family would pack up the car and go just to get a good night's sleep at a higher elevation. During this period, no official temperature readings were taken in the Amargosa Desert, but the official readings taken in Death Valley provide an idea of how hot it could get. The highest temperature officially recorded in Death Valley occurred on July 10, 1913, when the thermometer reached 134 degrees Fahrenheit, making it the hottest place on Earth. In 1917, official readings showed forty-three consecutive days of temperatures of 120 degrees or higher. The temperatures in the Amargosa Desert are slightly lower than in Death Valley, which is a long, narrow valley hemmed in by very high mountains that magnify the heat on the very low valley floor. The Amargosa Desert lacks Death Valley's extreme geography; even so, temperatures in July can exceed 120 degrees. When the T & T was under construction in 1906, it was so hot that the Pacific Coast Borax Company could not keep workers, the joke being that there were always three construction crews in the field: the first one was returning after having quit, the second one was beginning to work, and the third one was on its way to replace the second, which was already preparing to quit.

We learned to endure heat, falling asleep at nighttime temperatures well above 100 degrees in the summer because we had no choice. In the foothills, a drop of ten, even five, degrees Fahrenheit was a blessing—enough to enable sleep. We used to drive to the foothills at least half a dozen times a summer. Winters were more comfortable; a sheepskin coat, at least for my father, and long underwear afforded adequate protection most days. No sleeping bags of course. And no shoes unless it was extremely cold. My brother and I went barefoot all winter long, developing thick calluses on the soles of our feet. In strong winds, the windchill factor could dip below zero; it wasn't the temperature that made it feel so cold but the wind velocity. It was misery.

After a particularly frigid January night spent parked in Death Valley Junction, Nona wrote in a letter, "And cold! Oh boy. It freezes most all day. And the nights are as cold as Greenland." Occasionally, there was even snow, as a photo of Harry being held by Nona at the Silver Lake siding attests. "It was the winter of '28–29 when I was six months old. My mother appears with me on the deck of the water car right next to the caboose. This was my first snow flurry."

As to how life was lived on the outfit, food included dried beans, canned goods, and plenty of potatoes. Canned milk was much more common than regular milk, which could only be gotten in some of the larger towns. Fresh vegetables and fruit were so rare that on those few occasions when the children had fruit, they never forgot. "One of the reasons Lloyd and I liked it when the outfit parked in Shoshone was that Charlie Brown, who virtually owned the town, would give us bananas. That was a treat for us." Because the crew had to be fed, the outfit usually had a cook, but when for some reason, the crew was very small, Nona cooked with the assistance of Harry Sr., who did the heavy lifting and helped clean up. In a letter dated February 28, 1934, and written at the Riggs siding, Nona wrote that there were no men with the outfit (all help having been temporarily laid off), so she was doing the cooking for the family, including five-year-old Harry, serving them mostly omelets, canned fruit, and salad that were easy to prepare. "I have been real ambitious lately and have been making cakes. Think I will go and try a devils food for today. We are out of potatoes, vegs, meat and bread, so will have a nice dessert to go with the tin cans." Even so, her younger sister Stella Proctor Rook felt that Nona "had stepped right into the lap of luxury," compared to life at Cronese because meats, such as beef, lamb, and pork were available via the railroad, not just the occasional chicken and rabbit. (Two Proctor sisters married two Rook brothers. Stella married Carl Rook, and Millie married Harry Rook. In 1933, Stella and Carl lived in the caboose with the Rosenbergs while Carl was employed by the T & T.)

Through the eyes of a child, Harry was not aware of any shortage of food. However, he was cognizant of the work required to get and prepare food because even though the cook car was replenished with ice on a weekly basis, meat had to be eaten quickly or dried into jerky, a job he learned how to do early on.[23]

> *My father was a hunter who rarely returned empty-handed*
> *from a trip to the high country where mountain sheep and*

mule deer roamed. Between those quarterly forays, he also knew where to find rabbits, dove, quail, and migrating ducks. Biweekly local hunts were standard except when we parked in remote places like Val Jean or Riggs. A mountain sheep could easily yield fifty pounds of meat, and since there was no refrigeration, you had to jerk it. We sliced it very thin and made rods or ribbons. Then we put salt on it and wrapped coarse-grain linen around it to keep off the flies. Then we put it out to dry thoroughly. Jerky will keep. The Paiutes and Shoshones could go a long way with just jerky and pine nuts collected up in the mountains in the fall. We collected pine nuts too, flour-sacks full of them. I liked them raw, but roasted a bit, they were better.

Injuries and sickness were also common. On the outfit, mercurochrome and iodine along with castor oil, milk of magnesia, and soda were the only medicines available. Harry also remembers his grandmother using old folk remedies, such as mustard plasters, to treat colds and kerosene dribbled on sugar to treat croup. "The recipe was a spoonful of kerosene on a dab of sugar!" The nearest doctor was in Yermo, California, which, depending on where the outfit was located, could be up to 160 miles away. If the outfit was parked near the Leeland or Beatty stations in Nevada, then Las Vegas was also an option.

I remember being deathly sick at Evelyn siding when I was four or so. Evelyn was just south of Eagle Mountain near the banks of the Amargosa. Very remote. The doctor came from Yermo, a distance of approximately 120 miles, driving on washboard dirt roads for at least half the way. I lived. His price? The princely sum of ten dollars of which he bought the needed gas for all of two dollars. People helped one another, although Indian and Mexican families were not always helped as much as they should have been. In the desert, they were always living on the edge.

Because hospitals were hours distant, rarely was anyone taken to them. If an injury occurred, it was attended to onsite to the best of their ability. Such was the case with Carl Rook, Harry's uncle by marriage. Once when the outfit was working on a bridge, Carl was using an adze to notch out timber. An adze is an inherently dangerous tool, more so than most, because the movement of the blade is toward the body. By accident, Carl sunk the adze right into his foot just below his ankle. Harry remembers the men bandaging it up as best they could, but no one stitched it. Fortunately, Carl recovered.

Keeping children out of harm's way in such a dangerous environment was a never-ending challenge. When Millie and Harry Rook brought their children to visit the Rosenbergs while the outfit was parked at Ludlow, the children were not allowed to play outside because they did not know to stay off the tracks. Because Ludlow was a hub for both the Santa Fe and the T & T, it was very busy with trains passing through every few minutes. After the two-day visit, Nona wrote in a letter to her mother-in-law that the caboose was so crowded with both families that she felt like the old woman who lived in a shoe.

Stella Proctor Rook remembers that when she was a child, she played with a little girl whose father worked for the T & T in Crucero. One day, when they were playing, they heard the T & T approaching, and Stella wanted to go watch, but the little girl became very frightened and insisted that they hide because there was a mean man on the train who owned it. Later on, Stella told her mother about what had happened and May went to investigate. She learned that the little girl had been getting up on the shoulder of the roadbed with her doll buggy, pushing it between the wheels of the train and then jerking it back. The girl's mother had tried to stop her to no avail until one day Blackie, the conductor, saw her do it. He swung down from the train, whirled her around, gave her a little swat on the backside, and said, "You leave my train alone! Get back away from my train! Don't you come near my train again!" Years later, Stella asked Blackie about the incident, and he said, "You know I like children, and I could see, every time we came by, that mother frantically running and grabbing her child to keep her from doing that. I realized she wasn't making any progress so I decided to see to it."[24]

Mail came two or three times a week and provided a bit of excitement for the boys because the train delivering the mail did not stop. The exchange of letters was literally on the fly. The transfer would start when the engineer would blow the steam whistle to warn everyone up ahead to get ready.

When we heard the engineer toot on approach, we would scramble to grab the bamboo hoop kept for the purpose of transferring mail. The hoop was in the shape of a figure nine with a clamp strategically placed where the loop ended. As the train thundered by at thirty miles per hour, Blackie, the conductor, would reach out with his arm and spear it through the hoop. Once inside the caboose, he removed our mail and replaced it with any he had for us, simply addressed to us at Death Valley Junction. He then tossed the hoop out the door maybe two hundred yards down the line. It was always a great adventure running down the mail and bringing it back. Sometimes I would try to guess where he would throw it out so I could catch it. But I never connected.

There were no sanitary facilities beyond an outhouse and not even that at some sidings. According to Harry, distance was modesty. There was also no electricity. Only once did Harry Sr. try to rig the cook and sleeping cars with electric lights, taking a week to run the wire, hooking up a generator to a one-horse gasoline engine. For one night only, the outfit had light. "We thought, *Oh boy, this is the way to live!*" But the engine used far too much gas, so the next morning, Harry Sr. disconnected it. It was back to the soft glow of kerosene lamps the next night. However, the outfit did possess what to Harry was a true wonder—a telephone—which he recalls as a mysterious gizmo by the door of the cook car.

I was very curious about it, and it remained a mystery even after I learned how to unhook it when the outfit was preparing to move and hook it back up in our new location. The wire on the pole was the obvious thing. My father had this big safety belt and a pair of lineman's spikes. He used this equipment to climb up a telephone pole and hook up the phone wire—a single wire made of zinc-coated steel! It was years before I finally realized how the system really worked. The needed second wire out of the phone didn't go to thin air; it went to the wheel carriage on the siding rail, thence to the main rail to which all phones were connected in common along the line. It was a party line of course. Our signal was simply five straight rings, no pauses between rings. The telegraph system used the same circuit trick. In fact, it was the telegraph operator at Silver Lake who was our connection

to the rest of the world. Call him up, and he would call your
party on the Bell system and tap you in.

Sidings were located along the roadbed about every five to ten miles. Usually, every second or third siding, there was a stationed section crew, meaning the men lived there instead of moving constantly as the outfit did. Some of those sidings had wells, but others, such as Riggs, Evelyn, and Sperry, had cisterns in the ground that had to be filled once a month by a water car. If there was a well, there was also a gasoline engine to pump the water up.

The one-cylinder engine went put-put-put-hissahis-hissahis-
hissahis-put-put-put. The number of beats varied as the
engine revved up and then coasted down under load. As
a little child, I used to watch the engine run with the cam
follower oscillating back and forth by the hour. The intake
valve was lightly spring-loaded and easily opened under
atmospheric pressure while the cam follower opened and
held open the exhaust valve when the governor sensed top
speed. At that point, the cylinder firing stopped and the air
oscillating into and out of the exhaust pipe gave rise to the
hissahis-hissahis rhythm as the engine slowed under load.
At half-speed, the cam follower was activated by a governor
and the process would reverse into the put-put speed-up
mode again. The engine had no throttled carburetor, only a
venturi, so it was either wide open and working hard, or it
was off and slowing down, doing work either way. Another
thing about this engine: it had no spark plug! But it had a
wire going to an extension of the cam follower such that it
tripped a further cam on a spring-loaded rod going into the
head of the engine. The wire went into what looked like a
bucket sitting on the floor of the engine house. I was too young
to realize it then, but that bucket was a primitive battery.
Many years later, I remembered all this when I was studying
inertia and centrifugal force in a college physics class. How
the cam follower really worked became an aha moment for
me. The same thing happened for the ignition system that I
had also observed carefully as a child and remembered in

exact detail. Unfortunately, I had to wait years to understand these things because the adults around me when I was a child, including my father, often didn't know how they really worked. Observe, remember, and figure out—that became my modus operandi throughout my life.[25]

The issue of water brings up the problem of bathing. On the outfit, the clothes washtub doubled as a bathtub. "The only other option was to hose down in public under the water car. But that was no problem at sidings such as Val Jean and Dumont where there was no one around for miles." The exception was at Tecopa, well-known for its hot springs, the hottest being 105 degrees Fahrenheit. To Harry, bathing in the hot springs was a treat. "Sometime before I was five, my father and Jim Francis, a friend of his who owned the store in Tecopa, combined resources and put up corrugated metal walls around the biggest hot spring so families could bathe in privacy. The sign to others that the spring was occupied was a towel draped over the wall."

As for laundering clothes, the rule was that socks were not washed until they were so dirty and grimy they stood up on their own. Nona did the washing and rinsing in the washtub, and Harry Sr. did the wringing because he had much stronger hands. One of the most interesting photos from Harry's first year of life is of just such a task. Taken in the fall of 1928 at the remote Riggs siding, it shows his mother, who is holding him, standing next to his father who is gripping a galvanized rinse tub in his left hand, its bottom edge resting on his hip. The morning sunlight is full on their faces, the wind is blowing their hair, and it is cool, for Nona wears a jacket over her dress, Harry is wrapped in a blanket, and Harry Sr. wears a flannel shirt, jeans, and high boots. On the ground in front of them is a mound of laundry wrapped in a white sheet. There is also a tub for heating and a bucket to carry water from either the water car or the cistern. Just behind them is a large pile of discarded wagon wheels, crates, buckets, scoops, and harnesses that were probably used in the building of the railroad more than twenty years before. In the middle distance, there is an outhouse. Beyond that there is nothing but a vast emptiness that stretches for mile after desolate mile westward to the Avawatz Mountains. Barely visible to the right is the hazy summit of Telescope Peak on the far side of Death Valley.

*If you look closely at that black-and-white photo, you might
realize that there are no ashes under the water-heating tub.
But that is consistent with just having moved here after
being gone for a good spell. One or two wash days and we
would be off to the next washout or weakening bridge—to
return maybe years later. Camera? A Kodak pinhole box
camera. Yes, no lens. It was among my mother's effects
when she passed on six and a half years after this picture
was taken.*

Rasor, the first siding north of the Union Pacific crossing at Crucero,
had what Riggs lacked—water—which made it an essential stop because
steam engines refilling from its thirty-foot-tall, thirty-thousand-gallon
water tank could make it all the way north to Death Valley Junction. It had
a section crew as well as a full-time track walker whose job it was to check
every railroad tie for loose spikes. His name was Pablo Martinez, and he got
around on a three-wheeled velocipede that was powered by hand and foot.
Harry loved Rasor because after filling up with water, the steam engines
would blow out their pipes and cause a small shower filled with rainbows.

*The engineers had to blow out the water in the pipes so that
the engines could generate full steam. They would blow it
out about a hundred yards down the line after passing the
houses, causing a miniature rainstorm in the desert. Lloyd
and I and the other children would try to run through it. It
was a gleeful, if brief, experience. The engineers would enjoy
it too, watching us from the locomotive and laughing.*

Another reason for loving Rasor was that it was a little oasis like
Shoshone. Because there was plentiful water from the underground Mojave
River, there were two large cottonwoods that towered over the adobe
section house, several athel trees with their delicate bluish-green leaves
and massive trunks that provided shade, and numerous mesquite bushes
with edible bean pods, which in former times were used for food by the
Shoshone and Paiute. And there was one reason more for loving Rasor:
Pablo had a daughter for Harry and Lloyd to play with.

Pablo's wife had a baby practically every year, but they all died except my friend Cholie. It turns out Pablo's wife was feeding them bean juice immediately from birth. Most likely, she gave birth alone as the Paiutes did. Somehow, my mother found out and taught her how to use canned milk for her last baby. Cholie survived. Life was tough for us, but for the Mexicans, Shoshones, and Paiutes, it was tougher. Many of the men were gandy dancers, a picturesque term for tie changers and track layers, but they also did heavy pick-and-shovel work, such as clearing the rails of sand and gravel after a storm. Their wives sometimes worked as washerwomen. After my mother died, a Mexican woman washed our clothes. I remember her but not her name. And I remember the Mexican boys—very thin—getting water for their mothers out of the cistern. After the T & T closed down in 1940, most of the Mexicans left, and I lost track of Cholie. But I will never forget her or Rasor. I have a photo of Lloyd and me sitting on a sandy rise with our dog between us. It was the place where I learned to ride a bike. Rasor was also important to me because it and Crucero were the closest the T & T came to Cronese Cove where Lloyd and I lived with my grandparents after my mother's death, so when the outfit was parked there, it meant my father was nearby.

While life was definitely hard, the pay scale for the repair crews was excellent for the time and place, with laborers earning three dollars a day. Harry Sr. earned eight dollars a day, a princely sum for the Mojave Desert, which helps to explain why he put up with such terrible working conditions for himself and living conditions for his family.

For the entire crew, it was backbreaking work in often disagreeable weather. It took some ingenuity to handle heavy timbers by hand and have all repairs in such a state that trains could pass over slowly but safely, remaining on schedule. I don't really know how much an engine or car weighed, but they were on the order of one to two hundred tons for an engine, half that for loaded ore cars. A bent was a complete set of sills, posts, caps, and diagonal sway braces that supported stringers upon which ties and guardrails were mounted. Changing out an entire bent in a day was par for the course. As a little kid, I was in awe of how my father and the crew managed to remove and replace a bent, all by hand. After all, stringers were twenty feet long and six by sixteen inches. They weighed over three hundred pounds. So how do a couple of skinny guys manhandle stringers and put them in place between two bents? No cherry pickers or cranes available in those early days. The way it was done was two sets of blocks and falls were draped over the side guardrails hooking onto chains around the stringers. The free ends of the ropes were tied to the motorcar. An early memory is how the motorcar moved slowly along the rails under the five-to-one gear ratio until its wheels slipped a bit. At just about that moment, the stringer popped up from its resting place. Other than the help of the motorcar, everything was done by hand. Every piece of timber was sawed to length with proper bevel by hand. The bigger pieces required two-man saws. Saws were sharpened by hand also. Early on, I learned about "set" in the teeth to cut a groove wider than the saw blade so that the saw would not bind as it cut. Set was created by a special tool or more often by the whack of a hammer on the opposite sides of alternating teeth. Every bolt hole was drilled by hand with a big auger. Oh, and digging the trenches for the sills supporting the bent—that too was by hand with pick and shovel. The only thing that counted was muscles, sweat, and a starving stomach. What a life!

In most places, bridges were not built to cross running water but to bring the railbed up out of a wash onto the tableland. Depending on the conditions, some bridges had to be ballasted to provide more stability, including those at Sperry Wash in the Amargosa Canyon and Evelyn, south of Eagle Mountain, a siding near a small playa that was prone to flooding. In fact, a severe storm in August 1908, less than a year after completion of the railroad, had washed the tracks out and caused the southbound train to derail, killing three men, including the engineer, the fireman, and a tramp who had been riding on the brake beam. For railroads in other parts of the nation, ballast was often gravel, but for the T & T, it was the gleaming white tailings from the borax mill in Death Valley Junction. Ballast was usually unnecessary where the ground was covered with what was known as desert pavement, which was the case at Riggs and Val Jean.[26]

Sandstorms were another threat and were capable of undermining or burying the railbed. They would appear out of the blue as an obscuring brown haze and then would rapidly pick up strength, until the sky was roaring, forcing sand around the frames of doors and windows, clogging machinery, and making it difficult for people to breathe. Frequently, station agents and other railroad personnel along the line sent telegraph messages to the train dispatcher warning of "strong sandstorms" and "bad wind." The dispatcher in turn would take appropriate steps to warn trains. One memorandum written on Train Dispatcher Hugh McPhee's train sheet at Ludlow on May 5, 1933, notes: "This has been a cold, stormy day—wind a regular gale from the west to NW and at this hour, not moderating in its intensity. Crucero says it is a h— of a storm. Never worse here—it has... looked bad in distance but it is right here now, don't have to look out in distance—It is *right here*." These factors made the maintenance of a firm foundation for the tracks and bridges a daunting challenge.[27]

When the T & T was built, its owners had calculated that the cost of maintenance, no matter how high, could be covered by the huge profits made from the transportation of borax, copper (which proved nonexistent), lead, and other ores. But there had been doubters from the beginning. Writing about the construction through the Amargosa Canyon, a reporter for the newspaper the *Death Valley Chuck-Walla*, wrote in 1907 that Smith, the Borax King, "must wonder at odd moments when his road will begin to earn money and how much it can earn when running at full capacity." Presciently, the reporter asked whether the railroad would ever be able to find a firm foundation along the Amargosa River.[28] The answer was it never did. What Harry Sr. and his crew repaired one year had to be repaired again the next year.

A fatal accident that occurred as a result of a flood and washout on August 5, 1929, gives a clear picture of the maintenance problems the T & T repair crews had to handle. Late in the afternoon of the previous day, there had been a severe thunderstorm in the Soda Lake Mountains. Realizing that there was the potential for a safety problem with the railbed, the train dispatcher issued the following written train order to all trains operating on the line: "Run with care at all points where water would soften or wash track in event of thunder showers or cloudburst. Run slow and careful between mile post 30 and Soda where water has been running over track." A copy of this train order was delivered at Ludlow to the engineer of the northbound train, No. 25, which was comprised of fifteen freight cars and a combination baggage car and coach. Despite the warning, at 7:45 a.m., No. 25 derailed at bridge 36-A, which had been washed out in the storm. The engine came to rest on the north embankment with the tender in reverse position. The first four cars were scattered in the creek bed with the fifth car on the south embankment. The engineer and fireman were killed. In its report on the incident, the Interstate Commerce Commission concluded that the storm had "resulted in an unusual amount of water coming from the west and north, scouring out the stream bed and undermining the north bulkhead and the track embankment north of the bridge, causing the bridge to fall into the stream bed and float to a point about 50 feet east of the track." Repair work started immediately, with the first job being to lift out the badly damaged engine, tender, and cars from the creek bed and then to rebuild the bridge.[29] Harry Sr. wrote to his mother in October 1929 that, "I have the place where the wreak was all fixed and a nice new bridge there. I am working 8 men besides myself and cook but expect to cut forces to 6 in a few days."

Harry Jr. was only a year old at the time, so he has no direct memory of the accident, but he heard about it often during his childhood. "My grandfather, in his way of embellishing stories, used to say that the engine could have jumped the washout if it had been going faster, but my father scoffed. No train could jump a washout, no matter how fast it was going. My practical, hardworking father cleaned up the mess."

CHAPTER 3:
GREEK TRAGEDY, MOJAVE BACKDROP

In her classic book *The Land of Little Rain* published in 1903, Mary Austin described the Mojave as "a big mysterious land, a lonely, inhospitable land, beautiful, terrible." For her, it was a country of three seasons that she did not call by name but by duration: the first season lasted from June to November during which time the land "lies hot, still and unbearable, sick with violent unrelieving storms." The second stretched from December through March, "chill, quiescent, drinking its scant rain and scanter snows." Finally came the third in April and May, "blossoming, radiant, and seductive."[30]

Nona also loved that brief blooming season when the desert was carpeted with flowers under a temperate sun. She wrote a letter to June Boardman telling her that "the flowers are blooming wildly up on the canyons and on the hill slopes." One of the canyons in the Calico Hills looked like it had "a river of gold running through it."

Even as a young child, Harry knew that spring was a rare time that had to be appreciated for both its beauty and its brevity.

The Sierra Nevada mountains capture the moisture coming in off the Pacific, so little rain falls in their rain shadow. A wet year usually meant an inch or so of rain in February and March, that was all, with warm, blooming weather arriving in April. If we were lucky and the outfit landed in Rasor around Easter time, the wildflowers would be in blossom, carpeting the desert in a sequence of colors. Purple verbenas and white desert lilies. Tall and stately, they were in great demand for the rare bouquet hunter. Because it was on the banks of the Mojave River, Rasor also had a few cottonwoods, athels, and mesquite. Those scrubby trees of the desert have fallen on hard times now because the water table has dropped and Rasor is in permanent drought. But back then, they provided a little shade and a little softness to the eyes of a child.

Unfortunately, the Mojave's spring benevolence was short-lived. Soon, the heat returned, flowers shriveled, the ephemeral rivers sank deeper into the sand, and the water in the playas dried up, leaving only flat plains of cracked mud. But the rivers also gave life to the desert all year long, in some places abundantly, even though their largesse was hidden.

There is a photo of me sitting in the boxcar during my second summer on earth. Other than the light pouring through the open door, there is not much to see in that afternoon shot and that is the point. There wasn't much to see for the casual observer anywhere, not just in the picture. Except for a lot of rocks, a little sand, and a lot of sagebrush and creosote bushes, there seemed to be nothing at all. But if you looked close and thought about it, which was my way as I began to grow up, there were many interesting things to see and smell. Creosote, stinkbugs, and civet cats made up the odorous observations. Animal life was more abundant than one might imagine. Everywhere there seemed to be pack rats and chipmunks. So also scorpions and ants. The coyote, kit fox, and lynx cat dined on cottontail and jackrabbits. So did the horned owls. Bighorn sheep and mule deer roamed the highlands. Around the rare oases like Ash Meadows, Shoshone, and Tecopa, a new throat could be heard by night—that of the Tecopa bullfrog. Migratory birds, teal and mallard ducks, made the oases their stopover points. Pupfish made them their permanent home. Indigenous birds included the common sparrow, dove, quail, ravens, and the famous roadrunner. Lizards, horned toads, desert tortoise, red racers, sidewinders, and diamondback rattlesnakes flourished. And funny little bugs with orange fur I used to watch dig in the sand by the hour. Each of these species

enraptured me at times. But the biggest pests were the insects.
Mosquitoes seemed to live everywhere, as did horseflies,
gnats, and wasps. But one also saw butterflies, tarantula
hawks, and dragonflies.

In the land of light, as Austin wrote, there was "the beautiful and the terrible," or as Harry recalls, the butterfly and the sidewinder, the little orange bug and the scorpion. Even the laws of nature seem to function differently in the desert, giving it a contrary aura. For example, the desert is preternaturally quiet. The quietness is not totally due to lack of noise but to the direction the sound waves travel—curving upward into space instead of outward across the surface of the desert. This phenomenon is caused by the air near the ground being drier and hotter than the air higher up. Light waves from the horizon act in an analogous way, curving upward into cooler air after grazing the hot and dry surface, thereby creating mirages.

You can't take the desert for granted. It can be illusory.
My grandfather Elmo Proctor wrote a poem in which he
described how the devil in his playground tortures the foolish
visitor: "With mirages he fools the thirsty man's eyes." For
example, playas always have mirages that look like water
rippling reflectively on the horizon, so blue and alluring that
people who are dehydrated go toward them to their deaths.
And if it is not the lack of water that kills them, it is the
opposite. They drown in flash floods, as did my father—a
man who had battled the Amargosa most of his life and who
knew better than anyone its awesome power. The Mojave
Desert is beautiful, but it is also hostile and dangerous.

So deceiving were mirages that on arriving at Silver Lake in the early 1920s and seeing sparkling blue water in the distance with trees reflected along the shore, Edna Perkins and Charlotte Jordan would not believe the owner of the general store when he told them it wasn't real. Only an exploratory drive down the lake bed convinced them he was not lying: "Every day we watched the dream water increase and diminish at the base of the black mountain with the tongue of silver sand running up it." Conversely, they had a hard time believing the owner when he told them the lake actually had been full of water during the 1916 flood until he showed them photos of the lake with boats on it. Perkins concluded that the Mojave was magical. She and Charlotte did not learn how to differentiate between the real and the illusory until, accompanied by the obliging sheriff of Silver Lake, they managed with great difficulty to drive to Saratoga Springs at the southern end of Death Valley. There, the Amargosa River makes its last appearance above ground before disappearing forever, but the women were disappointed with the pool they found that was surrounded by green rushes in the angle of a dark red mountain. "Though this real lake in the desert was a pure and lovely blue, and dazzlingly bright, it had none of the magicalness of the dream-water by the three black hills. Somehow it just missed enchantment. Henceforth, we would be able to distinguish mirage by this indescribable quality."[31]

The enchantment was heightened by the elusiveness of the wildlife that survived by means of camouflage and stealth, hiding out during the heat and light of the day and hunting under the cooler cover of night. Alma Proctor wrote in a letter dated June 11, 1934, of a rare coyote attack.

> We have been following the goats every day. This morning Mr. Chislom was with them. He was sitting down with his eyes closed some distance from them when he heard the bell ring. He looked up just in time to see a big coyote spring on the back of one of the goats. The goat ran clear through the band with the coyote on its back. He was afraid of hitting the goat so aimed high. He either hit the coyote or else the goat bucked him off. It leaped for another goat and Chislom went to pumping lead. He shot six times (all he had) and hit the coyote once or twice. The coyote left and headed across the lake towards Bryons head. Chislom came back for shells and Dad. They took the car and chased all around over there but couldn't find anything. The coyote didn't even mark the goat. Ray Morgan shot at a coyote Sat. morning. He and Al chased it all forenoon and Al shot a leg off of it as it went over Babers Pass.

In 1927, four months after their wedding, Nona and Harry were with the outfit at Scranton. Nona wrote in a letter to June that the coyotes and foxes were holding a convention every night. Attracted by the smell of the cook car, the animals were gathering at its door looking for scraps. She wrote that the dog hated them, but there were too many for him. There were also tarantulas. "I never saw them before but now find three or four a day."

One predator came looking for prey in the middle of a summer night in 1931 when Harry was three years old and his family was sleeping on cots beside the caboose. The outfit was parked in Death Valley Junction on the spur to the east of the mill and the borax bins. Death Valley Junction, like Shoshone, was a favorite spot to stop because the Civic Center built by Pacific Coast Borax Company provided many things to do, even though by then the company had moved its headquarters to Boron. The Rosenbergs could wash their clothes, take regular showers, go for a swim in the ice-cold pool filled from a deep well, pick up their mail themselves instead of chasing after it down the rails, and shop in the general store for fresh milk and fruit. But for Harry, who at only three already knew about the weight of desert loneliness, the greatest highlight was the presence of other children to play with, Lloyd being only a baby.

The incident really started in the morning when my mother was frying bacon and eggs. Suddenly, the kerosene stove malfunctioned and caught fire. My mother screamed, and I ran for cover, scared for my life. My father found a pad from somewhere and smothered the flames. But the excitement was not over. That night began as usual under the stars after a long day of play, Death Valley Junction providing me with that rare commodity—children to play with. I was so tired I was asleep even before I was tucked into bed. Deep in the night, I was startled awake when my mother screamed. Having seen my first fire roar out of control, I hunkered down under the covers scared to death. Then a 30-ought-6 rifle exploded in my ear. That really scared me! It frightened me out of my wits. Wailing in terror, I was yanked out of my cot and pulled into my mother's bed where I spent the rest of the night. Next morning, I was shown what had happened. There was a big lynx cat dead on the ground near the foot of my cot. It had been preparing to attack me when my mother spotted it. As proof, there is the photo my mother took of the lynx with her pinhole camera. Typically, lynx roam many degrees farther north than Death Valley and they prefer mountainous areas. But this wasn't the first time. My grandfather also killed a lynx a few miles south of Baker, and, as my mother did, he took a photo. Both were undoubtedly lynx from their markings, size, and bobbed tails, and both were considerably larger than the domestic desert lynx available from modern breeders. I remember the yellow color vividly.

Not only was nature hostile and unpredictable in the Mojave, but so also were many of the people. Some were on the lam from the law; some were running away from personal problems; and some were deeply antisocial, hating human contact and culture. What the Mojave had to offer them was solitude but not solace. In the Death Valley region, monikers instead of names were common, some indicating a physical trait, such as Slim, Shorty, Deafie, and the Black Swede, while others indicated some fluke in a man's character or habits, such as Johnny-Behind-the-Gun or Cross-Country Mike.

Cross-Country Mike was well-known in Shoshone and Tecopa. His moniker came from his famous method of getting from here to there. Being a tramp miner and a drinker, he never owned a car. A tramp miner was the term for a man who worked in a series of different mines either because of a union strike that forced a mine to close or because the ore played out. Whatever the reason, he had to tramp to a new mine. When I knew Cross-Country Mike, he didn't have a burro as the old-time prospectors did to carry their grub and water. So when he couldn't hitch a ride, he would just take off and walk—tramp—straight as a crow could fly, cross-country. The story is told that he walked from the lead mine in Darwin to Tecopa, a distance of 150 miles. Unfortunately, he was badly burned in a fire in his shack that was on the road up to the mines. They took him to the hospital, but he never returned.

A moniker usually attaches itself to a person who has thrown off societal conventions and family ties, such as Seldom Seen Slim, whose real name was Charles Ferge and who was born in Illinois in 1881. Slim settled in Ballarat in the Panamint Mountains when it was already a mining ghost town and stayed there as a recluse until his death in 1968. His epitaph in the Ballarat cemetery reads "Me lonely? Hell no! I'm half coyote and half wild burro." In the earlier era of the boom camps, some women (always in the minority) also had monikers, such as Diamond Tooth Lil, a famous madam in Greenwater, who replaced a lost tooth with one in which a diamond was set. There was also "Ma" Preston who ran the saloon, store, and boardinghouse in Ludlow and who was said to swear like a sailor, have a voice as loud as a foghorn, and a shape like a hippopotamus.[32] But by Harry's time, what women there were in the towns along the T & T were raising families. These included Celestia Fairbanks and Stella Fairbanks Brown, who were called by their normal names (although Celestia was sometimes called Ma) and who tried to provide their children with normal lives in a place that by twentieth-century American standards was not normal.

> *Most desert women stayed in the background. But don't think their roles were unimportant. Their strength and devotion were the sinews upon which the desert country was built. A very few, like Helen Ogston, my high-school teacher at Death Valley Junction, were ahead of their time—educated, liberated, and psychologically independent. But then she had arrived in the desert with those attributes. Some, like my grandmother, were simply meek and busy having babies or burying money in the sand so robbers wouldn't find it. She and others doubtlessly felt trapped and probably were. Where would one go if one walked out? They lived in depressing times. No corner grocery. No relief from the heat. No phone for the most part. No doctor. No dentist either. Charlie Brown used a pair of pliers to pull abscessed teeth, free! For many, no car either. My grandmother never learned to drive or even use a motorized washing machine properly. She actually preferred the washboard, as I recall. She cooked on a kerosene stove. Her greatest luxury was a Servel refrigerator, purchased around 1935, which ran on kerosene.*

One of the exceptions to the homebody rule was Louise Grantham, who had a talc mine in Warm Spring Canyon in Death Valley and who, in the assertive mold of Ma Preston (tempered by greater education and civility), defended her claims assiduously against the US government and the Bureau of Indian Affairs after the designation of Death Valley as a national monument. In the article "She Mines Talc in Death Valley: The Story of Louise Grantham," Judy Palmer describes Grantham's arrival in the Mojave in 1926 when she came hunting for a prospector her father had grubstaked the previous year. "To the local people of Shoshone, she was a shocking individual, a woman with short hair who wore pants tucked into her boots; one who smoked, cussed and played poker, and one who carried a gun. She located the wayward prospector in Ash Meadows, not far from Death Valley, and used the gun to persuade him to quietly surrender the truck and mining equipment he had purchased with her father's money." Grantham remained a successful presence in Death Valley for almost fifty years; she earned the reputation of taking care of her miners as assiduously as she defended her claims. She never had a moniker, always being called simply Louise.[33]

Among the men in the Mojave, suicide was relatively common, whether by dramatic means, such as hanging, by less obvious means, such as walking off into the desert without any water, or by risky behavior that intentionally courted death.

> *For example, there was Short-Fuse Louie, a tramp miner, who got his moniker for his habit of conserving fuse when blasting out a round, which is roughly five to ten tons of ore. And true to life, he met his end via a short fuse—leading to a half stick of dynamite—in his mouth. He killed himself in the Western Talc bunkhouse. When I started to work at Western Talc following my high-school graduation, my bunk had been Louie's the year before. Suicide is always tragic, but the early days on the Amargosa had a per capita suicide incidence far in excess of the national average. Doubtless that was due to the bitter and often unstable people who tried to get away from it all by fleeing to the isolation of the desert. But the desert does not often comfort the disturbed personality.*

During the time Harry Sr. was responsible for the Leeland section of railroad track, a crew member committed suicide by hanging himself. Some forty years later, Harry Jr. returned to the sandy nothingness that is all that remains of Leeland. He found there two unmarked graves, just shallow depressions to the west of the T & T roadbed, only one of which he recalls his father digging after cutting the man down. "The man's name died with my father. To die in the desert often meant to lie in an unmarked grave for eternity." Harry has no idea who is buried in the other grave.

Alcohol was a huge problem, playing an exacerbating role in a number of suicides and murders. Until Prohibition ended in 1933, bootleg liquor was common. In fact, one of the largest stills in California was located south of Shoshone, which upon discovery was blown up by the authorities. But its destruction did not put the local moonshiners out of business. Henry "Hank" McGiveney and J. P. Madison were the most well-known. The author William Caruthers relates in his book *Loafing along Death Valley Trails* that the woman who ran the Shoshone dining room (in front of which was a long bench) told him that McGiveney came into town with his Ford pickup loaded with liquor. "Comes Wednesdays and Saturdays. Regular as a bread route. Always tell when he's due. Bench is crowded. Didn't you notice the tarpaulin over his truck? Always two kegs and a sack of empty pints and quarts. Rough roads around here. Siphons out what you want."[34]

The newspaper the *Inyo Independent* reported that a murder had occurred in Tecopa in December 1918 and that "liquor played an important part in the affair." Then in 1924, the bootlegger J. P. Madison, who was known as Jack, was convicted for supplying liquor for a party that turned violent resulting in the murder of Al Lambert by Dan Foley.[35] The most famous murder and suicide in Tecopa took place on August 22, 1931, when Franklin A. Hall, a deranged storekeeper, shot Harry Stimler and then killed himself. Stimler was a well-known prospector who had been involved in the Goldfield strike early in the century, the Palmetto bonanza, Old John's mine, and the Gold Ace near Carrara, among others. At the time of his death, he had a small mining camp in the Black Hills south of Tecopa.[36]

Harry recalls being told as a child about a murder and suicide that took place when a man killed his wife in the Kingston Mountains east of Dumont Dunes and then killed himself, an incident that probably stuck in his mind because of the death of a woman. Occasionally, bodies would turn up without identity, such as the body, purported to be that of a mobster, dumped in an abandoned T & T freight shed.[37]

The Snake Room in Tecopa was notorious for drinking and fights. Mary Lou Walbergh, the daughter of Jim Francis, who owned the Tecopa Trading Post and who ran the hot springs, remembers that "consumption of alcohol was about the most important activity in town" there being no other form of entertainment. She writes in her memoir *Tales of Tecopa* that "especially on Saturday the drinking went on all night long" and that the next morning the drunks would be stretched out on the porch asleep.[38] Many of the women drank too, but they tended to do it privately because the bars were a man's world.

For Harry Sr., alcohol became more and more of a problem as he got older, and Harry and Lloyd saw its depredations in their own lives.

> *My father drank on and on off through the 1930s and '40s.*
> *He'd go on what we'd call a drunk, then he'd sleep it off and*
> *get back to work. Fortunately, he was never a mean drunk.*
> *But by the 1950s, he had become a full alcoholic. His third*
> *wife, Grace, died of cirrhosis of the liver. Jim Francis also*
> *struggled with alcoholism. No one was keeping statistics*
> *back then, but it was often a factor in automobile accidents.*
> *My father was drunk the night he drowned. Otherwise, he*
> *wouldn't have been tempted to cross the raging Amargosa.*
> *He would have known better.*

There were good solid people as well, including "Dad" Fairbanks, Charlie Brown, and their wives. Dad was called Long Man by the Paiutes and Shoshones because he was tall and thin. Charlie was even taller and much larger. Both men literally and figuratively cast lengthy shadows in the Amargosa area, establishing a family dynasty that survives to this day. When the automobile came along, they saw a further opportunity than just providing food to the T & T crews and passengers and decided to open service stations. Harry remembers that Dad Fairbanks, who left Shoshone and moved to Baker in 1927 to build a service station on the newly built Arrowhead Trail, always tried to take good care of his customers. "They usually needed it since the road from Los Angeles to Las Vegas was nothing but an oiled two-lane country road and Baker was a desolate spot near Soda Lake. I have a photo taken around 1928 of Dad Fairbanks's Big Blue Service Station. Besides two hand-powered gas pumps you can clearly see two oil dispensers, necessary because most cars used at least a quart or more of oil every fifty to five hundred miles or so." For both Charlie and Dad, as was also true of Harry's grandfather Elmo at his station in Cronese, sometimes taking good care of customers meant organizing search parties to find those who had wandered into the desert and gotten lost. Sometimes, it meant notifying the authorities, who notified the next of kin.

Besides the gas station, Charlie's businesses in Shoshone included the general store and the post office. He also supplied foodstuffs, diesel fuel, and dynamite to the local miners and prospectors, although by the 1930s, prospecting was an old man's game that wiser folk knew couldn't be won. That being the case, Charlie was as much a philanthropist as a proprietor, making loans, finding small jobs for broken-down tramp miners and prospectors to work off their debt, and driving them long distances to see a doctor when their luck (what there was of it) ran out. Meeting Charlie for the first time at his store in 1926, Caruthers described him in *Loafing along Death Valley Trails* as follows:

> *He was slow in his movements, slow in his speech and I had the feeling that his keen, calm eyes had already counted the number of buttons on my shirt and the eyelets in my shoes. I asked about the road to Baker.*
>
> *"Washed out. Won't be open for two weeks."*
>
> *"Two weeks?" I gasped. "Long enough to kill a fellow, isn't it?"*
>
> *"Well, there's a little cemetery handy. Just up the gulch."*
>
> *Impulsively I thrust out my hand. "Shake. You win. Now that we understand each other, have you a cabin for rent for these two weeks?"*
>
> *"Yes, but you'd better take it longer," he chuckled. "In two weeks you'll be a native and won't want to get out."*[39]

Caruthers stayed friends with Charlie for the rest of his life, often visiting Shoshone and the Amargosa region and devoting an entire chapter of his book to him and another to Dad Fairbanks. But according to Harry, Caruthers failed to write about the best thing Charlie ever did: he built a swimming pool in Shoshone that was fed by a natural spring and allowed everyone to use it. It was a unique experience for a desert child.

> *Shoshone was one of my favorite places for the outfit to park—although that didn't happen often enough—and the pool was one reason. It was six-feet deep in the far end and cool, just warm enough to swim. Another reason was*

that the Fourth of July celebrations, organized by Charlie Brown, always began a day early and stretched a day late, no matter the day of the week. Still another reason for liking Shoshone was the boardinghouse and restaurant, although nobody called it a restaurant. When food was ready, the cook clanged this big triangle and the town came running. Roast beef, potatoes, and dessert were primary fare. I was always hungry. Charlie never cheated anyone and was forever doing something for someone. His few enemies were mostly the ne'r-do-wells full of sour grapes. Charlie was a big man, over six feet tall and well over two hundred pounds. He had an unforgettable resonant voice pitched on the tenor side. In 1938, Charlie was elected state senator. He represented not just Shoshone but the whole of Inyo, Mono, and Alpine counties ably and well for twenty-four years. Charlie was a success story in another way. He never graduated from high school. An inspiration? You bet.

Julia Weed Ross was a Paiute woman who lived with her two children, George and Stella, in the first house built in the Shoshone area in the late 1800s. George would become a lifelong friend of Harry's, their closest connection being baseball, the local pastime, as teammates on the baseball team the Shoshone Indians. Nona Rosenberg and Julia knew each other well, and as a token of that friendship, Julia gave Nona a small decorative basket that she had woven. Her mother had been a basket weaver, and Julia carried on the tradition until the late 1930s. Nona was deeply pleased with the gift, showing it with pride to her sisters and mother at the gas station in Cronese. She hoped to make a collection of Julia's baskets, as well as other Shoshone and Paiute artifacts that she had discovered in the desert, being like the rest of her family, an inveterate collector. Looking back over many years, George Ross recalled: "I remember Mother making baskets. She would gather with other women and they would sit on their haunches while they made them, maybe to be closer to the earth." Julia worked with a bowl of water set on the ground next to her to keep the reeds wet and used a small hook to work the material in and out. Principal materials were willow and the devil's claw plant that grew at Chappo Spring, which provided the color black.[40]

Eddie Main was another benevolent character in Harry's childhood. He was a bachelor who was loved by all the children in Shoshone for the simple reason that Eddie loved them back. As a result, he was the town's self-appointed babysitter when one was needed. Eddie was so solicitous of all the children that he taught several of them to swim in Charlie Brown's pool by supporting them with a long-handled rake, walking back and forth the length of the pool as they paddled and kicked. Eddie was not a gambler, but he watched over the doings of the Mesquite Club, supplying firewood for the establishment in the winter. He also acted as a self-appointed bouncer when drunks got out of control, even though he was in his sixties. Since alcohol, money, cards, and men don't make a passive mix, Eddie's skills at breaking up adult fights were as appreciated in Shoshone as his skills with children.[41]

> *I never saw that aspect of Eddie's character. I was too little and the outfit stopped in Shoshone rarely. Then too when I knew him as an adult, he was slight of build, silver-haired, and slowing down a bit. I suspect it was his kindly nature that commanded respect, allowing him to intervene when fisticuffs were nigh. It was said he came from wealth, was educated, and liked to read. All I know was that the kids were safe with him. They were happier with him than with their mothers. And that stuck in my memory. He was saintly in the way he dealt with people.*

Harry's parents were a mix of stability and instability, of strength and frailty. The extremity of trying to raise two boys on a beat-up railroad line surrounded by emptiness without the company of other women and the supportive institutions of schools, churches, and community groups did not always bring out the best in his mother. The fact that they lived with the outfit, meaning there was no separation between work and family, did not always bring out the best in his father.

> *My mother had five sisters and one brother, so she naturally enough wanted a girl instead of the boy she got when I was born. A second boy only compounded her disappointment. She delayed my first haircut because she liked my long, curly hair. Somewhere around the age of three or four, I received my first haircut. And my first toys were dolls. She even*

taught me to crochet. But it was a losing battle for her—I really was a boy. Maybe because of that, she was a bit hard on me, even as she was the more nurturing parent on a daily basis. Like the day I put rocks on the rails just to see what would happen when the train came by. As mothers do, she had a sixth sense about what I was up to so she kept her eye on me. As soon as I completed the rock job, she appeared and made me remove them, but she didn't explain why. She was stern, judging, and made me feel guilty. It wasn't until much later that I realized the rocks would likely derail the motorcar with my dad and crew on it.

Harry remembers his father as very skilled and hardworking but at times given to brief outbursts of violence, the type of man who wanted to be a good father but sometimes failed in his efforts. Harry loved him, respected him, and feared him, all at the same time. Unlike his wife, Harry Sr. wanted only sons and tended to be lenient with Harry and Lloyd, but he was also capable of overreaction when one of the boys stepped over the line. Harry Jr. had a temper and used to throw tantrums to get his way. Unfortunately, Harry Sr. also had a temper, and when the two tempers sparked at the same time, the result could be explosive. One such explosion marked Harry Jr. for the rest of his life. As most incidents do, it started out small. When the boys were old enough to watch out for themselves and not get underfoot, occasionally, they would go with their father to the work site, riding on the rail motorcar.

We could pretty much decide for ourselves whether to go or not. On the day I remember vividly, Lloyd wanted to go to work with my father, but I did not and I wanted Lloyd to stay home. The rail motorcar was ready to leave, and Lloyd and the crew were already on board when I threw a fit to end all fits. My father lost his temper because I was embarrassing him in front of his crew. When I saw his reaction, I ran and crawled under the boxcar. He pulled me out, took me inside, and gave me a much-too-hard spanking, and then he left with Lloyd and the crew. My mother was furious. Come evening, when everyone returned, my mother had a surprise for my father. She had the Model A packed. All she had to

*do was gather up Lloyd and leave for San Fernando where
June, her only aunt, lived. The trip was painful; my butt was
sore, like real sore. It took a week for me to feel okay again.
Eventually, my father convinced my mother to come back,
and years later, he confessed to me that he was ashamed
of himself for such a violent reaction. But the upshot of the
beating was that I unconsciously became fearful of powerful
men, a fear that stayed with me well into adulthood. Anyone
in a uniform or with a superior social or economic position
could intimidate me, and many did.*

Harry was also faced with the problem of learning how to interact
with other children, given that the opportunities to play with anyone
other than Lloyd were few. From the start, self-reliance and independence
were drilled into the boys, as was the importance of looking out for each
other. "Playmates beyond my little brother were a rare treat, and that only
happened when a bridge went out near a settlement. Friends or enemies
rarely had to put up with me long. Since it might be years before we stopped
in again, I could always look forward to a new set of both whenever we
parked near people." Even the family pets were independent-minded. Once
their dog named Perro, a German shepherd mix, could not be found when
the outfit pulled out of Beatty. "He was one smart dog. He saw the train
leave and took out after it. Imagine how he must have felt chasing after his
own home! He lost the sprint but not the race. Yep, next day, here came
Perro wagging his tail, having traveled miles and miles."

When there were children around, Harry and Lloyd had to figure out
how to play cooperatively with them, since out in the desert, they could
do what they pleased. Harry remembers himself as a spoiled brat who got
his own way. He certainly was not spoiled in terms of material possessions,
and in fact, he generally did get his own way because there was no one
else to insist on theirs, other than Lloyd who was two years younger and
more easygoing.

*When I was four or five, the outfit was parked at Beatty,
Nevada. Beatty was the end of the line. It was a lively town
socially. Mining and ranching in the isolated outlying districts
kept the town alive in the same manner as Shoshone. It was a
fun place for the outfit to park because there were other kids*

> *to play with or fight if the occasion arose. It was there that I became aware of thievery as one human trait. A boy, older than I, stole my favorite toy that I had just gotten for Christmas. My mother would not believe me, nor would she try to get it back. I was very disillusioned. The other incident involved my father's radio that had three different batteries in it. It was AM and could run for three or four hours. My playmates got into the boxcar and ran the batteries down. My father was mad. It is possible I would have had an easier time the year we lived in Long Beach and would not have been bullied so much if I had had more experience playing with other children. I just didn't know how the world beyond the outfit worked.*

Birthday parties with other children, playing games, such as pin-the-tail-on-the-donkey, opening gaily wrapped gifts, and eating birthday cake and ice cream were unknown. Instead, birthdays and holidays were usually spent with the Proctors at Cronese. Or if that were out of the question because of distance, they were celebrated with the outfit. Some adjustments were made to traditions, such as having rabbit instead of turkey for Thanksgiving, making wreaths out of desert holly, and using a mesquite bush for a Christmas tree if a pine were not available. There was even an adjustment in the protocol for Santa Claus.

> *I must have been three or four when my parents told me Santa Claus was going to come the next day and that he would land his sleigh and reindeer during the night on the top of the boxcar. I was a practical child who needed to know how everything worked, so the prospect of a roof-landing strained credulity. But the next day, there were the presents, so I had to believe it was true.*

Mary Proctor Huff, Nona's younger sister, remembered the Proctors spending one Christmas with the Rosenbergs in the caboose when she was about twelve or thirteen years old. That year, the outfit was parked at Rasor, which was easily reachable by car from the gas station at Cronese, although the road was very sandy and care had to be taken not to get stuck. Christmas dinner included delicious pies and fruitcake that Nona had made long before and wrapped in a brandy-soaked cloth to mellow.

Mary wrote the following in a letter to Harry about a pensive moment in time that occurred after dinner:

> *At Rasor I sat on the floor showing you a book. My mother and your mother sat across the table from each other. They seemed very content. They talked of everything and nothing, as a mother and daughter will. I watched rather fascinated as your mother indulged in a habit I'd seen her perform time unnumbered—she had her left arm up on the back of her chair, her hand dropping down as she played with a strand of hair. It was shiny and the color of dark honey and it curled a little and with her fingers and thumb she pulled the smooth curl through her fingers and I'd watch it come through straight and snap back into the curl, but at the time it seemed to me to show she was content and relaxed after a successful day with those she loved.*[42]

Whatever contentedness Nona possessed was about to come to an end. There were few schools along the rail line, so in 1934, when Harry was six years old, it was decided that Nona and the boys would move to Long Beach, California, where relatives of Harry Sr. lived and where he owned two small houses and an apartment rental that he had inherited after the death of his father in 1933. The plan was to spend the school year in Long Beach (a six-and-a-half-hour drive from Death Valley Junction), returning to the T & T for holidays and school vacations. Long Beach was a port city and an oil boomtown with oil derricks rising on nearby Signal Hill like trees in a dense forest. It was noisy and crowded compared with the desert. But what was oddest to Harry was that it smelled like hot tar instead of creosote and sage. At the time of their arrival, the city was reeling from the Great Depression. "I remember that collecting rents was a problem for my parents because the times were so bad, but at least they had rents to try to collect." The city was also struggling to recover from a devastating earthquake that had occurred the year before in 1933, damaging and destroying the majority of the city's brick schools and killing 120 people.

> *The frame houses belonging to my father's family were not damaged, but the brick garage adjacent to the apartments we rented out on Anaheim Street collapsed on the backside.*

Both of the schools I would eventually attend, Willard Elementary—for one miserable year—and Franklin Junior High, for grade nine during World War II, had to be closed and rebuilt. But the house we lived in was fine and it had a telephone, electricity, running water, and a bathroom with a toilet, sink, and tub. Our bathwater heater was totally manual. Light the burner, and when you could hear a low boil, turn it off. I never found out what would happen if you didn't. My imagination was enough because I had often been told the story of the T & T engineer, with the appropriate moniker of Low-Water Floyd, who liked to race his train full-throttle into Death Valley Junction like a hot rodder. He could get more speed if he ran the water dangerously low in his engine boiler. One day, he ran it too low, below the crown sheet. The engine blew up and killed him and the fireman. With that story drilled into our heads, no one ever forgot to turn off the burner under the water heater![43]

Even had everything else been perfect, the transition to city life in Long Beach was traumatic for the boys, who knew nothing of traffic on busy downtown thoroughfares, department stores, sidewalks, factories, oil derricks, and noise. In August before school had started, Nona wrote to her sister Stella in Cronese that "the boys like it here most of the time, but they are kind of homesick." In Long Beach, there was no Low-Water Floyd, no Short-Fuse Louie, no sidewinders under the cot, and—most missed of all—no T & T train. Its massive physical presence had been like the sun and the moon, holding within itself the same awesome capacity to appear and reappear with regularity, seen first as a tiny black speck in the rippling heat waves and then growing larger and larger, eating up the rails, until it flew by two little boys waving to the engineer who blew the whistle in response.

In Long Beach, everything was strange and scary. It was like being dropped out of the sky into an alien world with no one to explain a thing and no one to protect Lloyd and me. In the Mojave Desert, I rarely wore shoes, not even in the winter except to an important function, such as a wedding. My feet were so calloused it was hard to get shoes on, and when I did,

> *they hurt. I had never been in a classroom before, never been*
> *with that many children before, never been separated from*
> *Lloyd. From the first day in first grade, I struggled to learn*
> *to read, for there were few books where I came from. I don't*
> *remember actually owning a book until I was ten years old.*
> *I didn't know what a library was because there weren't any.*

Nona did not want to move to Long Beach either, at least not without Harry Sr. She had pleaded with him either to find a job in Long Beach or to take a section job in Tecopa so Harry Jr. could go to school there, but he refused. Being a section head on the railroad lacked the professional challenge of rebuilding the line after disasters. Furthermore, it would entail a major cut in salary. A few years before, in 1932, Nona had written to June about the prospect of leaving the desert and buying a small farm in Salinas, giving as a reason the need to send Harry to school.

Complicating the decision as to whether to stay in the Mojave Desert or move to Long Beach was a more serious problem than a salary cut: Nona was very sick with pulmonary tuberculosis with recurring bouts of fever, coughing, and fatigue. The signs of illness had been there for a long time, unrecognized by the boys and unacknowledged by the adults. On February 28, 1934, she wrote to June Proctor Boardman about being sick again. "I have a temp every day and my eyes are sure on the bum. Harry insisted I go to the Dr. out here but he did not seem to know what was wrong either." However, Harry vividly recalls her going away to what turned out to be a sanatorium when he was three or four and returning no better.

> *I was not told what the word* sanatorium *meant. I knew my*
> *mother was sick. We all did. But no one knew just how sick.*
> *What I recall most were the piles of containers in the closet*
> *near her hospital room for her to spit into. I have always*
> *noted the odd things, and these were odd and scary to me.*

At the time, the prevailing belief was that living in the desert helped alleviate the symptoms of tuberculosis. As a result, sanatoriums were often built in desert regions. However, the beneficial nature of desert air was not absolute, especially in places, such as Crucero and Riggs, where the long sweep of wind made sand airborne, exacerbating lung conditions. There was also the notion that if desert air didn't help, then salt air might.

But what Long Beach really had that the Mojave Desert did not have were physicians, although they had little to offer in their black bags—streptomycin being years away from discovery.

If Nona was hopeful that Long Beach would provide a cure or at least a respite, it was not to be. Her condition deteriorated rapidly. The first entry in her diary for the year 1935 was written on January 1 at the desolate siding of Val Jean where she and the boys had returned for the Christmas holiday: "Seems good to be back in the little red caboose where I spent seven years." On January 3, she wrote, "Washed. Did not feel well, read all afternoon. Got together some notes on Mountain sheep and hope to write a book about them." The entry nine days later on January 12 after she and the boys had returned to Long Beach is the first time her sickness is mentioned: "Went uptown this morning. Made appointment for a TB test next Friday." It wasn't until January 28, after taking a second test, that she found out the results were positive. In brief entries over the next five months, she complained of fever, pains in her side, trouble with her eyes, a sore throat, and heavy fatigue. By May, she had to hire women to help clean house and take care of the boys. On May 9, she went to the hospital to have her tonsils out, but her throat continued to hurt. She wrote on May 16 that she "had the blues bad." Unable to attend church, she listened to church programs on the radio. More and more of the entries are similar to the following: "May 23 1935 Felt very bad today. Congested lungs and 102 temp. Laid around all day. House terrible." On May 24, 1935, she wrote that Harry had come home from school with the chicken pox, noting that he was "not very sick but cross. (Oh dear)." Her last entry was written on May 27, 1935, "Sure sick all day. Sort of a flu. Dr. came this morning. Called Sophe but she could not come. Must have someone tomorrow. Boys fine." Harry remembers that her last few months were filled with home visits by a doctor.

> *She became totally bedridden. She had a spittoon she coughed into day and night. Alma, her younger sister, came to help, as did other ladies. The foot of her bed was elevated maybe six inches. I remember well when it was leveled. "That feels so good," my mother said. But I was not prepared for what came next. An ambulance arrived, with shiny bars outside. I knew they had come for her. So as was still my habit, I threw a tantrum. But my mother calmed me down in her usual manner. "Don't you want me to get well and come home nice*

and fat?" Who could argue with that? Those words were the
last I ever heard from her. They still ring in my ears.

After she was admitted to the hospital, Harry and Lloyd were taken back to Cronese by their uncle Solly Rosenberg and his wife, Alpha, to stay with their grandparents. Nona died on June 27 at the age of thirty following an operation to remove a lung abscess, which may have resulted in the formation of a blood clot. On that day, Harry Sr. wrote an entry in Nona's diary: "June 27 1935, Our mommie passed away this day with lung abscess. An awful blow to Daddie and little boys. We loved her very much." Overwhelmed by his loss, Harry Sr. later wrote one more entry on an empty page: "My love was greater than I knew for Nona. My grief has been immense but will try to carry on in way she would want me to."

Back at Cronese, Elmo went to the old homestead in Crucero, climbed the dune the family always called Lookout (the one where Nona liked to sit when she was growing up), and gathered desert holly to put on her casket.[44]

On the day she died, I remember my grandfather sitting
on the curb at his gas station in the cove. He had tried to
give blood to no avail. I did not comprehend the discussion.
About noon, my father drove in. He was crying and broke
the news to Lloyd and me. He cried all the way back to San
Fernando. My terror was so stark I could not cry. My brother
and I were both frozen with fear. In her casket, she had been
made up to look tan and rosy, just as she did in real life.
Somewhere in those few days, my father said to me, "Take
care of Lloyd!" I had just turned seven, and I was scared to
death. But I was given a responsibility and had not a clue
how to do that. It added to my problems.

Compounding Harry's feelings of grief, guilt, and confusion was an incident involving a neighborhood playmate named Becky just a few months before his mother's death.

She was a cute little blonde about my age. She was fun to
play with. Her many games included one game she called,
"See my butt!" She wore a skirt and twirled around like a

ballet dancer. But I never saw anything, nor did I even know there might be something to look for. I was not aroused, only amused. My innocence was total. Since it was her only play of its kind, I remained innocent. I think Becky was as innocent as I was. It was just another child's game. After all, we were both only six. Anyway, my mother found out about the game but did not realize its innocent nature. My mother promptly reacted much as my father had when he beat me so severely. She dragged Lloyd and me to the doctor's and had us circumcised. I was sore for a week. Her punishment was out of proportion physically and a guilt trip was laid on me beyond all reason. Adding to that guilt trip was the treatment I immediately received from my peers who of course noticed the change during trips to the lavatory.

As with all psychological trauma, Harry's perception may differ a little from what actually took place or was intended; for example, it is possible that Nona did not consider the circumcision to be a form of punishment. In retrospect, he sees his parents as good people who meant well. Even so, he negatively internalized his mother's action. "What I know for sure was that my world had turned against me and I felt powerless, which indeed I was." His father's brutality had resulted in Harry becoming afraid of males. His mother's action resulted in his being afraid of females.

I didn't know why until almost four decades later when my wife Kris—who was a psychologist—helped me to call up the incident from my unconscious and put all the pieces together. But once I did, I immediately realized that my mother's punishing me severely and making me feel very guilty, then promising to get well, then dying, was the second of two betrayals felt by my inner being—by the very person most important to me at the time. I had developed a dual hang-up, not apparent to others perhaps, but over the long haul most serious to me nevertheless.

As if this was not enough tragedy for a lifetime, just two weeks after his mother's passing, there was another death in the family and another funeral to attend. Harry's three-year-old cousin Elmo, who lived in Salinas, drowned in a hole that his father had dug in preparation to plant a tree. Between the digging and the planting, a heavy thunderstorm had filled the hole with water. When no one was watching, Elmo fell in headfirst and could not get out. "When Elmo died, I was petrified. I was sure, absolutely sure, I would die next." On looking back at his early years, Harry sees them as similar to Greek drama. "Modern cinema often works hard to achieve a happy-ever-after ending, while the Greeks worked hard to bring about the ultimate in tragedy. Nineteen thirty-five was the worst year of my life, and I carried its darkness into adulthood."

CHAPTER 4:
GROWING UP IN THE DESERT

The immediate problem was what to do with Harry and Lloyd. June Proctor Boardman, their great-aunt who lived in San Fernando, was willing to take Lloyd but definitely not Harry.

She didn't want me. I was too hard to handle. Lloyd was not the pest that I was. Alpha Rosenberg, who was married to my Uncle Solly, my father's brother, wanted me but thought two kids might be too much. She was the most worldly-wise of the family, and I always liked her. She and I clicked at an early age. Furthermore, she and Uncle Solly had no children. The other option was to keep us together with our grandparents back in Cronese. Three of their children were still living at home, my aunts: Alma, who was eighteen years old; Mary, who was fifteen; and Ethel, who was thirteen. It might have worked out with Lloyd being raised by June and me by Alpha. There's no way of knowing. But the decision was made to send us to our grandparents, probably so that our father could visit us much more regularly, which he did faithfully. So Uncle Solly and Aunt Alpha drove the two of us to Cronese. I remember that long journey well. For the next five and a half years, we lived with our grandparents during the school year and with our father and the outfit during the summer.

As a small child, Harry had longed to live with his parents and brother in what he called a "stuck in" house in one of the settlements along the

T & T, such as Shoshone or Death Valley Junction, instead of in a red caboose parked in the fiery emptiness of a railroad siding miles away from civilization. However, when it actually occurred, the reality fell far short of his dreams. For one thing, there was no house, only the gas station; no neighborhood, only the desert; no parents, only Lloyd.

> *My grandparents were in their fifties when we came to live with them first in Cronese and then in nearby Cronese Cove. My grandmother was tall and skinny with a leathery, wrinkled face. I think that, like my mother, she preferred daughters to sons or grandsons, not that she ever said so out loud. My grandfather was big and fat and was a teller of tall tales that he passed off as truth. They took us in out of necessity. They provided for us physically—food and shelter—but not emotionally. Neither one was a nurturing person to me. I'm sure I gave them a hard time. Mary and Ethel were the ones who were supportive, for which I am forever grateful. It was an austere life in which every drop of water was used, every scrap of food was eaten. Dinner plates had to be slick and clean, not a crumb of food left after a meal—another ingrained habit still with me today. When my grandfather would fill a customer's automobile with oil, he would later turn the empty can upside down and drain the last drops into a small bucket. Eventually, he would have enough oil to put in his own car. Nothing was wasted.*

Cronese and Cronese Cove are located to the east of the Cronese Mountains and to the south of Death Valley. They are about five miles from Crucero, which was at that time the southern terminus of the T & T. Their geographic mark of distinction is the dune on the side of the mountain that looks like a sitting cat with a twitching tail. Formed by prevailing westerly winds, the dune can be seen clearly from the road. Elmo Proctor maintained that the word *Cronese* meant cat and that he had a hand in naming it, but in fact, the name seems to have predated his arrival, and the word is not found in Spanish or Paiute. The cove, so named because it is similar to a small inlet on a lake, is off to one side of the valley, defined by low brown hills covered by gravel and rock. Just behind the cove to the southwest is Cave Mountain, rising to a height of 3,585 feet, beyond which is Afton Canyon through which runs both the Mojave River and the Union Pacific Railroad.

East Cronese and West Cronese lakes are two interconnected playas that occasionally fill during flooding of the Mojave River. During the Pleistocene epoch that ended about twelve thousand years ago, Lake Mojave, fed by the Mojave River, filled the Cronese lakes as well as Soda Lake and Silver Lake. Afton Canyon was formed approximately six thousand years earlier when Lake Manix overflowed, cutting a new west-to-east passage through the mountains for the river. At about the same time and in a similar fashion, the Amargosa Canyon to the north was created. Much is unknown about the complex interplay between meteorology and hydrology that brought about these enormous changes; for example, even if the Mojave River were to have carried ten times its present volume, rainfall would have had to be much greater and evaporative conditions much lower to create and sustain such large lakes. In fact, multicolored sediments in Afton Canyon reveal cool and wet conditions followed by warm and dry. Slowly, the ancient lakes evaporated, shrinking first to marshes and finally to playas. With that change, the flora and fauna also changed as indicated by numerous fossils and artifacts, such as the remains of bison, wampum, arrowheads, spear points, and pottery shards, which are abundant along the borders of the pluvial lakes, giving clear evidence that the ancestors of the Shoshone and the Paiute tribes had lived there and flourished.

Because of the invisible presence of the Mojave River as well as groundwater, the basins support two varieties of native mesquite along with creosote, desert holly, and grasses. Nonnative athel trees are common where there is groundwater or natural depressions that can collect and retain some of the rare rainfall. Where there is no groundwater, such as on the alluvial fans along the foot of each mountain, the native vegetation is dominant.

Several years before the Proctors settled there, some families had tried to homestead in Cronese under the federal government's Desert Land Entry Act.[45] Encouraged by a brief period of increased rainfall in the second decade of the twentieth century, they had built an earthen dam to the east of the cove to retain water with the hope of using it for irrigation, but their hope was misplaced—the area was too dry and windy to farm. Forced to give up, they left only the dam as evidence of their efforts.

Fortunately for the Proctors, there was an eighty-six-foot-deep well at Cronese Cove that had been dug by the State of California for use by the road crews that were relocating the highway. It produced copious amounts of fresh water instead of the barely potable brackish water that came from the well at the old station. Located just below the abandoned dam and adjacent to the roadbed, the well never ran dry, though the family was careful to use the water sparingly.

> One of my chores at Cronese Cove was to check the level of water in the four-thousand-gallon water tank that my grandfather had installed. It was eight feet by eight feet and located about eighty feet up the hill to the east of the station. The tank had a float and rope system and a marker on the outside that showed the water level. After it fell into disrepair, Elmo, by then obese, may have realized it was easier to send Lloyd and me to check the level than to fix it himself. On a hot day in the summer, to keep from burning my feet, I'd run like hell from creosote bush to creosote bush for shade up the slope to the tank. Good thing the skin on my feet was good and thick. I'd place my hands on the outside of the corrugated steel to feel the temperature; where it changed from cool to warm, that was the water level. When it got low, we would start the pump and let it run until the gas ran out. The only problem was that the water was very high in fluoride. Children growing new teeth found they were brownish-yellow from drinking it. Years later, when I was in graduate school, I understood why. Now you would not be allowed to drink water having thirty parts per million fluoride; back then, we didn't know any better. We were just happy to have a cold drink of water.[46]

Elmo Proctor's Union Oil gas station was set back in the cove about 150 feet from the highway, which was on higher ground than Cronese valley. The previous year, Route 91, known as the Arrowhead Trail, had been rerouted across the valley, raising it above the playa. The section of road on which the old station had been located was abandoned, leaving Elmo no option but to move and rebuild. In the spring of 1934, Nona wrote to June that "the station at Cronese is going up. Should be ready to plaster next Sunday although the roof will not be on." At the beginning, the cove seemed an ideal site for the new station because of the presence of the deep well as well as two empty boxcars with their undercarriages removed. Far from any rails, the boxcars had been hauled there by tractor to serve as a temporary public school.

To a degree, the location in the cove was readymade because it had a reliable source of water and two useable structures. However, it had one major drawback: while it was in plain sight to automobiles traveling from the northeast, it was hidden by a small ridge from automobiles traveling from the southwest. Elmo's plans included building the gas station first and then building a garage directly across the road where his son Al would repair automobiles. That garage would help solve the cove's sightline problem. Unfortunately, it was a good idea that came to nothing because of the Great Depression. Ethel Proctor Talbot recalls the day clearly when her father found out he could not go through with his plans. The construction of the new station was well underway when Elmo drove to Barstow to cash a check given to him. When he got there, he found to his dismay that the bank was locked and a sign on the door announced it had gone bankrupt. "When my father returned to Cronese, he sat in his car for the longest time. When he finally managed to come inside, he was obviously devastated." Not only was Elmo wiped out, but he also had unpaid bills at the builder's supply store. Fortunately, the store extended credit so he could complete the gas station, but there was no money to construct the repair garage. Ethel remembers that at that point, the family had no option but to hunker down in poverty in the cove.

Too young to know anything about the family's economic straits or the reasons for them, Harry's memories are of the effort Elmo made to attract motorists.

> *Much of the traffic we got came from the northeast. To get business, my grandfather parked a 1929 Plymouth by the highway and hung two big signs on it that said, "Please give us a brake." He meant break! Or did he? Drivers had to apply brakes sharply going east to avoid driving past his station. He did have a sense of humor! There was a perfectly good location about a mile away at the intersection of what is now Basin Road. If he had built the new station there, he would have done very well. You could have seen it from both directions. For its day, it was a good station, but business was never good. The next nearest gas station was quite a distance away at Beacon Hill, so called because one of the*

beacons for flight lines from Las Vegas to Los Angeles was located there. That station could be seen from the highway, and they did okay though they had to haul water from my grandfather's well because they had none. But they made a go of it. That station is still in business today. Nothing remains of my grandfather's station except the water tank. Even the thick cement foundation is gone. Only some athel trees remain as evidence of human habitation.

Built of hand-made adobe blocks with a wide overhanging roof, the station did double-duty as a one-room house. On entering the front door, a customer would see a wooden counter jutting out from the right wall that separated the front business space from the rear living space. On the counter sat a box of candy, mainly Hershey bars, Baby Ruth, Life Savers, and Snooker bars costing between a penny and an extravagant dime. Next to the candy was a big brass cash register with its keys, pull-down handle, and pop-out drawer. Immediately behind the counter was an icebox for soda pop, such as Coca-Cola, orange soda, fruit-flavored Delaware Punch, and ginger ale, and behind that was a small kitchen table with four chairs. Finally, along the back wall there was a sink and kerosene stove, with a twin bed in the far left corner where Elmo slept.

Of greatest interest to Harry was the little refrigerator standing on the floor to the left of the counter that had a volume of six cubic feet. This type of refrigerator, which worked on the Servel principle, was very popular in the 1930s and '40s in areas not served by electric power.

By making heat, you could make cold. Maybe other children would not have been interested, but that is just the kind of thing that got my attention. I wanted to know exactly how it worked but no one could explain it to me. It wasn't until I was in college that I learned the details. What made it work was a closed loop of hydrogen that changed the equilibrium between pure ammonia and water so that its heat of vaporization could be used to cool an evaporator within the refrigerator interior. And the process was totally quiet.

The only other furniture in the station was a small desk to the left of the front door where Elmo did his bookkeeping and an old picnic table to the right by the window on which were displayed collections of Indian artifacts, shards of pottery, pieces of purple glass colored by manganese, fossils, and rocks collected by Elmo. One rock that everyone in the family prized highly and which fascinated visitors to the station was known as the musical geode. It was far and away the rarest find in all the Mojave. Dull and oval, about the size of a small watermelon, it was nothing to look at, but when a person picked it up and gently rocked it back and forth, it made a tinkling musical sound, caused by loose crystal striking against other crystal within the geode. Those who heard it described the sound as ethereal.[47]

> My grandfather was quite a rockhound, often collecting specimens when he was out prospecting. Among his specimens was an iron meteorite that looked like a flat rusty blob. He said he found it in the detritus left from the rerouting of the highway. Of course, he had a story to match, which was that a friend saw a similar one land on the ground just ahead of his wagon. There were also pieces of quartz, chalcedony, amethyst, and the like on display that he found in a place he called Menagerie Canyon near Afton Gorge. Menagerie Canyon was his name for it because you could actually see a number of rock forms that reminded you of people and animals. He took the painter John Hilton there once when the latter was writing an article on places to visit in the Mojave for Desert Magazine.

There was one thing more in the station: out of sight beneath the counter was a loaded six-shooter that Elmo kept ready. Harry does not remember his grandfather ever having to use it, although he does remember Gypsies stealing candy once, but the theft was not discovered until the caravan had moved on.

For about a year after the boys arrived, the family lived in the old station two miles distant, keeping the new station for business only, but it made more sense to live and work in the same location, so in 1936, the old station was abandoned and whatever could be salvaged was moved to the cove. The problem of there being no sleeping space at the new station was easily solved. Everyone but Elmo slept in the two unpainted boxcars incongruously perched on the gravel-covered hill behind the station. When used for what was called an emergency school, one boxcar had functioned as the schoolroom and the other as the living quarters for the teacher.

Emergency schools were, as the name implies, stopgap efforts by the State of California to supply education to children who lived far away from established communities. A daily attendance of six children had to be maintained, or else the teacher would be reassigned and the schoolhouse closed or abandoned, which was what occurred with the two left-behind boxcars at the cove. At nine feet wide and either thirty-six feet or forty feet long, a boxcar was spacious, and when equipped with a few wooden desks, a blackboard, and a roll-down map, it functioned quite well as a schoolroom. Ethel remembers with fondness going to the boxcar school that had been parked first in Crucero before being hauled to Cronese for the 1930–31 and 1931–32 school years. Being a shy child who had never had playmates except her sisters, she liked the small size that enabled the teacher to give everyone special attention. "She did a great job teaching all grades. I don't know how she did it." When the school was held in Crucero in 1929–30, Stella, who had been attending high school in San Fernando while living with her grandparents, was kept home to drive Ethel, Mary, and Alma each day. "The year we drove to Crucero must have been quite a worry for my parents. The road was just two tracks in the sand and Stella just a teenager and three little girls. The car couldn't have been very reliable, and no one else traveled the road. We were on our own."

By the time Harry and Lloyd were living in Cronese, the construction of better roads and the advent of school buses made emergency schools unnecessary and most of them were abandoned, at which point they filled numerous other functions, in this case, that of bedrooms. Harry's grandmother slept in one of the boxcars that was also used for laundry and storage. Ethel, Mary, and the boys slept in the other. Elmo slept in the station itself. But usually in the summer, everyone slept outside on cots, just as was done when living with the outfit. Even in the winter, they did not sleep in the boxcars unless it was very cold.

Out front, the new gas station in the cove had a corrugated metal awning supported by wood posts anchored on a cement platform upon which were three manual pumps with glass tanks on the top, forming an island. Cars could drive in and park on the highway side or on the station side under the awning. High-octane ethyl with lead (about 85 to 90 octane) *was colored red. Regular gas (about 80 to 85 octane) was colored orange, and the cheap gas with no lead (about 75 to 80 octane) was white. That was standard throughout the industry. Ethyl cost twenty-one cents a gallon, regular was eighteen cents, and cheap was sixteen cents. That was the price for a period of eight or nine years. It never changed. The pumps were hand-operated, so one of my chores after a car had been filled with gas was to pump the gas level back up to the zero point on the glass-bowl top. Once every two or three months, a gasoline truck would come and fill the tanks. Other trucks made regular deliveries of ice and foodstuffs. At the northern end of the sidewalk that ran in front of the main door and along the sides was a water faucet to fill up the cars. There were two flush toilets with no sinks behind the northern and southern extensions of the sidewalk. There was even a pay phone in a booth on the front walk; a call cost $1.36 a minute, which was pretty expensive, the equivalent of somewhere around $20.00 per minute today. On the northeastern side of the station was a water fountain for drinking. My grandfather's creativity appeared here. When pouring the cement foundation, he provided a lateral cement-lined trench some four-feet deep and twenty-feet long beneath the foundation. He ran the water pipe to the fountain both ways through the bottom of this trench and returned all overflow to the trench. By providing openings to the trench, he was able to take advantage of evaporative cooling of the water supplying the fountain. Thirsty tourists were often amazed by the water's coolness, and thankful too. Wild bees frequently visited the fountain to tank up on water. One had to run a bit of water through the vertical spout to get rid of the bees before taking a drink.*

There wasn't much repair work done at the new station, because most people were just passing by and auto reliability and speed were increasing dramatically; nor was there a local community to supply steady business. Even so, Elmo dug a hole and lined it with wood to use as a repair pit. Ethel recalls that her father was a gifted mechanic, but prior to digging the pit, if he had to get under a car, he had to lie on his back and wiggle underneath, which was nearly impossible for a man of his size to do.

To Elmo, the automobile meant more than just business and a convenient means of getting to a town. He found that it opened up the desert, enabling him to reach places previously beyond his reach. He captured his feeling about the coming of the automobile and the changes it made in the following poem. He even made up a tune for the poem and would sing it to himself while driving.

ME MYSELF

I've always been a desert rat,
The truth to you I'll spiel,
But I've given up the burro pack
To get behind a wheel;
The hills they come to meet me
Before I'm halfway there,
Nice little smooth hills, pretty little rough hills,
I'm rolling past on air,
This modern transportation
Is about alright I vow,
It gets me there and back again
In almost no time now,
Through mountains, hills and gulches,
It takes this desert rat,
So fast the country is all a blur,
What do you think of that?[48]

The one problem automobiles presented that burros did not was getting stuck in the deep sand, which meant that pulling travelers out was a regular activity for Elmo. It wasn't just the tourists; even the locals could and did get stuck sometimes. Tourists used to swear there was quicksand in the region, but the real culprit was the wind that had the power to shift dunes and conceal rocks. On April 28, 1927, Elmo wrote a letter to the newspaper the *Barstow Printers* telling of an incident where he had been hired to find a woman and her friend who had set out from Yermo in a Ford coupe and had gone missing. "The only road to Crucero is deep sand practically all the way," he wrote. He found the abandoned automobile stuck in the sand with tracks leading away from it. He followed the tracks and found the women, who were "completely all in from the heat, exertion, and thirst."

However, getting back was so tough Elmo burned out the low gear of his Ford and had to return the next day with a tow truck to retrieve the coupe. Similar mishaps forced him to conclude that "driving the Cronese-Baxter-King-Crucero route should never be attempted except in case of life or death and then with a light car, balloon tires, sand equipment and a good sand driver; also plenty of water."

For the task of getting automobiles out of deep sand, Elmo used sections of the broad flat belts used in industry for power transmission, a technique he taught to Harry Jr.

He bought two ten-foot sections of these belts. He would jack up the stuck car and put them under each side of the rear drive wheels. This spread the load and gave the drive wheels a firm footing. After he drove the car out, he would tell the people not to drive off the road again. He did it for nothing or took a tip. In the desert without pavement, over time, roads turned into washboards. You had to drive slow or really fast. It was hard on the car no matter how you drove. Besides washboarding, there were rocks that could blow out a tire. The state and county road crews would use a grader to resmooth a gravel road. But a week later, the washboarding would be back. It was tough on cars; tough on passengers too. By the 1930s, roads and highways were being paved at about the same pace that the auto industry grew. The romantic era of the Model T was largely memory.

While Elmo was pumping gas and pulling out stuck cars—playing solitaire hour by endless hour in the interim—May was tending to daily necessities involving the family. Harry's perception of his grandmother differs from that of Ethel in large measure because the death of his mother and the complete disruption of his life put him in an utterly different emotional world with significant unmet needs. He and Lloyd lived with their grandparents from 1935 until 1940 when Harry was twelve years old and Lloyd ten. Had he lived with them through his teenage years, he may have developed a more rounded understanding, seeing the situation from their perspective. On the other hand, Ethel was born in Crucero and raised in Cronese and had never known any other way of life. She lived for a few years with her Proctor grandparents in San Fernando while she attended high school (as had her older brother and sisters), there being no high school anywhere near Cronese. In her senior year, a school bus route was established between Cronese and Barstow, so she returned from San Fernando and attended Barstow High School, a distance of forty-nine miles one way. Other than those few years in San Fernando, Cronese was her home until she left for a job in Los Angeles in 1941. Therefore, Ethel's description of her mother is both illuminative and balancing:

> *Mother was a very private person. It was difficult to get her to talk about her family and more so about herself. She was the youngest in her family. Her brother James died when he was two so she never knew him. She was two when her mother died. An aunt helped raise her. Her father was very stern and dominating, but she was devoted to him. When he became estranged from his other daughter because she had married against his wishes, he forbade mother from contacting her sister and as far as I know she never did. Looking back, I realize my mother was very lonely. After all, she had no social contacts. I remember her seeming brighter and happier after a visit with another woman—when a tourist spent extra time at the station or someone from a neighboring station or town would stop by for an hour or so, or when one of her grown and married daughters visited. She liked poetry and could quote from Longfellow and Whittier. She also liked rocks—one almost had to have that interest to live with my dad. Her main focus was her family and getting through each day. She had a hard life. She didn't have a washing machine until six months after the boys came there to live. She did her washing by hand on a washboard.*

Because she never learned to drive, May never went anywhere. The Model T that had opened up Elmo's world, giving him the freedom to head out on his own to prospect or just to explore, did not bring freedom to May. Even when Elmo drove to Yermo or Barstow for supplies, she would stay at the gas station attending to customers and family. Clothes were purchased from either the Sears or the Montgomery Ward catalogs. In fact, Ethel recalls only two times that her mother actually left Cronese Cove: once when the family had Christmas dinner with the outfit, conveniently parked at nearby Baker the first year after the boys arrived, and the second time when her daughter Millie and her family became ill and May's son-in-law Carl Rook drove her and Ethel to Salinas. "After a day or so, she and Carl went back to the cove and I was left to care for the sick family. I was about seventeen."

Just as Harry's memories of his grandmother are colored by the circumstances of his life, so also are his impressions of his grandfather, who was known to everyone as a bit of a character. Again, Ethel's recollections as well as those of a few friends help to paint a more balanced portrait. "Dad was a storyteller and poet. He had a great sense of humor. He was strictly honest in all his dealings. He had a very soft heart for those less fortunate. He was a gentle father and grandfather." If there were any statement about Elmo with which everyone could agree, it would be that he loved the desert, especially being out in it by himself. His moniker was "Desert Rat," which he signed as his name on some of his poems and advertising handouts for the gas station. One such advertisement encouraged travelers to "visit with the Desert Rat who wears holes in shoes and socks as on sore feet he wanders over sharp and ragged rocks." It ends with the following humorous request: "Do your friends a favor. Tell them about us. Do your enemies dirt—Don't tell them."

The Desert Rat loved nothing better than to be out in the vastness prospecting, hunting for arrowheads, or simply exploring. In an era before there was much awareness of the environment, he was concerned for the desert's preservation. For example, when Elmo took the writer and painter John Hilton to Menagerie Canyon, he asked him whether prior magazine articles had led to an increase in litter at the highlighted sites. Hilton assured him that they had not. At the end of the trip, on which Mary and Ethel had gone along, they all returned to the gas station to spend the evening sorting the stones they had collected and to tell May about the day's adventures. Hilton wrote: "I could not help but compare the pleasures and contentment of this home where its occupants have really *learned* to live on the desert, with other desert homes I have known which were occupied by people who merely were *staying* on the desert." Hilton concluded that Elmo had little to show for his prospecting and collecting except a "cabinet of rocks and an intimate knowledge of the desert—but he feels well paid."[49]

Elmo also served as a reference on desert flowers to Lucile Harris for her botanical articles in *Desert Magazine.* In one article in the May 1939 issue titled "Botany Class: Wildflower Parade," Elmo is quoted as follows: "The lily season will, I believe, cover a longer period this spring than at any time within my memory. And they give promise of covering all the sandy places profusely, another rare condition. The heavy, luxuriant growth of the octopus like leaves indicates extra large, well shaded flowers."[50]

Elmo collected his poems into a booklet titled *Rhymes of the Mighty Mohave*, which he sold as a souvenir in the gas station for fifty cents. The following poem (read years later at his funeral) sums up his love for the desert:

BEAUTIES OF THE WESTERN DESERTS

Mosaic carpets of living colors
Shading into rare designs;
Turquoise skies—far horizons,
Vast wide reaches—level mesas,
Winding valleys—rolling hills,
Veiled blue mountains—tinted peaks,
Deep and craggy purple canyons,
Flaming sunsets—star crowned nights:
Still and clear majestic mornings,
Sun filled days of golden glory,
Wonders of such gentle mystery.
Listen! In the shrouding silence,
Still, small voices—from hidden depths
Speak most wondrous, wordless wisdom,
To receptive souls of men.

The local historian and Mojave Desert explorer Dennis G. Casebier writes of Elmo that his fame spread far and wide as an expert on the local desert and that he guided "all kinds of folks through the desert country." Casebier notes that it was probably Elmo who first described and named what is called Spooky Canyon, which at that time still had rough-hewn ladders wedged in the rocks, probably of Shoshone or Paiute origin. "Today it is sometimes called Proctor Canyon. It is a steep and dangerous canyon carved in many places through solid rock down the west side of Old Dad Mountain. Anyone athletically inclined and experienced in rock climbing can ascend the canyon. There are watering places for bighorn sheep high above. It is not uncommon to see them watching you from above when you are in or near the canyon."[51]

Elmo liked to prospect every chance he got, but he had no luck other than in collecting interesting samples. He even tried to invent a dry washer that he thought could be used to separate gold in a dry streambed. "My grandfather designed that thing by instinct not by scientific principle. I was only about nine, but I could tell it would never work. For the first time, but definitely not for the last, it made me question the judgment of my elders." Once Elmo staked a claim with a future son-in-law on a small outcrop of manganese not far from the cove. To do so, he built a monument with rocks, put up a pole, and nailed a tobacco can on top. In it, he put a document stating the claim and the landmarks. Then he filed a copy in the county seat. "That's the way you had to do it, but my grandfather's claim turned out to be worthless. There was not much manganese there." Early on, Harry came to realize that prospectors had the gift of gab, as did his grandfather, but rarely did they have the knowledge capable of turning their finds into anything significant.

> The prospectors would go to a beer hall and talk about bonanzas they were prospecting. They'd throw out a line of baloney, mostly hot air. They'd talk it up so that someone would give them a grubstake for a certain share. They claimed they were going to make a fortune in a gold mine. Most of the time, they didn't know what they were doing. Many of them walked past millions of dollars of gold and never saw it because sometimes gold ore doesn't look like gold ore; the particles are too tiny to be seen, and they are spread uniformly throughout the entire formation. The prospectors panned for larger nuggets and granules down to their visual limits. Years later, I learned that you needed to know geology. You needed to assay a sample to know what you had. I realized that exploitation mixed with avarice mixed with exuberance and wishful thinking led to grubstakes and useless forays.

Prospecting had virtually come to an end by the 1930s, although there were still old-timers hanging on, several living in the caves in Dublin Gulch near Shoshone or in crumbling adobe huts, who dreamed of finding a mother lode. What mattered was the hunt. It was in their blood. One of them was named Jim Hyten.

> *Jim was a prospecting buddy of my grandfather's. He had a gold mine in the Halloran Hill area called the Wanderer that never came to much, but that was before my time. When I knew him he was in his late seventies, early eighties, and was all skin and bones. But he still went out looking, hoping to stake a claim. He lived for a time in the last house in an empty road camp. The road camp was a row of rooms with a kitchen at one end used to house the highway road crews that first paved the Arrowhead Trail between San Bernardino and Salt Lake City. Each camp functioned as the staging area for the building of the next section of highway. Once that section was done, the crew moved on and built a new one. Only the camps at Yermo and Baker became permanent state highway facilities. Jim Hyten lived for a time in the abandoned Cronese road camp all by himself. A kitchen—that was all there was to it. He had an old ramshackle car, but he didn't get around very much. Once when I went to visit he was eating out of a can. I asked him what he was eating, and he said, "Dog food." It was the first time I realized that was possible. He could get dog food cheap at five cents a can. I was put off by it. I had some empathy, but nevertheless it was kind of revolting.*

Herman Jones was a hunting companion of Harry Sr.'s who also prospected. He had the reputation of always carrying a gun, having a short temper, and frequenting the Mesquite Club in Shoshone where legend has it he threatened Dad Fairbanks's son one evening over an argument concerning a poker game. Dad drew a gun and fired, hitting him in the belt buckle, which deflected the bullet. True or not, the story is indicative of the type of man Jones was. Harry remembers being told that Jones, who came from Texas, had gotten in trouble with the law as a young man.

> *Herman prospected some like my grandfather. He also knew all the Indian waterholes, could find wampum and arrowheads. Missing three fingers on one hand, he ended up*

working for the county on the road as a grader and bulldozer operator. Then he retired and had a ranch in the Spring Mountains with a radio, water running into the house, even a power generator. One day, Herman got appendicitis. He made it to Shoshone and was driven to Loma Linda Hospital in Southern California. In a rare event, he survived a ruptured appendix. One tough nut? You bet! Herman was one of my father's favorite friends. When I got to know him well in the late 1940s, he lived in Shoshone and loved to play Panguingue with Carl Rook and anyone else who wanted to join the game. Panguingue was a rummy card game that was popular in the California gold fields and mining areas. Herman was one of the most colorful characters in the desert, a true-to-life old-timer. He and his wife, Etta, were buried together in the Shoshone cemetery in 1951.

For all the fascinating aspects of the lives of Elmo's friends and of his own life—prospecting endlessly among the dry hills, collecting rocks and Indian artifacts to display in the station, writing poetry about fiery sunsets, guiding artists to high vistas overlooking dry playas, taking tourists to gemstone sites, advising botanists on where to find the desert lily in bloom—the one thing he seemed not to be interested in having was a warm, supportive relationship with his grandsons.

If I asked him how something worked, he would tell me not to bother him. But if it came to telling a story, well then, he had plenty of time. He could make up an interesting story. Then it got better and better in the retelling. For example, we had a lot of horned owls in the desert especially after floods that would drive animals up out of the ground, and the owls would come in and feast. He told us that he had spotted one at night with a flashlight, then he dropped the flashlight, pulled out his pistol, and shot it between the eyes. Everyone he told that story to at the station believed it; only problem was no one in the family had ever seen him shoot except at a helpless animal for slaughter. That was another one of my grandfather's stories that my father scoffed at because my father was a real-live crack shot, and his exploits with a gun needed no embellishment.

In the fall of 1935, less than three months after his mother's death, Harry started to attend elementary school in Yermo where he found the emotional support and a measure of stability for which he hungered. His teacher was Miss McCarthy. She taught the combined first, second, and third grades while also serving as the principal of the school, which had approximately seventy students altogether. "From the first day that I walked into her classroom, Miss McCarthy was very patient with me. During all my years in Yermo, she was always in my corner. As a result, I tried to do the best I could for her. She treated me better emotionally than my grandparents." The prior year, Harry had not done well in first grade in Long Beach, partially because of his mother's declining health and the upheaval in the family. At the end of the school year before his mother died, his first-grade teacher had given his father two books for Harry to learn to read over the summer. One of them was the *Wide Awake Reader*, a standard graded text of the era that was the forerunner to the Dick and Jane series. If he succeeded in reading the books by the opening of school in September, he would be allowed to enter second grade in Long Beach. If not, he would have to repeat first grade. After his mother died, those two books traveled with him to Cronese like heavy stones weighing down his small bag of belongings. There, the job of teaching him to read fell to his reluctant young aunts Mary and Ethel. The word *dyslexia* did not exist in the mid-1930s, but looking back, Harry is sure he was, and still is, afflicted with it, necessitating careful reading and rereading to fully understand the meaning of sentences.

> *Miss Butts, my first-grade teacher in Long Beach, tried hard to teach me to read. She'd show me a picture of a duck and then the word* duck, *but I just could not get it. She also tried to teach me to write with the same poor results. In frustration, I tried to rely on rote memory, but that didn't work either. How I hated Mary and Ethel for making me learn to read the summer after my mother died. It was pure torment, and it seemed to me to be relentless. Only years later did I learn from Ethel that she hated teaching me as much as I hated learning. But by September, I could read those two books. Decades later, I discovered that the only "cure" for dyslexia is drill, drill, drill, and more drill. My torturers were drillers before their time.*

Being only thirteen years old, Ethel remembers the struggle well. There was a seventeen-year difference between her and Nona, but only six between her and Harry. Nona was an adult whom Ethel had worshipped from afar and who had left home when Ethel was only five. "After she married and came home for short visits, I was busy off playing. I always thought she was beautiful, and I wanted to be like her, but my memories of her are sketchy. Her health problems were kept from me for the most part until the very last." In Nona's place, there were two children suddenly underfoot, and at least one of them had learning problems Ethel could not comprehend. "Teaching Harry to read was almost as frustrating to me as it was to him. I was an excellent reader and found reading very easy," she explained. "I didn't understand anyone who found it difficult. In the beginning, each session ended in tears. He allowed his to flow freely. I squelched mine. In time, we seemed to find it easier for both of us. I learned to be more patient, and he learned to keep trying when he failed. We both grew together."[52]

Harry felt a profound sense of relief in entering Miss McCarthy's classroom in the Yermo elementary school, his struggles to read behind him.

> *I was fortunate in school. Though none of my early schools were any good academically, a few of my teachers gave me room. I lived and died for them. I endured the rest. I remember hitting my first home run when I was in Miss McCarthy's third-grade class. Until that time, I couldn't do a thing. Physically, I was all thumbs. But Miss McCarthy would always come out at recess to watch us play baseball and to encourage us. I rarely hit the ball, but on this particular day, I hit a home run—more than a home run—it went clear over the trees into the street. In my mind, I can still hear Miss McCarthy cheering. From that day on, suddenly everything jelled, and I had eye-hand coordination. It happened all at once—a strange phenomenon that would reoccur in my life many times. From there on, I played with the big boys and I got on base as often as they did.*

The phenomenon of a skill appearing fully and abruptly, as if a gear had suddenly slipped into place, happened also with arithmetic. Harry had a toy game that gave answers to addition and subtraction problems that he liked to play with in the gas station, but he did not consider himself to be a good arithmetic student. Then one day, in fourth grade, he took an arithmetic test in class. Shortly thereafter, his teacher announced to everyone with incredulity in her voice that one student had received a perfect score. "It was me, but the whole class wouldn't believe it because I had always had trouble up to that point. For the rest of the year, they always expected me to get perfect scores, and I think I did." Proficiency in spelling occurred the same way with the same suddenness in seventh grade. "One day, I was mediocre, and the next, I could spell everything. It was an aha moment, a sudden and inexplicable breakthrough." The one skill that would be slow in coming was understanding what he read. "There is a difference between reading the words and getting the full meaning. That ability came much later in my life. I have my late wife, Kris, who was an English major and a psychologist, to thank for that slow-to-arrive ability."

The boys traveled to school by bus, an hour and a half each way on the Arrowhead Trail. At various times during the 1930s, their grandfather and their uncle Al drove (although Al never drove during the years that the boys were being transported), acting as both drivers and on-board mechanics, because the bus, the first of its kind in the desert, had many problems.

> *That bus was hardly up to the challenges of desert driving. Once, a front tire blew out, but fortunately, the bus did not wreck. Also, it had constant maintenance problems stemming from a design flaw with the Ford engine that was exacerbated by the desert heat. The engine had a fuel pump above the manifold, and when the engine got hot, the fuel would turn to vapor and then the fuel pump wouldn't pump and the engine would die, so there we would sit—out on the road miles from anywhere—until the engine had cooled sufficiently.*

During his first year at Yermo, Harry missed a month of school when he and Lloyd came down with pneumonia right after Christmas, which they had spent with their father on the outfit. Because there were no doctors anywhere near Cronese, their father drove them to June's house in San

Fernando where a nurse and a doctor came every day to give the boys shots and to take their temperatures. "After three days without a temperature, we were considered on the mend. Then Dad took us back to Baker where the outfit was parked repairing the section house. We did not go right back to our grandparents. I think Dad wanted to watch over us. He had lost his wife six months before; he did not want to lose his sons."

The section house was adobe with an overhanging tin roof. It had three small rooms, each one housing a family. There was no heat except from the cookstoves. But Baker had compensating amenities even for two children who were not allowed to do much but recuperate. Although it was a little town, it was the intersection of two roads: the Arrowhead Trail heading northeast to Las Vegas and Route 127 heading north toward Death Valley. It had a level of economic activity not seen elsewhere in the region partially because of the construction of Hoover Dam (then known as Boulder Dam) in Nevada. As a result of the presence of construction and service workers, there were two competing service stations, two cafés, and even motel cabins.

The one thing I remember at Baker, besides its liveliness compared to Cronese Cove, was finding two hobos in a ditch just to the west of the T & T section house. I don't recall if it was when Lloyd and I were recuperating from pneumonia or the following summer when we rejoined our dad on the outfit. It was morning, and the hobos were making coffee in a rusty tin can over a little fire. That's all they had. The can was so bad I didn't know how they could heat anything in it let alone drink its contents. It was 1936, the very depth of the Depression. The Dust Bowl was still going on, driving desperate people into California, although their route was usually farther to the south. All of the hobos I met were men walking west. No women. They would stop at the station in Cronese and ask for food. My grandmother would give them some, but she would also give them a job to do to earn it. One guy came by who had worn out his heels to the point that they were at right angles to the soles. I didn't know how he could even walk, but when I asked him, he said he could walk three miles an hour. I have to wonder how many hobos ever made it to where they were going, or whether the desert got them.

Because of Baker's liveliness and the chance to be with the outfit again, Harry and Lloyd would have liked to stay longer, but with their returning strength, they had to return to Cronese Cove and school at Yermo. So with reluctance, their father drove them back to their grandparents.

Besides a few good teachers, Yermo provided the boys with good friends who came from families spread out over a large area, sometimes several miles distant from the school bus stop. It was the first time that the boys had steady friends.

> *There were my friends Steve Hoag and Paul Lathum. Paul's father was a tap dancer and tried to teach me to dance to no avail. There was Joyce Miller, the prettiest girl in school, and Rowena, the first flaming redhead I ever knew. Jenero Trujillo was a heavyset Mexican boy. I remember he made baloney sandwiches for school lunch. He bought the baloney and bread at a store in Yermo each day. Lloyd and I thought it was great and were envious because we had to carry our lunch and we felt poor. Jenero had several brothers and sisters, and they all rode the bus from Afton Canyon where his father worked for the Union Pacific. There was Barbara Williams, whose family had a farm in the Mojave, one of the few. We all rode the school bus together, and that was one long ride! The kids would razz each other but were pretty well behaved. I remember them kidding me because I was a pack rat—still am. Every day, I'd take all my schoolbooks home with me, every last one. The boys and girls all kidded me, "Are you going to read all those books tonight?" I wasn't going to, but I took them home anyway. I really don't know why. The other thing I always carried with me on the bus was marbles. In the schoolyard at Yermo, we played for keeps, and I was better than anyone. At the gas station in Cronese Cove, I had a big coffee-can full. If I took five marbles with me in the morning, I would return with ten or so at the end of the day.*

One personality characteristic that sustained Harry while also getting him into trouble was his constant curiosity. The summer after his mother died, he discovered he could see double by holding up a pencil close to one eye. Unfortunately, he mentioned his findings to his father, who misunderstood and thought there was something wrong with his vision. He took him to an eye doctor in San Fernando who fitted him for glasses that had no correction whatsoever. "My vision was really fine. I was just experimenting." He wore those useless glasses for a year out of loyalty to his father before putting them away permanently.

If I asked my father a question as to how something worked, he would give it a shot, but his explanations were generally superficial, just enough for the situation. For example, he had sulfuric acid, hydrochloric acid, and nitric acid in the tool car. He would put a few drops of nitric acid on a piece of wood to show me that it ate wood, but he didn't really know why. He knew what the different acids were used for on the outfit; for example, the sulfuric acid was used in lead acid batteries and the hydrochloric acid was used to pickle off wire before you soldered it. But that was the limit of his education. But later on, even after I had my master's degree and knew how and why things worked, he would still argue with me. He was pretty set in his ways.

Harry's curiosity extended far beyond the mechanical and chemical to the natural world; for example, he wanted to know where the honeybees in Cronese Cove came from. The bees would come to the fountain at the station for water and would get down into the three-eighths-inch steel pipe that rose up into the basin. When a person turned on the water to take a drink, out the bees would come in a buzzing frenzy. Sometimes, there were only two or three; at other times, there was a swarm. Harry wondered in what cave in the mountains behind the station their hive was located. Squinting into the sunlight, he traced them for hundreds of yards through the air and then tried to follow on foot over the rough terrain, always losing sight of them and having to return to the station to begin again. He did this repeatedly but failed to find the hive, much to his regret. However, in the process, he learned a great deal about the behavior of honeybees as well as the value of intense observation. Harry's curiosity and ingenuity is epitomized in the following story about his pitched battle with the fire ants:

I don't know much about ants, except that the big red ants that live on the Mojave Desert can give you a healthy sting when you step on them with your bare foot. When I was about nine, I went to war against the ants in our backyard in the cove. First, I caved in all the anthills. Of course, the next day in Antville, it was business as usual. So I found a shovel and dug deep, smashing all to be seen in blitzkrieg fashion. That worked better, but three days later, it was again as if nothing had happened. Then I got to thinking about how I might waylay them. This led to a crumbs-and-ambush technique that had no effect at all. When I asked for poison, the only kind available was some Flit that had to be rationed for killing flies, and wiser heads knew even ant poison was a losing game where we lived. Wearing shoes, the best strategy of course, would have avoided all the stings, but I didn't have a pair. So my war continued because being stung once or twice a day wreaked havoc with my playtime. I began watching my nemeses carefully everywhere I found them. After several days, I realized that they had trouble climbing glass windows. So I put an old Coleman lantern glass over an anthill as a barrier they couldn't climb over. The next morning, I discovered they had tunneled under it to continue their mischief. So I gave up. Then one day, it came to me out of nowhere. I found an empty Coke bottle in the dump, polished its top and throat, and buried it in a strategic place at the foot of the anthill. I leveled the sand exactly flush with the lip of the bottle. Then I watched. Sure enough, an ant on the run couldn't stop in time and wound up in the bottle and couldn't climb out. The next day, there were only a few ants left from the six or so nests I had ambushed. Soon, I had a dozen Coke bottles, each nearly full of red fire ants. I never completely won that war, but ant stings went down to once a week or so. My need, curiosity, and persistence combined toward a creative result. No way could I be as persistent as the ants were—a lesson in itself. But the lasting effect was that free-thinking had become a permanent habit.

When not plotting the demise of fire ants, there were chores to do, such as checking the water level on the tank, zeroing out the gas tanks, and—once—chasing a skunk that had been cornered by the dogs in among the fifty-five-gallon drums that were standing against the boxcars. Ethel remembers that nighttime incident clearly. Awakened by the commotion, Harry and Mary climbed "on top of the drums and used a long-handled sledgehammer to try to scare the poor skunk away" while Ethel and Lloyd held back the dogs. By the time it escaped, the whole area reeked. The next morning, May had to burn the children's pajamas. A more frequent chore was searching for and killing rattlers so customers wouldn't be threatened.

> *Sidewinders are around in the early morning when they are hunting kangaroo rats and chipmunks, which they swallow whole. They also will come out onto the road in the evening after dark, especially in the spring and fall when the road is warm. Each morning, I would go out with my grandmother and patrol the sandy areas near the gas station. My grandmother had a mesquite branch, thicker on one end, thinner where she held it. She was afraid of snakes, and once she found one, she beat that guy fifty times more than it took to kill him. She dispatched him thoroughly. My method was less dramatic: I dropped big rocks on them.*

For fun, the boys concocted their own games, praying for rain so they could ride their bikes down the hill behind the station on sand compacted enough with moisture so their bikes wouldn't sink. They liked to climb mountains, explore canyons, and look for Indian artifacts and pottery. "Also, Lloyd and I played catch on the gravel road to the station—played till it was very dark and we could not see the ball. We played chess. We played marbles. We had yoyos and tops, and most wonderful of all, I had a gyroscope that I loved. I played with it by the hour. If we got bored, we caught chipmunks, kangaroo rats, and turtles."

The best fun of all was kite-flying, for if blue sky, constant wind, and no trees make for perfect kite-flying, then Cronese valley had to be a contender for the spot on the globe with the ideal year-round conditions. The kites Harry and Lloyd flew in the valley for hours on end were not the kind bought in stores made of red or blue tissue paper with balsa-wood struts. The boys did not have money to purchase kites such as those, even if there had been a store that stocked them. Instead, Lloyd and Harry made the kites themselves using sticks broken off the greasewood bush for struts, which Harry remembers as a wood "pretty heavy for a kite but it would still fly." They also used old sheets of newspaper glued together for the airfoil to which they would tie a tail made of torn-up rags. Harry loved his creations, not so much for how they looked against the brilliant sky catching the sunlight or for how they danced on the wind but more out of awe that they flew at all. "I didn't know the word *aerodynamics*—I was too little—but I had an intuitive sense of how to make them fly." Harry's interest had begun when the Yermo elementary school held a contest to see who could design, build, and fly the best kite, with a prize for the winner.

That day, my first design would not fly; nothing I could do would get it to stay up, but I won the fourth-grade prize anyway because I was the only one to bring a kite to school. I won by default, but it still got me enthusiastic. I taught myself by trial and error to make a kite that could fly in a gale or in a light breeze, experimenting with any material I could get my hands on. For a gale, I would use a long tail on a small x-shaped kite. For light air, I would use a short tail, just enough to keep a large irregular pentagonal design oriented. I also experimented with other shapes, but I was never able to make a box-type. My kites were all flat. I never decorated them, but they did have fancy tails. To this day, I enjoy watching kids fly kites.

There was one more experience that got Harry excited: learning to steer his father's car even though he was only eight. It occurred one day when the outfit was parked in the vicinity of Cronese and Harry Sr. came to visit the boys. He took them hunting for Indian artifacts at a site in the valley where Elmo had found signs of an early Paiute campground. The day was a rare one: calm and cool, making it ideal for collecting.

A strong wind driving sand into one's eyes and abrading any exposed flesh was torture to be avoided if at all possible when collecting. But that day was perfect. My father promptly found an arrowhead, and so did Lloyd. They each found beads. We did not dig and screen in proper fashion. Neither did we keep any record of what we found or where. Civilized? Scientific? Not exactly, and not at all. But I was still empty-handed, and when it came time to go home, I was in a foul

mood. My father loaded us into his new 1936 Plymouth.
Perhaps to console me, he pulled me up into his lap. Only a
pair of ruts through the sand connected us with the highway.
But he let me steer all the way. Not once did we get stuck.
Getting out from being stuck was always a problem, and
sometimes dangerous. Proud? I was out of my gourd!

CHAPTER 5:
THE END OF THE LINE

The year 1938, when Harry turned ten and Lloyd eight, was one of strange occurrences, near catastrophes, and growing up before one's time, all precipitated by an unusual weather event. The great flood of 1938 began in late February and early March when two Pacific Coast storms dumped eight to ten inches of rain over Southern California and Nevada. There was also heavy snow in the mountains. The catastrophe was most severe in the Los Angeles and San Bernardino areas where more than one hundred people died and thousands of homes were damaged or destroyed.

Little is written about the flooding of the Mojave and Amargosa Rivers other than in the account books of the two railroads that were seriously affected: the Union Pacific and the T & T. For a while, the Mojave region was virtually cut off from the rest of Southern California because of roads and tracks being washed out. By far the heaviest damage was on the Union Pacific line in Afton Canyon where the Mojave River pinches down and cuts through a deep chasm. Three major trestle bridges were reduced to splinters, and the 542-foot tunnel in the canyon was weakened beyond repair.[53] Ties and debris were washed into the Mojave floodplain all the way to the junction of the Union Pacific and T & T at Crucero. Operations of both railroads were brought to a halt until repairs were made. The 1916 flood of the Mojave River had also done extensive damage, but at that time, the T & T trains had been able to keep going by diverting east from Crucero on the Salt Lake Route to Las Vegas, north on the rails of the Las Vegas and Tonopah Railroad to Beatty, and then south on T & T's own rails. But in 1938, that diversionary route was no longer available because a mile of track between Rasor and Crucero had been washed out by the flood. As for the stretch of track between Crucero and Ludlow, it had been "abandoned in place" by the T & T in 1933 and had so degraded in just five years that it was unsafe for the passage of trains even at slow speeds.

Silver Lake, the playa at the lowest elevation along the T & T, filled to a depth of several feet with an estimated length of twelve miles and a width of over two miles. So also did the Cronese lakes near where the Proctor gas station was located. Suddenly the cove had become lakefront property. Lloyd and Harry had never seen the playas that full, and neither had the adults.

> *During the flood, Lloyd and I walked out to take a look at the dam in Cronese that had been built before my grandparents had arrived by some families who hoped to farm the valley if they could store enough water. The families were long-gone, but the dam was still there, usually holding back nothing but wind. It had a rock foundation with an earthen overlay. For the first time in our lives, the basin behind the dam was full of water. We didn't see any danger, so we started to walk across the dam, but as we did so, it began to collapse. We took off running with me in front and Lloyd behind. Just as we got across, it washed out, with about fifteen to twenty feet of backed-up water going down the line. We could have gone along with it. I remember distinctly looking back and seeing Lloyd running hard and the earth behind him slowly beginning to give way. It scared us because neither of us could swim. We couldn't go back by the route we had come so we had to wait until the local flood from the dam break subsided to hike down to where the water was shallow enough to wade across.*

That was the second time in only a few months that Lloyd had nearly lost his life. The first occurred when he and Harry were riding in the backseat of an automobile owned and driven by a friend of their father's; Harry was on the left side, Lloyd on the right. In the style of the day, the automobile had rear doors that were hinged to the back instead of to the front. As the car reached a speed of about fifty miles an hour on the highway, Lloyd realized that the door on his side was not latched securely. He leaned forward and grabbed the handle to pull the door closed when suddenly it blew open, taking him with it. Harry Sr., who was sitting in the front passenger seat, swung around and caught Lloyd by the wrist just as he was flying out. "Had Father not been so strong and so fast, Lloyd would have been killed. It really scared us. An identical accident had killed the sister of one of our friends at Yermo Grammar School." It was only in the hindsight of adulthood that Harry came to realize how important Lloyd was to him, writing to him in 1990 at the time that Lloyd was dying of cancer that he was "the best brother I ever had or even could have." Two of his memories he shared in that letter were crossing the collapsing dam and the "time the old man caught your arm as you were flying out the rear car door after you opened it to close it right at high speed." Harry ended that last letter to Lloyd by writing, "I have spent a lifetime running away from death I think. So I didn't call, as I should have. Again I am sorry. My brother taught me more than he knows. I am the better for it—by a lot."

As summer came on, the playas remained full. Some took upward of a year or two to return to their normally desiccated states, so the exploration opportunities for Harry and Lloyd were of the once-in-a-lifetime variety. The playas were not only overflowing with water but also alive with strange ephemeral creatures that only appeared during extraordinarily wet conditions. One day, the boys went to Cronese Lake, took off their shoes, rolled up their pants, and waded far out, following the reflection of the sun on the water, straight as a die. Their quarry was a pinkish aquatic creature, probably a form of fairy shrimp. "It swims rather gracefully in the water. During dry periods, its eggs are like a hermetic ball down in the silt at the bottom of the lake. Its eggs survive periods of drought as long as twenty to thirty years until the next big storm. Then they hatch out in a day." The problem for the boys was that they got so involved in catching shrimp they lost track of time and distance; when they turned around and followed their shadows back, their calculations as to where they had left their belongings were way off. "We could not find our shoes for the longest time. Lloyd and I laughed about that for years."

Word spread rapidly far beyond the Mojave Desert that the playas were sparkling with miles of water, bringing boaters from the Los Angeles area to race on Silver Lake for the sheer novelty of it. No one in the desert owned a boat, and most had never seen a race, so it was a big draw when it was announced that boating clubs were going to host sanctioned races with demonstrations of water-skiing. People drove from up and down the railroad line to watch this unique event.

Talk about excitement! Silt and clay usually made up the dry surface of Silver Lake. Usually whirlwinds stirred up fine dust funnels that dispersed high in the air. And suddenly there were outboard motorboats speeding across the surface! They were one-man open boats with small outboard motors. There were two classes separated by size of engine. The bigger boats were not really that much faster. The guy who won the little-boat race had a boat made of cloth. He horned in on the big-boat race, and he came within inches of beating the big-boat winner. For us desert kids for whom water was prized because it was scarce, to see it in abundance and used for sport was a rare experience. To underscore just how vast the contrast was between wet and dry conditions, during World War II, an airbase for pilot training was built on Silver Lake. Just after the start of World War II, a B-17 got lost at night. We were in Death Valley Junction at the time, and I remember hearing it come overhead going north and a little while later fly over again going south. The pilot, who was lost, contacted the radio operator at Silver Lake, which was then being used as an emergency airstrip. The operator, who was nicknamed Fog, turned on the runway lights, and the plane landed safely, taking off early the next morning. By the time we arrived, all we saw were its tracks in the sunbaked crust.

The other pastime, reaching an apex each summer, was baseball. Harry remembers it as "a community addiction." At over 120 degrees in the shade in the summer, it also took an unusual set of survival skills to play. "No one ever slid into second! The ground was like 160 to 180 degrees. I know because I measured those temperatures many times about ten years later when I was working at the mines using the thermometer for the diesels that had a significantly higher degree range than a normal thermometer. When I was older and played on a team, I played first base and wore two layers of wool socks in shoes with thick soles to keep from burning my feet." In 1938, at the famous Fourth of July celebration in Shoshone, which according to custom lasted three days, the Death Valley Giants played the Shoshone Indians—an apt team name because at least half the players were Native American. The Indians won by a wide margin.

After the game, there was a greased pole competition that I took part in. One of my Indian friends, I think it was either Bud Clemens or George Ross, was systematically climbing the pole. His strategy was simply to clean the pole an inch or two at a time, making several attempts. On top was a five-dollar bill, which was about a hundred dollars in today's money. Townfolk were gathered all around as my friend prepared for one more, hopefully last, try. As he wiped his hands for a victorious climb, one of the Death Valley Giants, still in baseball gear, leaped at the pole and—using his strong legs in clean trousers for traction and gripping with his big clean hands—easily won the prize. To say the least, the euphoria the Shoshone Indians had experienced on the diamond sort of evaporated. But the event I remember most vividly came later in the evening. One of the Giants was something of a bully who didn't take losing games lightly. Pitchers made all the difference on the sand lot, and only Shoshone had a good one. After a few drinks, the bully challenged the Shoshone pitcher, an Indian, to a fight outside. Unlike his mastery on the mound, where he fanned the bully three times, the pitcher became defensive, parried blow after blow for some minutes without punching back. He used both arms folded with fists down. By ducking his head down, he gave the bully a tough and bony target. A crowd gathered around, as crowds do, cheering on the pitcher. Then suddenly, out of nowhere, it came. Like a rifle shot, heard as well as seen, the bully's jaw was snapped back and to the side from a fist as fast as a fastball. He fell straight backward in a heap. As the pitcher's family rejoiced in their second victory in one day, the bully finally came to his senses. Spitting out teeth, he immediately started yelling, "Brownie, Brownie!" Will Brown, the constable, was nowhere to be found. Brownie later said he thought justice was served. I thought so too.

Back in Cronese Cove, the boys were also exposed to other, older activities, the teacher being John Hilton, the painter and writer who occasionally stopped at the gas station to visit their grandfather. One day, he dropped by unannounced, this time not to ask Elmo to help him scout out a gemstone-hunting itinerary for *Desert Magazine* but to see if anyone wanted to accompany him up to the top of the hill on which the water tank was located to paint a canvas of the Devil's Playground, the region that stretched from Cronese all the way to the Kelso Dunes. Elmo had written a poem about the Playground called "The Mojave Sink" that was a favorite among customers at the gas station. In it, the devil asks God if he has land to spare to be used for a hell. God obliges by giving him the sink, an area so poor God doubts it will suffice even for the devil's purposes. Delighted, the devil calls it his playground and populates it with tarantulas, scorpions, and snakes. He puts thorns on the foliage and horns on the toads. He also lures prospectors to the playground, and they get lost in the waste and die of thirst, cluttering the ground with their bones. The boys had memorized the poem (to this day, Harry can recite it), but they had never heard of Hilton, nor could they understand why he would want to paint a picture of the Devil's Playground. What captivated them was that Hilton was as good a tall-tale spinner as their grandfather.

Lloyd, Mary, and I were spellbound by the stories they swapped that day. I had heard my grandfather's versions countless times, but now they were all spruced up to match those John was telling. But John had the more serious business of painting the Devil's Playground to attend to. He invited Mary to go, but Lloyd and I tagged along. So off we went with easel, paints, and a canteen. About halfway through the paint job, Mary sent Lloyd and me on a lengthy errand. Now I was the type of kid who never missed a thing if I could possibly help it, and John was the most fascinating man I had ever encountered. He even explained his techniques to us. He used a pallet knife! Glory be! So run we did to do the errand and return in a hurry. And what did we discover? Mary and John hugging and kissing passionately! Their surprise was matched only by Mary's embarrassment. John was of a different stock. He laughed. The painting? It hung on the station wall for a year or so, until Mary left Cronese. It hung in her own home for the rest of her life. Maybe there was something to the legend of the Devil's Playground after all.[54]

Meanwhile, repair work progressed on the T & T, including rebuilding the weakened wooden water tank at Rasor, which was crucial to the operation of the steam engines because it was the only tank at the southern end of the line. Harry tried to pitch in with flood repairs. Mounds of sand had been deposited by the water on the upstream side of one of the bridges near Crucero. Thinking that if he dug a two-foot wide channel through the sand, the bridge would not wash out again, Harry borrowed a shovel that was not being used and immediately set to work, digging purposefully for several hours. But when he returned a few weeks later, all signs of his efforts were gone, the wind having filled up the channel and shifted the mound of sand to the other side of the bridge; the only thing that came of Harry's labor was a greater appreciation of the indomitable power of wind, sand, and water—the forces against which his father had to struggle. "The damage from the flood took a long time to fix. Finally, the repairs to the T & T came to an end with a slow and careful transit of a train over the newly built railbed. I can still recall the triumphant look on Mickey Devine's face from the engineer's seat as he rolled by at about one mile per hour."

But there really wasn't any reason for triumph. At the time of the storms, the T & T was already in dire financial shape, so the flood was its death blow. As soon as repairs were finished, fifteen to twenty men had to be laid off. It was an early lesson for Harry in placing an accurate value on human beings because he was enamored with a well-built young worker who he thought resembled the nationally renowned bodybuilder Charles Atlas. "He had big muscles and a big sense of humor. Myself being not yet five feet tall and as scrawny as they come, I admired him." But when it came time for layoffs, only a thin man in his fifties was kept on. Harry was incredulous and challenged his father's judgment, asking why he had made that choice. "He was always working when the others took time off," replied Harry Sr., matter-of-factly. Years later, when Harry worked at Titanium Metals Corporation of America and was the only one retained in a big layoff because he worked hard and could get to the bottom of things, he recalled my father's words. "They also served me well when I was in a position to hire, mentor, and occasionally fire someone."

Later, in 1938, Harry Sr., then forty-two, married a woman named Audrey Stocko, who was in her early twenties. For a very brief time, Harry and Lloyd lived with them in Baker instead of with their grandparents. Unfortunately, that union ended abruptly.

The rest of the family made fun of him behind his back, like he was too old for a young beauty. But I was there when it all came apart and I knew the inside story. Audrey tried hard to be a good stepmother. Once, a kid from Baker wanted Lloyd and me to go see an old pioneer settlement that was about an hour away by bike. She helped us plan it and fixed us the best picnic lunch I'd ever had. I guess I remember it because I wasn't used to that kind of attention. They broke up because she took off to Los Angeles with money my father had given her to buy clothes for Lloyd and me but she used it for dope instead. That was what really ended their union.

Perhaps to escape the magnitude of a mile of railroad washed away, or perhaps being frustrated at being single again, my father loaded us into the car one Saturday evening when the outfit was working at Rasor. There was a bar in Baker, and that was our destination. I remember nothing about the evening until after the bar closed. He was drunk as a skunk but could still walk. He drove slowly, unlike so many drunk males who drive without thought or foresight. That was until at about ten miles from Baker; he turned off onto the dusty ruts passing for a road leading to Rasor. Then he stopped the car, got out, and climbed into the backseat. Before he went to sleep, he said to me, "Drive us home." Never did I have such responsibility before. I was only ten. Too excited to be scared, I realized I probably could. After all, I knew how the gear shifting went. And the clutch, while different, followed the same principle as the one on the railroad motorcar—the one that went on the tracks that I had driven many times with the outfit. The motorcar throttle was of the hand variety, but it too followed the same basic principle as the car throttle. Easy does it. I already knew how to steer, and I was just big enough to see the road ahead. Lloyd got into the front seat with me, obviously anxious about what was to come. My only real worry was the sand dune I would have to traverse at Rasor. I approached the sand dune at the same speed that Father used. And made it we did; I had never seen Lloyd so happy about reaching home. Our forward motion never faltered. We had to wake

*up the drunk in the backseat who missed all the drama. The
aftermath? There was none—neither the next day or any day
thereafter. My father was slow with compliments. "Pretty
good" was about as superlative as he ever got.*

That was also the summer that Harry and Lloyd began to learn how
to shoot and hunt, although they had accompanied their father on hunts
almost as soon as they could walk. With the time to practice, there not
being much else to do, and having miles and miles of emptiness as a target
range, the boys became excellent shots, hunting badger, rabbits, ducks,
deer, and quail. When they got the chance, they went with their father into
the mountains to hunt bighorn sheep, the most majestic of animals and the
one that took the most hunting skill because of its elusiveness. He taught
them about how guns worked and how they should be taken care of. Most
of all he stressed safety.

*The .22 rifle that I first shot had not been used in a long time
and wasn't any good for shooting anymore. It was full of pits
in the barrel, and the grooves were destroyed. Father cleaned
it up and put a beer can on a post. He said, "Now draw a
bead on that and pull the trigger real slow." I hit it dead
center. He was astonished. He told me I wasn't supposed to
be able to do that. He showed me that the bullet had gone
through the can sideways because the pits in the rifle had
destroyed the grooves. Not long after, he bought me a single-
shot .22 with an adjustable scope. Lloyd and I competed in
target practice with my father. Once when we were parked
at Riggs siding, Father and I had a shooting match using tin
cans. The rule was that I could use the scope and he was to
use only the iron sights, but just as he was about to beat me,
I caught him cheating by using the scope. He erupted into
laughter. Since he missed, he called it a draw. He was easy
to forgive; cheating was not his way of doing things. I now
think his real purpose was to teach me to be on the lookout
at all times for chicanery.*

Although he rarely praised them, Harry Sr. was proud of his sons'
abilities and was not above showing them off when an opportunity arose.

Such was the case when a man joined the outfit who had a habit of bragging about his hunting prowess. Longing to show him up a little and aware that his eleven-year-old son already had a fair amount of skill, Harry Sr. took Harry Jr. hunting with them, traveling via the motorcar to a little known and very remote waterhole that attracted waterfowl in the early spring after the winter rains. After they had hiked down the canyon and had hidden in the tall grasses that surrounded the waterhole, Harry's father whispered to him to do his best. That day, with his 410 repeating shotgun, he got one bird on the water and six in the air, while the man with his twelve-gauge got only one. From then on, Harry had a reputation as a hunter and a little more standing in his father's eyes.

> *I was never the crack shot that my father was, but I was plenty good enough. I didn't give up hunting until my second marriage many years later. Kris was opposed to guns, and I came around to her way of thinking. Lloyd kept hunting until one day he was out before dawn with three guys who always hunted together. One of the guys accidentally killed one of the others. That was it for Lloyd. My father always said to us in regard to gun safety that we must never shoot at the shaking of the leaves or at something that you think is there. You had to be absolutely sure. "Keep the barrel pointed up, always."*
> *My father's words still ring in my ear.*

At the end of 1938, the Pacific Coast Borax Company filed an application with the Interstate Commerce Commission to cease operations of the T & T. David Myrick writes in *Railroads of Nevada and Eastern California Vol. II* that a proposal was made to leave the track in place and to maintain the equipment in good order so that operations could be resumed should conditions warrant. The maintenance expense was not expected to be high because the 1939 roster of T & T equipment listed only four locomotives, the Goose, twenty-nine freight cars, and four passenger cars.[55]

That Christmas at the cove, a greasewood Christmas tree was set up in the station as usual, but that was the only sign of holiday spirit. The Great Depression was ongoing, and the news from Europe was growing ominous. However, the big problem was the awareness that the T & T's days were numbered and that Harry Sr. might be facing unemployment. It was bittersweet for Harry Jr. as well because of two related incidents: one bad, one good. The first involved his playing the part of a wise man in the school play in Yermo. Instead of going barefoot (as he and Lloyd usually did unless it was extremely cold), he was supposed to bring shoes to the performance to wear with the gold crown and robe. He had two white pairs at the station, but one no longer fit. "By accident, I brought the pair that was way too small. So that day, standing in front of everyone, I did the part barefoot, but my teacher was embarrassed and I was embarrassed too. I guess I looked poor." He was still smarting from that event when a few days later, his father, needing a drink, took the boys to a beer hall in Halloran Springs, about fifteen miles east of Baker at an elevation of over three thousand feet. It was a clear, crystalline night—a typical desert night glittering from horizon to horizon with stars undimmed by city lights. Usually, the boys waited in the car dozing under blankets when their father went drinking, but this time, the night was cold, so they climbed out of the car and accompanied him inside. The beer hall was warm and dark with a haze of cigarette smoke around the dim lights, and the men hunkered at the bar were not in the Christmas mood—if anyone was.

> At about 11:00 or 12:00 at night, Father mentioned to the men at the bar that we could sing, and someone said, "Well, let's hear it." So that got me and Lloyd started. My brother and I stood up and sang, "We Three Kings," the song we had done in the school play, to an audience of mostly prospectors, highway people, and men down on their luck. We sang all the verses a cappella and then sang them again. Got a big hand. Some said, "Bravo." I doubt they were wildly enthusiastic, but the performance was important to me as was singing with Lloyd. This time, I wasn't embarrassed as I had been in Yermo. When we were done, Father finished his last drink and we headed out into the night and returned to the outfit.

As the new year of 1939 arrived, protests delayed closure of the T & T. Most of the protestors were the owners of talc mines who were worried about shipping costs increasing substantially if they were forced to use trucks. Finally, on June 14, 1940, the line came to an end. Because it was "abandoned in place," Harry Sr. continued to work, making regular inspections, doing repairs, and pumping water into the wooden tanks at the sidings because if they were allowed to dry out, they would shrink in the desiccating air and become useless. It was all part of keeping the line minimally useable at least by slow trains. But these tasks did not require Harry Sr. to live in the red caboose as he had done since the early 1920s. He rented a house in Death Valley Junction, married a woman named Grace, and brought Harry and Lloyd to live with them. Their years living with their grandparents, sleeping in the boxcar on the hill behind the gas station, were over. "That marriage worked well, at least at the beginning. Unfortunately, Grace was an alcoholic who got worse over time. She died of cirrhosis of the liver after she and my father opened the motel and café in Tecopa after the war. By then, I was pretty much grown. But for three or four years in Death Valley Junction, Long Beach, and Tecopa, she was a halfway decent stepmother."

Harry had just turned twelve and was entering seventh grade. Lloyd was ten and entering fifth. They liked being able to ride bikes to school—no more hour-and-a-half-long trips to Yermo on a school bus prone to overheating. They also liked the presence of friends with whom they could play. There were even enough boys to start a club with Tony Castillo as president. "He was a natural leader, and we were best friends, but when it came to building a clubhouse or a soapbox racer, he turned to me because I was the one who knew how to make things work." Once Harry and Tony got a job together cleaning out the large swimming pool. "It was sixty feet long, and the wooden walls would get moss on them, so we had to drain it, scrub it down, and refill it. The water came from a well that had an electric pump run from power from the mill. It was in that pool that Lloyd and I learned to swim. No one taught us." Besides the pool, there were all sorts of peculiar amenities in Death Valley Junction that were attractive to children. For one, there was the towering mill tailings dump that was one of their favorite playgrounds. "It had a nice slope, about thirty-five to forty feet high, and in 1941, Tony Castillo and I raced our winning soapbox derby racer on it, beating out my brother, Lloyd, and our mutual friend Duffy Chisholm whose father also worked for the railroad." They also occasionally got into trouble once starting a fire by accident, an incident none of the boys owned up to.

> The water used to cool the big diesels at the mill came to
> the surface for a half mile or so past the mill, flowing hot
> at the start and then cooling down. It always had some
> lubricating oil floating on it. One of our pastimes was to
> rework old clothespins, notching them such that the spring

*became the trigger that snapped into a gap between pieces
of wood that served as a barrel. We loaded matches in them
with the match head inward. We could launch match heads
as flaming missiles that would burn for a second or two
simply by pulling the trigger. But this one time, we were
careless. The grass along the bank started burning, and the
fire picked up speed and approached the dump that was just
outside town. By then, it had jumped to the oil slick on the
water. Old ties and old boxes in the town dump also started
burning. Fortunately, the men from the mill saw the fire
and put it out and there was no real damage. But fires were
serious in the desert. Any fire in a house meant the house was
gone because the wood was always tinder-dry, the humidity
was in the single-digits, and there was often a wind. There
were no fire departments and usually no hydrants, although
in Death Valley Junction, there was one up near the civic
center, but there wasn't enough hose to reach anything but
the civic center itself. How the dump fire started was never
discovered because no one ever squealed.*

There were also the normal temptations for boys on the verge of
adulthood; for example, learning how to smoke, sneaking cigarettes from
their father, being found out, and discovering they didn't like to smoke
anyway. There were also girls—strange and fascinating creatures.

*In terms of the opposite sex, Annette Gil was the first beacon.
A brown-eyed beauty, at least to me. It happened for three
glorious days in Shoshone at Charlie Brown's famous Fourth
of July celebration that was attended by just about everyone
up and down the line. No sex involved. What mattered was
being together. She brought awareness of my potential in a
direction I had never felt before and only rarely over some
decades afterward. Being eleven years old and in love for the
first time is a common enough event—except when it happens
for the first time. I'm not sure if Annette had been smitten
before. What I am sure of is that she was miles ahead of me in
maturity, which did us in. By the age of twelve, we still knew
each other, but she was no longer infatuated. I had a much*

harder time shaking it loose. My infatuation hung on literally for years while Annette went artfully on with her life. I didn't know it at the time, but Annette became a sort of standard by which I eventually measured subsequent relationships.

Then came the morning of December 7, 1941, which brought upheaval into everyone's life. That Sunday, the Rosenbergs were on their way to China Ranch near Tecopa, one of the few places in the region that was an oasis with palm trees and sufficient water to grow crops. "Our 1939 Dodge had a radio, but you could only get a signal early in the morning or in the evening. The rest of the time, we were kind of cut off from world news. That early morning, we were headed for Bill Greer's place at China Ranch, which is just above the Amargosa Canyon where my father had done so much repair work over the years. Dad turned the radio on, and it was getting a good signal. That was when we heard the announcement come over about the Japanese attack on Pearl Harbor. That changed everything." Subsequently, the War Department requisitioned the T & T line, and in July 18, 1942, Sharp and Fellows, a railroad contractor, began tearing up the rails, starting from Beatty and heading south. "Before the demolition began, I remember going with my father to count the rails all the way from Ludlow to Beatty. It was the last time." Harry was told by his father that the rails were to be shipped to Egypt to be used to build a rail line to help the Allies fight the Germans under the command of General Rommel. Some of the locomotives were scrapped; others were sold, with one ending up at to the San Bernardino Air Base. The pine railroad ties were left lying by the thousands on the sand and were available to anyone who needed lumber, which in the Mojave Desert was just about everyone.[56]

In the summer of 1942, Harry Sr. worked for a while for Sharp and Fellows building a railroad spur in Amarillo, Texas. Then that September, he, Grace, and the boys moved to Long Beach where he got a job with the Craig Shipyard as a carpenter working on the construction of minesweepers for the US Navy. Unlike other naval vessels, minesweepers had to be built of wood to prevent the mines from sensing magnetically the presence of a metal hull and detonating automatically. Therefore, master carpenters, such as Harry Sr., were in high demand. But before the Rosenbergs left for the city and all that entailed—crowds, traffic, large schools, and painful memories of Nona's death—Harry and his father went to hunt bighorn sheep one last time.

It was in the Funeral Mountains that form the northeast wall of Death Valley. There are no springs there. It's pretty barren. However, on the eastern side there is a tank, which is a rocky declination that holds what little rainwater there is. The water tastes bad, but it won't hurt you. It's called Scranton Tank and is at the foot of a vertical cliff. Only the mountain sheep have the ability to climb down that sheer wall to drink from the tank. The Indians often hunted them there and had left a blind built from rocks so the sheep couldn't see them. On this particular day, a ram bighorn sheep was high up on a ledge. My father and I hunched down and took bead with our 30 ought 6s. When my bullet hit him, the ram flinched and began to run; after my father shot, he stopped for a half-second before he pitched off into thin air, crashed down hard near the tank, and then rolled. He looked so majestic in death. I asked myself, What am I doing? *Years later, when I was a miner at the Noonday Mine, I went back there with a friend and found the old skull with my bullet hole through the horn. My father and I had cut off the head to lighten the load back to the car.*

Fortunately, the move to Long Beach was not as traumatic as it had been when Harry was only six and his mother had been dying, although academically it was hard. Harry wrote to his grandparents in Cronese in May 1943 that he and Lloyd were in junior high school "and the going is pretty tough for me, especially in algebra, which is all Greek to me." He quickly made friends with a boy named Keithley Smith, who invited him and Lloyd to join the Boy Scouts, the first organization to which they had ever belonged and which gave them a sense of direction and purpose while living in Long Beach. Troop #49 met weekly at Eastside Christian Church where Phil Smith (no relation to Keithley) was scoutmaster and Jed Crane was junior assistant scoutmaster. Daniel Boone completed a quartet of close friends. They went swimming in the Pacific and hiked in the San Bernardino Mountains covered with thick forests of oaks, cedars, and pines. While being in the wilderness was not a novelty for Lloyd and Harry, camping amid towering Ponderosa pines whispering in the wind at 6,500 feet elevation was. Back in Long Beach, the boys worked on earning merit badges as well as collecting paper and cardboard for the war effort.

Keithley was smart as well as mechanically and electrically skilled. He got both Harry and Lloyd interested in building radio sets.

> *At Wilson High School we were both in an electrical class. We made crystal radio sets and worked on joint projects. In the attic of our house, I found wondrous artifacts from the time that my grandfather lived there, including an Edison cylinder player and an early battery-driven radio that still worked. There was even a jar of canned blackberries up there. I spent hours figuring out how the player and radio worked with Keithley's help. He was skilled with a soldering iron and had a corner of his father's garage where he kept his things. My brother stayed interested and became a proficient ham radio operator. I was proud of him for that. But I went on to other projects. I wanted to build the radio sets, but I wasn't interested in operating them or in learning the code beyond the merit badge level. It was no surprise that Keithley eventually went to college and became an electrical engineer. I had always thought I was going to be an engineer too—the kind that drove the choo-choo train. Now I started thinking about the other kind. Meanwhile, being in need of money, I delivered newspapers and got a part-time job on Saturdays at Barker Brothers, a furniture store in downtown Long Beach to which I rode my bike.*

Harry also played tennis and ran track but was lackluster in both. His first year in Long Beach when he was fourteen years old, he had competed in a track meet for Franklin Junior High School about which he wrote his grandparents that he "kind of saved their face" because he was the only one who placed, coming in second in high jumping by leaping five feet two inches. In high school, he qualified for the Southern California divisional track meet because another boy, whom he'd beaten only once, dropped out of the 880 and decided to run the mile instead. Even so, Harry did not go, figuring he'd lose. His main competitive sport was much more sedentary— chess. He and Lloyd started a chess club at Wilson High School that held regular meetings and had a tournament with a rival school.

My father had taught us when we were little boys. He had learned the game from a man named Judge Rolles who owned a store and served as the Tecopa postmaster in the early 1920s. It was a good way to pass the time in the desert. We'd play it at night in the caboose by the light of the kerosene lamp. It wasn't until I was about fourteen years old that I became good enough to beat my father. The day I first realized what his strategy was and made the correct countermove, he roared with laughter. Lloyd became nearly as good as me. At Long Beach, I taught at least a dozen kids how to play.

As to the events of the war, other than radio broadcasts and black-and-white newsreels at the Saturday movie matinees showing the battles in which American troops were engaged, Harry didn't know much about what was happening except that Long Beach was heavily involved in shipbuilding for the US Navy with sailors and workers everywhere. Also oil was being pumped out of the ground as fast as possible with 126 new wells drilled in the harbor in 1943 alone. The Great Depression was a thing of the past.

I didn't understand about what was going on in World War II—the politics, the economy, the history, the trends. I was naive and narrow in my thinking. I remember listening to the Richford Reporter on the radio every night. My friend Danny Boone read Freud and Karl Marx and tried to explain them to me. I was interested, but I found them scary, especially his tales of the Socialist Norman Thomas. I was fifteen years old and didn't have a much clearer idea of how the world worked than I had possessed back in the Mojave Desert. My only hands-on experience with the war effort, other than collecting cardboard with the Boy Scouts, was during the summer of 1944 when I worked at Douglas Aircraft on the B-17 model G installing rubber gas tanks on the wings.

In 1945, after the war ended, the Rosenbergs returned to Tecopa where Harry Sr. had purchased 120 acres of land from Charlie Brown on which to build a motel and café. With the help of Jimmy Gil, Annette's father, and Joe Fisher, a carpenter friend at the shipyard, the Rosenbergs started building in December 1945 using the T & T's abandoned railroad ties for lumber.[57]

> *I drove my pickup truck down through the badlands to China Ranch and then kept going, dropping down into the Amargosa Canyon itself following the route of the old gypsum spur. At the bottom on the abandoned railroad bed, there were many ties lying there for the taking—and take them everyone did, not just me. I think half of the buildings newly erected up and down the Amargosa were built of those pine ties in the late 1940s and early 1950s. Most were in good shape. Call it a postmortem gift of the T & T. The only other things needed for construction of the motel were stucco, lean-mix cement, and a lot of sweat. There still wasn't any electric power in the area.*

The motel and café run by Grace opened for business five months later in May 1946. "It was never a great motel. Nor was the café anything special. They were okay by 1940s standards, which means pretty basic. But neither was there any competition around, so they did okay." The hope was that with the war over, the hot springs would attract tourists and people with health problems because the hot mineralized water was considered curative. With that goal in mind, Harry Sr. dug and enlarged a spring of his own and named the motel the Tecopa Hot Springs Resort, giving an upscale name to a rustic operation. Hidden by tulles that grew thickly around the edges, the mineral-rich hot springs had been highly esteemed first by the Shoshone and Paiute, and later on by the miners in the region who came to soak away their pain. Harry remembers that his hot spring was his father's pride and joy. "It was the reason his clientele kept coming back and why he bought the place in the first place. Temperature was 109 degrees right out of the ground, but the flow rate wasn't high enough to keep the pool anywhere near that, more like 100 to 102 degrees Fahrenheit maybe."

To help make ends meet, Harry Sr. served as the town barber and also became the constable for Tecopa, which meant the jail—a small brick building with two cells—was his responsibility. "The Tecopa jail was no place to be: a cage of iron bars out in the open; no sanitary facility; not even a decent bunk. Doubling its capacity came later. My father had a big railroad car lock on the door. Fortunately, it was never occupied for long, mostly just long enough to cool off a temper or sober up." The bars on the windows were narrow enough to keep a man in but not so narrow they could keep wine bottles out. George Ross recalls that there were more wine bottles below the jailhouse windows than any other single place in town, drunkenness at the Snake Room being the chief reason for arrests. According to Ross, once a drunken husband and wife got into a heated argument in the Snake Room, leading to the husband's arrest and incarceration in the jail. Harry Sr. locked the front door of the building but not the cell door itself, the upshot being that the man escaped out the attic vent, headed straight back to the Snake Room, and resumed the argument before being apprehended by Harry Sr. a second time.[58]

If an incident was more serious than drunkenness at the Snake Room, Harry Sr. turned for help to a man with the moniker the "Black Swede," who impressed Harry Jr. as "quite another sort of man. Trouble often came his way because he knew how to handle it. He knew his way around in fast company. When a warrant came in for a real baddie on the lam from the big-city cops or the FBI, my father would deputize the Black Swede. Together they made many an arrest."

Harry's senior year was completed at Death Valley Junction High School located in the old T & T depot alongside the roadbed. The commute from Tecopa was thirty-eight miles one way and took about an hour. The school had only thirteen students who were bused in from all over the region, including Furnace Creek, Shoshone, Pahrump, and Tecopa. It was so small, the kids and teachers were on a first-name basis. There were no classes in science or mathematics classes beyond the basic level, and the only language offered (other than English) was Latin. Even so, the two teachers brought to their students an unusual knowledge of a larger world. Valeria "Val" Dotterer was the principal and also taught typing, Latin, history, home economics, and basic math. A graduate of Oregon State University, she had lived in Hawaii prior to the war writing a food column for a local newspaper; in fact, she was in her Waikiki beach house just below Diamond Head on the morning of December 7 when she and her roommate were awakened by someone who had heard voices of US Army pilots coming over the radio. Shocked by what happened, immediately after the attack on Pearl Harbor, she helped set up a makeshift cafeteria in Honolulu for people who were working around the clock. Later on, she joined the Women's Air Raid Defense (WARD) group under the Seventh Fighter Command and was authorized to wear captain's bars on her uniform. WARD assignments included handling the plotting boards for tracking the location of planes and ships and also staffing the air defense centers. Dotterer's WARD service ended in 1943, and sometime thereafter, she got married, moved to California, and began to teach. Moving from the lushness of the Hawaiian Islands to the desiccation of the Mojave Desert, she tried to bring a touch of the tropics to Death Valley Junction High School by setting aside a small room for the girls that she named the Kane Kapu room, which meant no men allowed. From Val, Harry learned to type, finding it a useful skill in the years ahead, but he didn't do as well in learning Latin because of his basic distaste for the routine drilling that mastery of a language requires.[59]

Music and English were taught by another unusual woman named Helen Ogston who taught three days a week.

More than anyone else until then, Helen opened my eyes and made me feel worthy. She went out of her way to help me launch my life. How vivid my first memory of her! Upon first encounter, she had seemed to be just another schoolteacher, at thirty years my senior. Helen played beautifully on the piano, and part of our class time was to be spent singing. I don't remember the first song we sang as a class of maybe ten of the thirteen kids enrolled in all four grades. I was standing to the right of the piano and could just make out the wrinkles forming on Helen's forehead and around her eyes. Nevertheless, her aging fingers could still dance across the keyboard. She is really old, *I thought to myself. After some formalities about the music, we all labored through it. Then came the thunderbolt, for me anyway. As soon as the singing stopped, Helen turned to me and said enthusiastically:* "You can sing!" *In that instant, I fell in love with a worldly woman almost old enough to be my grandmother. I was all of seventeen, but no woman had ever issued such a heartfelt compliment to me before. I was on air for a week! I barely remember another thing she did in class for that whole semester. But she came into my inner life as a permanent alter ego. A hang-up about women laid on by my mother just days before she died had created a tough veneer, a thick skin, between me and other females, especially pretty ones.*

That became particularly acute as I passed through puberty. Yes, my aunts, Mary and Ethel, taught me that females could care for me—watch out for me—love me. And there was my crush on Annette Gil. But Helen was different. She poked through my shell as no one ever had before and began to repair my psyche. It was decades before I developed the insight to know just how important the encounter really was.

Helen was married to Edward E. "Ted" Ogston, the chief park ranger for the US Forest Service, who had come to the desert after being stationed for many years in Alaska and at Yellowstone.[60] Helen was urbane and smart and had connections with the larger world. No matter where her husband was stationed, she took her piano with her. She was a writer and was working on a book that was published in 1948 titled *Piney Bear* about a bear cub in Yellowstone. Somehow, in her travels, she had become a friend of George Putnam, the grandson of the founder of the New York–based publisher G. P. Putnam's Sons. Once when he was vacationing in the area, he was invited by Helen to speak to her students. Then sixty years old, Putnam had just published a book titled *Death Valley and Its Country* and was writing a novel about the 49ers titled *Hickory Shirt*. Putnam was the epitome of the man-of-the-world. He had led expeditions to the Arctic and Greenland for the American Museum of Natural History before entering the family business where he was responsible for the publication of Charles Lindbergh's autobiography. But his greatest claim to fame was helping to build the reputation of Amelia Earhart, whom he married in 1931. Not long after she was declared dead in 1939, he moved to California.[61]

That afternoon in Death Valley Junction, Putnam spun tale after tale about Amelia Earhart, whom Helen also knew. That alone left an indelible impression on all of us. It was an eye-opener. To whom do I give credit? George for his willingness to take time out on vacation to visit an old friend in the desert or Helen, who had the magnetism to induce him to spend an afternoon with us desert kids instead of sightseeing. It was both of course. It was the high point of my time at Death Valley Junction High School, and it stuck with me for the rest of my life.

On May 23, 1946, Harry graduated from high school, one of only two seniors, the other being Betty Ford from Pahrump. He was valedictorian, and by default, Betty was salutatorian. Everyone attended the ceremony held at Corkill Hall at which Harry gave a speech titled "My Education." In fact, a few weeks earlier, everyone in the school had attended the senior prom held at the luxurious Furnace Creek Inn in Death Valley; had they not all come, Harry and Betty would have been stuck dancing with each other all evening. In his yearbook (actually a newsletter only four pages in length), of which he was the editor, he listed his high school activities as track, chess, Spanish Club, and slide-rule club, an impressive list that must have included his activities at Wilson High School in Long Beach. One of the snapshots in the yearbook shows him standing on top of Mushroom Rock, an appropriately named basalt outcropping in Death Valley.

Harry had no idea what to do after graduation. That fall, he went to Long Beach City College for one semester, having been encouraged to do so by Helen Ogston, but he was not prepared either scholastically or emotionally. "I wanted to follow my friend Keithley Smith into electrical engineering, but I was too immature, and my education was not up to college standards. I withdrew without credit and went back to the desert and married my girlfriend Geri Davis in Las Vegas." A senior in high school, Geri was only seventeen years old. She came from a broken family and had been raised since the age of twelve by her father because her mother was abusive. She graduated in 1948, there being only one other student in her class, and that was Lloyd.

> Geri's father Luther Davis, a.k.a. Johnny—no one called him Luther except his parents—was a truck driver and a diesel power plant operator when I knew him. He was a good and very decent man whose heart was in the right place. He helped us financially at critical times. Unfortunately, besides inheriting some of Johnny's excellent attributes, Geri inherited her mother's flash temper. As for me, I had a quick temper too, although I didn't realize it. I was in no way suited to life, not just married life. I could only take it one day at a time. I had some quirks that didn't blend with her personality. Geri and I were just different people—too different to keep the early bloom going. But we were also too conventional to let go when perhaps we should have.

In the meantime, Harry had to find employment. Occasionally, he helped out at the motel, and for a while, he worked part-time as a rod man for a US Geological team as well as for a private surveyor. It was boring, and it didn't pay much, but at least it was something to do while looking for a better opportunity.

> *The guys on the surveying team with me didn't know the area. I was the only local person. One day, they came across a sidewinder, and I guess they were afraid. They threw gasoline on it, and then threw a match. It started to writhe and writhe, then it buried its fangs in itself. I'll never forget that. I don't think the men meant to be cruel. After all, I'd killed many a snake in my day but never like that. It increased my empathy, for here was an animal that killed itself the pain was so bad. I'd had the same feeling sweep over me when my father and I killed the magnificent bighorn sheep at Scranton Tank.*

One of the few industries in the region that was hiring was mining, specifically talc and lead. It was a hard, dangerous profession, and Harry did not have the right build. "I was too tall, too skinny." But the job paid, so Harry reluctantly headed for the mines.

CHAPTER 6:
WORKING IN THE HOLE

The first mine in which Harry worked briefly was the Gerstley borax mine northeast of Shoshone, which had begun shipping ore in 1924, getting it down to the T & T by means of a three-mile-long baby gauge railroad. Its profitability had been short-lived because, like all the other borax mines in the area, it had been closed following the big borate discovery in 1926 in the Kramer District of the Mojave Desert. That strike had severely drained the vitality of Death Valley Junction because Consolidated Borax moved its headquarters—lock, stock, and barrel—out of its recently built Civic Center to the new town of Boron. It had also been the beginning of the end for the T & T since the railroad's profitability had been heavily dependent on borax shipments. However, after World War II, broadening industrial markets had made all three types of borax produced in the region marketable again, with unit prices rising nationwide from $80.5 per metric ton in 1945 to $91.3 in 1948.[62] The mine at Boron produced kernite; the mines at Ryan produced colmanite; and the Gerstley mine produced primarily ulexite. As a result, Consolidated Borax sent sampling crews of engineers and geologists into the closed mines to reassess them. Harry began his mining career by working with just such a crew.

The truth is we weren't mining. We just sampled the entire mine. A prospector's pick and sample sacks were our only equipment. No dynamite was needed. Abandoned mines are inherently dangerous, but the Gerstley was well-timbered, the ground solid, and it had never had a cave-in. The strange thing was the air. Most of the stopes at the Gerstley had outlets for air, but two or three did not. The unventilated ones were hot and stinky with odors arising from God knows what—quite unlike any odors in lead and talc mines. I was also surprised that the stopes were so hot, yet their walls were cool. I never encountered that smell in any other mine.

The Gerstley ore had been discovered by Johnny Sheridan, a prospector who was also a legendary character, as were so many prospectors. When he was not out staking claims and then drinking and gambling away his grubstake at the Snake Room in Tecopa or some other desert watering hole, folklore has it that he lived in a cave with chuckwallas (a chunky black-and-brown lizard common in the Mojave Desert) and hydrophobic skunks (a critter that shows up often in Western tall tales and may have had some slight basis in fact in terms of a rabies epidemic). At least the part about living in the cave is true. There are seven caves built by humans in Dublin Gulch near Shoshone, and their occupancy goes far back. Cut into caleche (a sedimentary calcium carbonate), the caves were a favorite abode for down-on-their-luck prospectors because they were rent-free, warm in the winter, and cool in the summer. Other prospectors who lived there at various times were Joe Volmer, who incongruously wore a white sailor's hat and walked with a cane, and Shorty Harris, one of the most famous prospectors of the Mojave Desert; he discovered the gold that started the great rush to the Bullfrog-Rhyolite area.[63]

One day, Sheridan was out prospecting for clay, but he found borax instead and immediately made a claim. Subsequently, he sold the claim for $50,000 to Clarence M. Rasor, the field engineer for Consolidated Borax Company. Financially, Sheridan should have been set for life, but he was like most prospectors, who were notoriously bad at holding onto their money. The story is told that Sheridan grubstaked a swindler named Smoky Dixon who gave him bad whiskey that killed him.[64] There is only one indisputable fact, which is that the mine Sheridan sold Rasor was a good one. Rasor bought it for himself and then made a deal with his employer, Consolidated Borax, to sell the ore to them, perhaps putting subtle pressure on the company to do so by naming the mine after one of its directors, James Gerstley. Rasor built a baby gauge railroad to connect the mine with the T & T and began shipping ore in 1924. Ironically, it was Rasor who discovered the borate in the Kramer District that resulted in the closure of the Gerstley mine in 1927.

It was twenty years later, in 1947, that Harry went to work for Jimmy

Gill (the father of his first girlfriend, Annette), who had been retained by Consolidated Borax to sample the Gerstley mine to determine whether it should be reopened.

> *Jimmy was quite a character. In tune with the industry, his vocabulary was full of four-letter, one-or-two-syllable variety words, strung together in novel ways with tone inflections and an animated face to complete his thoughts. As far as the male animal was concerned he was quite insightful in his descriptions, no doubt because of his life of hard knocks and betrayals coupled with his own base instincts. Miners meeting him for the first time usually misread him morally. He was always tender in defending his wife and three daughters. But he was hard for them to live with, often taking needless chances in their eyes. But the chances he took in my presence were always calculated, the kind I might have taken myself at the time.*

The crew found significant ore reserves in the Gerstley, but once the sampling was done, Harry had to find other employment. He took the first permanent job offered to him: working as a miner in the Western Talc mine in the mountains about twelve miles east of Tecopa. It was called simply "the hole" by all the men who worked there.

The discovery of talc in 1909 by the owners of China Ranch never fired up prospectors' blood as did gold or silver. Newspaper reporters were not interested in writing stories about talc strikes. Plain white talc was ordinary next to gold and its industrial uses too mundane. Talc was sprinkled on a baby's bottom while gold adorned the hands of kings. However, it would be talc, as well as equally drab borax, that would be the real bonanzas in the Death Valley region.

The Western Talc mine was opened in 1912 by Lycurgus Lindsay, a mine speculator and owner of Western Art Tile Works and the Independent Sewer Pipe Company near Los Angeles. Lindsay hauled out one thousand tons of talc that first year and then steadily increased the amount until by 1920, the mine was producing twelve thousand tons a year. With an ego as big as the talc seam, Lindsay had visions of becoming "the Talc King," just as Francis Smith had become the "Borax King" and Williams Andrews Clark "the Copper King." But L. Lindsay (who did not care for his Greek first name so used only the initial) was heavily in debt, and in 1921, he went bankrupt. Eventually, the mine was leased to the Western Talc Company. It continued to be a steady producer, using the T & T to ship its ore until the railroad stopped operations, after which it shipped by truck.[65]

Talc has a host of uses in cosmetics, pharmaceuticals, ceramic tile, ceramic pipe, paper manufacturing, industrial lubricants, and paint. The uptick in the postwar economy gave the mining of talc a boost, particularly in the Mojave region.[66] An enormous belt of dolomite containing seams of high-grade talc extends from the Panamint Range on the west side of Death Valley (the Crystal Springs Formation) eastward to the Alexander and Silurian Hills. Formed under a shallow sea, some of the dolomite was altered into talc wherever it contacted the intrusion of diabase sills about one billion years ago.[67]

> *In the Western Talc mine, talc came in two varieties: hard on the footwall against the diabase sill; and soft—called steatite—on the dolomite hanging wall. The footwall is below the ore body, and the hanging wall is above. Most of it was shipped to a company called Gladding, McBean in the Los Angeles area for firing into tile. Gladding, McBean made much of the beautiful red roof tile for Stanford University, my future alma mater.*

The Noonday dolomite overlying the Western Talc seam, which was located in what is known as the Noonday area, is approximately one thousand feet thick. Besides white, it can occur in various colors, including gray and a light-to medium brown. From a distance, the white talc tailings from the mine stand out clearly against the darker stone. Talc is the softest mineral known, listed as one on the Mohs hardness scale (by way of comparison, a diamond has a hardness of ten), and can easily be scratched with a fingernail. Its slipperiness is caused by weak bonds holding the platelets together, enabling them to slide by one another. In this feature, it is similar to graphite. The result is a greasy or soapy feel, hence the name for soapstone, which is largely composed of talc. This presented a unique safety problem in mines.

> *One of the first things I had to learn, and learn fast, was that in a talc mine, footing can be slippery, sometimes too*

slippery. It was easy to lose your footing and end up sliding down the chute used to remove ore. Mining of all kinds is grueling and dangerous work, but this hazard was unique to talc. For footing, we used planks about a foot wide to stand on. Spikes driven into the footwall on each end of the plank made footing secure.

Because dolomite is fairly soft (3.5 Mohs) and talc is even softer, mines required extensive timbering for support in the adits (main entrances), shafts (vertical or angled from vertical), drifts (horizontal dead ends off a shaft or adit), tunnels (generally open to the surface at both ends), and stopes (the space above the drift made by the blasting and the removal of ore). Drilling and blasting can fracture and destabilize the rock beyond the area intended, so even when care was taken, collapses could occur. A third risk not unique to talc was that without ear protection, which miners did not wear in the 1940s, the sound of pneumatic jackhammers and blasting underground resulted in hearing loss.

When I started working in Western Talc, my partner was already very hard of hearing. We had to use sign language down below because the noise was so great. The same thing happened to me. By the time I quit the mines, my hearing had been affected. I have tinnitus, a disability I've had to deal with ever since. It is possible that cells in my brain receiving input from some of my auditory nerves—hammered by endless hours of battering—locked into a steady-state of reporting sound even when none was there. And I've worn hearing aids for years. Sometimes people ask me what I most loved about living in the desert. What I most loved was the incredible quietness. Unfortunately, working at the Western Talc and then at the Noonday mines stole that quietness and put a forever ring in my ears. Trying to understand others, when I hear only one word in three, has been the bane of my existence. I hear virtually nothing of frequencies two octaves above middle C. Vowel sounds are distinguishable, but consonants can only be guessed at, even when context is apparent. Timbre, resonance, and color in sound go largely unrecognized.

A further risk arises from certain similarities between talc and asbestos. Although it was not recognized at the time, prolonged exposure can cause lung damage resulting in diseases, such as silicosis and chronic obstructive pulmonary disease. However, the deleterious effects were more marked in the mill workers than in the miners, because the grinding of the ore produced great clouds of dust.

Two-man crews were standard in talc mines at the time. A typical morning started with mucking out the previous day's round, loading it in an ore car that was pushed by hand along the horizontal haulage way to the shaft where it was dumped into a skip (two feet wide by three feet tall by three and a half feet long) and hoisted to the surface on rails on an inclined shaft when a signal was sent from the miner below to the hoist operator above. Once on the surface, the ore was dumped into a bin and finally trucked out for processing elsewhere. Waste from the footwall or the hanging wall exited the mine in the same way and was piled in the dump. Mucking was usually completed by noon. The typical afternoon was spent timbering as necessary and then drilling out the next round for blasting.[68]

The experienced miner to whom Harry was assigned was a Polish immigrant who had come to the United States just a few years earlier following World War II and who sent money from every paycheck back to his family. In his mid-forties, he lived in the bunkhouse at Western Talc. He was fluent in English and spoke with only a moderate accent, but when it came to cussing, he was multilingual.

> Bohunk was the slang word we used for an Eastern European. Unfortunately, I don't remember his real name. But I got to know him well and he would not mind me calling him Bohunk even though it could be considered derogatory. My first task working for him was to muck out the pit at the bottom of the inclined shaft driven into a hillside to reach a thick deposit of soft talc, known as steatite, next to the hanging wall. Boulders fell regularly down the shaft from the mismatch between the skip that hauled the ore to the surface and the ore cars dumping ore into it from the upper levels of the mine. Sometimes boulders split into rocks and gravel, but the hard talc and waste remained boulder-size. My only defense was a hard hat and my pick and shovel. I dodged falling boulders for several days before Bohunk deemed me fit for real mining.

One of the things I learned from Bohunk was the matter of strength. I'm tall, but my build is slight. Head to head, I was never a match for the endomorphic bulldogs who made mining their careers. Bohunk was such a bulldog, in some ways bigger than life. But we got on okay after he realized I could hold up my end of the shoveling by using leverage. I think he also appreciated my stubbornness to stay with it, a legacy from working with my father, also a bulldog.

While Harry may have had the wrong physiology for mining (too tall and thin), at least he was not claustrophobic. But when he first started, he had to adjust to what he called "a new reality—black—just there and I am here, like a presence you could not get away from." It was disconcerting to step from the intense aboveground light into the equally intense underground dark. The carbide lamp (a.k.a. acetylene gas lamp) that attached to Harry's hardhat produced a brighter light than a candle and, with a metal reflector, provided sufficient illumination, particularly in a talc mine in which some of the walls, floors, and ceilings gleamed white. But it gave adequate light in only one direction; when Harry turned toward it, the darkness vanished, but when he turned away, it whelmed up, physically pressing against his back as if it were not a thing of absence but of presence.

To keep his lamp going, every four hours, Harry had to refill the bottom container with calcium carbide chips. These were stored at the mine portal so miners could pick up a supply on their way in at the beginning of their shift. The chips were also available at each level. Water in the upper container of the lamp dripped slowly onto the chips, reacting chemically to produce acetylene gas that came out through an orifice in the center of the metal reflector. A lever regulated the amount of water dripped, thereby controlling the brightness.

To start the lamp, you opened the valve and when you smelled the acetylene, you put your hand over the reflector to concentrate the gas, then you would drag your hand off quickly over the thumb wheel rubbing on a flint rod that created sparks. About the time your hand got clear, the lamp would light with a pop—that is if the flint was in good order, which it not always was. Another problem was that the tiny orifice through which the gas flowed often plugged, putting the light out. With your partner's light, you would use a thin hard wire attached to your light to unplug the orifice. Managing your light was sometimes touch and go.

The more modern Noonday mines, operated by Anaconda Copper Mining Co., had already switched to battery-powered headlamps, but not Western Talc, where things were done the old way. At least a carbide lamp was generally safe, easy to use, and usually reliable, although only a brand-new lamp gave a good beam. The polished metal reflectors corroded quickly so that after a few weeks, the lights were little better than candles. "If the lamp gave out for some reason, you could always follow the rails by feel through the blackness to the main shaft. That happened to me when I was working in the Gerstley. It was eerie but not scary." There was one added advantage to the lamp: its flame was used to light the fuses for the dynamite.[69]

Bohunk taught Harry everything he needed to know, although Harry already possessed some carpentry skills from working with his father on the T & T. The day that Harry finally won Bohunk's respect was when he was ordered topside to cut a section of timber called a "stull" to support the roof. Since the stope ceiling was not square, Harry asked Bohunk how much bevel he wanted, and he replied derisively, "It'll have enough when you get through with it," not realizing that Harry knew all about bevel from building railroad bridges with his father.

Threading the needle to win respect in the rough-and-tumble world sometimes requires chicanery, and this was one of those times. Well, Bohunk got his piece of timber cut to exact length, but with both ends perfectly square, with absolutely no bevel. I can still hear him cussing a blue streak, which he was very, very good at. After he cooled off, he laughed, and we were on the road to becoming friends.

Harry and Bohunk worked in the stope, a shaft following the seam of steatite going up at an angle from the main haulage tunnel working at 365 feet down, the lowest level of the mine. Their job included drilling holes in the talc face for dynamite (*powder* in the common usage). Jackhammers mounted on a bar and arm were used to drill out each round if the face was vertical. Stopers (named after the stope shaft and pronounced *stow per*) were jackhammers mounted on air pistons with compressed air piped from the surface. As their name indicates, they were used to drill holes for blasting in the stopes.

> *How to drill each blasting round was critical. Bohunk could be arrogant, even disrespectful, but he was careful, and he taught me well. The first holes were drilled downward from about chest height at an angle with the ore face. These were the "cutters." Then "upper" holes were drilled deep straight in just below the ceiling or hanging wall. The final holes were drilled in deep near the bottom, maybe angling down a tiny bit. These were the "lifters." Once this was all accomplished, the equipment was moved to a safe place out of the way. The holes were loaded in a specific nine-hole pattern with a certain sequence of explosions in mind. It is still so real to me, I am going to use present tense to explain it:*

> 1. *Powder, caps and fuse cords are fetched. [By way of background, the powder was Amodyne dynamite, a "safe" mixture of nitroglycerine and diatomaceous earth wrapped up securely in tough oily paper in several layers. The caps were the igniters. In essence, caps were powerful firecrackers in light copper or aluminum cartridges. They were stored in places separate from the powder in magazines. Each cap had a hole in one end for a fuse. The fuse consisted of a core of slow, hot-burning powder wrapped up in tough cloth in the form of a cord. It was designed to burn at exactly one foot per minute. Upon reaching the cap, the cap would explode like a strong firecracker. It had more than enough explosive force to make the powder explode.]*
> 2. *Using a wooden tamping rod, tamp in all but the last stick of powder into each hole. Tamp them firmly, but not too firmly!*
> 3. *Then cut fresh sections of fuse, say five feet long, one for each hole.*

4. *Insert one end of a fuse into a cap, and crimp it on securely.*

5. *Break through the side wall of a stick of powder, midway between each end. Insert the cap/fuse assembly into the stick securely.*

6. *Tamp the loaded stick and fuse into each of the holes. (You now have nine holes with fuses hanging out.)*

7. *Slit each fuse at an angle near its end so as to expose the ignitable core.*

8. *Light the fuses in sequence, with a few seconds in between, starting with the cutters, continuing through the uppers, with the lifters last. Use your carbide light to ignite the fuses, always having a backup light for escape purposes if needed.*

9. *Timing is all important, for it provides a known amount of burning time to ignite the round and retreat to a safe distance. From the stope, this means sliding down the chute into the main drift and moving down the drift fifty to a hundred feet or so.*

10. *When the last fuse is lit, it's time to "haul ass"—mining vernacular. You've got only about four minutes to get out. Once in the safety of the haulage drift, wait to count the blasts. By so doing, you will know the likelihood of finding unexploded powder come mucking time on the morrow. Hitting a cap buried in a stick of unexploded powder has killed many a miner.*

11. *Listen to the important sequence of explosions. The cutters will go off first. They create a cavity in the ore face. Then the top holes, the uppers, will go off, exploding ore into the cavity and advancing the ceiling. Finally, the lifters do the heavy work by literally lifting the lower part of the ore face into the opening above. The net result is a mound of crushed ore back a bit from the face of the ore body ready to be mucked out next shift.*

Because a miner's sense of hearing was diminished by the constant barrage of loud noise from the jackhammers and the blasting, he had to sharpen his sense of touch to compensate. Miners also relied on intuition based on experience, for which Harry, being new, had to trust Bohunk. Many miners were superstitious, because even with safety precautions, they did not have complete control over their dangerous environment, far from it. A mine collapse or hitting an unexploded stick of dynamite with a pick when mucking out could occur in the next second. However, their superstitions had less to do with the supernatural than with the *hypernatural*: what senses they *did* possess were heightened, such as the ability to perceive a tiny change in air pressure, a faint tremor deep in the mine, or an unusual smell—just enough to provide warning that something was amiss. In the higher order of mental states, such awareness can be interpreted as intuition; in the lower order, it can take the shape of superstition. Either way, the heightening of awareness was so gradual that most experienced miners did not realize how exquisitely attuned they were to their surroundings. Unfortunately, many mine disasters occurred without warning, and no amount of intuition, superstition, or plain-old experience could prevent them.

I was really nervous about a spot on the hanging wall that might be dangerous, but Bohunk told me not to worry. On Sunday afternoon, the day before he died, Bohunk let me give him a haircut. His coarse black hair was laced here and there with the gray of age. The hand-powered clippers I used were a present from my father, who expected me to fill his shoes as town barber one day. That was not to be. The next day began as just another day in the hole. By noon, we had mucked out Friday's round and sent it topside. As was our custom, I went topside for lunch while Bohunk stayed in the hole with his packaged lunch. I was just finishing my sandwich with Sam, the hoist-man, when the emergency rings came from 365. Quickly, Sam lowered the skip to 365. Up came the other miners. They had bad news. At the spot about which I was nervous, the entire roof had caved in on Bohunk. They had found him as they walked back from lunch on the skip-loading platform. I was shaken to my bones hours later when his crushed remains were finally laid out on the hoist-room floor. The coroner picked up Bohunk the next morning. He told us there was no one claiming his body. As it happened, it was Sam's last day on the job. The mine superintendent pointed to the hoist while looking at me. And so I was emancipated from the hole and given a safer job as hoist-man while Bohunk, my friend whose hair I had cut the day before, was dead. I shall never forget that miracle of irony.

There were three holes being worked at Western Talc, and shortly thereafter, Harry was transferred from the newest to the oldest, an out-of-the-way mine being stripped of its last ore by a pair of old-timers. Because only one stope was active, as hoist-man, Harry had time on his hands. It was then that the most important chance encounter of his life occurred. He met a young geologist surveying in the area who would redirect Harry's life by explaining to him about the region's geology and recommending that he leave the mine and go to college. Harry remembers that first meeting well:

One day, a couple of guys appeared and parked their pickup near my hoist. They took off with drawing boards and charting equipment, which I recognized from earlier brief stints as a rodman for the US Geological Survey and for a private engineer in the business of staking out mining claims around other people's mines. Two days later, one of them reappeared accompanied by a different man. The man I'd seen earlier—a good-looking guy not that much older than I was in appearance—was at the wheel. We struck up a brief conversation, long enough for me to discover that he and his friend were mapping the talc deposits of the Mojave Desert. He came several more times, sometimes joining me for lunch at the cookhouse provided by the company. As we got acquainted, I became more and more interested in the geology and formation of talc as a result of molten rock from the earth's interior coming into contact with sediments laid down long ago beneath a sea or ocean. Subsequent continental uplift exposed the rock formations involved. These were all wondrous things, and I could hardly imagine the events, even though I could visualize them. My new friend's name was Lauren Wright. He gave me a professional goal. Exciting? You bet. Geology, here I come! I shouted to myself. Then reality set in.

Running the risk of hyperbole, Harry's meeting with Wright while working a hoist is analogous to a janitor at the Institute for Advanced Study at Princeton chatting with somebody named Einstein while leaning on a broom and subsequently becoming a physicist at his casual suggestion. Only a graduate student at the time of their meeting, Wright would go on to become one of two great pioneers in continental extensional tectonics, the other man being his friend and colleague Bennie W. Troxel. By means of meticulous mapping of well-exposed basin-and-range areas, the two men recognized the fundamental importance of shallowly dipping normal faults. This had enormous influence on concepts of continental dynamics. Wright's interest in Death Valley and the Amargosa region had begun when he was a geology major at the University of Southern California in the 1930s. His fascination turned into a lifelong passion when at a seminar in 1942, he read a paper written a year before by Levi F. Noble on the Amargosa chaos, so named for its peculiar geological complexity.[70] Noble was a highly respected geologist, who was in the twilight of his career. His work on the geology of the Grand Canyon, the San Andreas Fault, and Death Valley had shaped the thinking of generations of geologists. This particular paper was destined to become a classic because in it he set forth a hypothesis on how the Virgin Spring phase of the chaos had formed. However, Noble was stymied in gaining a full understanding of the chaos by inadequate topographic base maps.

A decade later (serving in the interim as one of the advisers on Wright's PhD thesis), Noble encouraged Wright and Troxel to undertake the systematic stratigraphy that was critical in gaining a full understanding of the chaos, joining them in the field when he was able. Wright wrote in an essay titled "Acknowledgements of a Professional Lifetime" that in the early 1950s, "the three of us entered the Virgin Spring area, the type locality of the Virgin Spring chaos, where Bennie and I would follow predetermined traverses, while Levi, in his seventies, stayed close to our vehicle taking notes on critical features. To have been able to 'stand on his shoulders' in this manner I continue to be grateful."[71] Before Wright was able to turn his attention to what would become known as extensional tectonics, he had to finish up his doctoral thesis on talc deposits that had been delayed by his military service in World War II. Wright's interest in talc had begun in the summer of 1942 when he worked as an assistant to Ben Page, a faculty member at Southern California University and later at Stanford, on the strategic minerals program of the US Geological Survey. (It was Page who had been with Wright when he and Harry had first met at Western Talc.) They assessed high-quality steatite talc, a critical ingredient in high-frequency insulators used in military equipment. After the war, Wright picked up where he had left off, returning to the Amargosa region to construct a plane table map of the Silver Lake talc deposits. While working for the California Division of Mines, he spent as much time as possible on talc-related excursions.

It was during this period that Wright met Harry working the hoist at Western Talc and took the time to explain to him what he was doing, stretching the maps out on the hood of his pickup truck or on the table in the cookhouse, thereby opening up a vast new world.

But if Harry were ever to get the chance to enter the new world Wright had revealed, he had to find a better-paying job. "The Western Talc paid all their employees a flat rate of $8.60 per day; barely enough to live on if you had a family out in the sticks. Every two weeks, I would put part of my $122 paycheck toward our debt at the local grocery store. But that left nothing toward what we would need to leave the desert and go to college." Harry soon found a better job at $10.20 per day at the Noonday lead mines east of Tecopa where he and Geri were living at the time. The downside of the new job was that he had to start over at the bottom as a mucker.

CHAPTER 7:
THE NOONDAY MINES

The name Noonday conjures up images of glaring sunlight and blazing heat. It is an appropriate name—so appropriate that it has adhered to several landmarks: an area east of Tecopa at the southern end of the Nopah Range and Alexander Hills; the rock beneath that area (the Noonday dolomite formation); and one particular lead-zinc mine within that area. The mine claimed the name first. Other lead-zinc mines in the vicinity were the War Eagle, the Columbia, and the Gunsight—not to be confused with the legendary Lost Gunsight, which to this day, remains lost. All were known jointly as the Noonday mines. To confuse outsiders even more, they were also called the Tecopa mines stemming from the Tecopa Consolidated Mining Company (TCM) that came into existence in 1906. However, by the time Harry began working, the confusion had dissipated somewhat because in 1947, Anaconda Copper Mining Co. had bought them all, including the Darwin mine to the west of Death Valley in the Alabama Hills. Anaconda was a behemoth of a company, one of the largest trusts of the twentieth century, with mines around the world, including the gigantic Chuquicamata copper mine in Chile.

In a way, Anaconda had been in the Noonday area since the beginning of the mining boom, at least in the person of George Hearst (father of newspaperman William Randolph Hearst), who had extensive interests throughout the West in gold, silver, and copper, specifically the great Anaconda Copper mine in Montana. Hearst had invested in the Balance mine in the Noonday formation as early as the 1870s, but he soon became convinced that it would never make a profit, so he sold out. The mines in the area then came under the control of Jonas P. Osbourne, who eventually reached the same conclusion after making numerous expensive improvements, including a smelter that didn't smelt, a pulverizer that didn't pulverize, and a stamp mill that milled but not very well. The mines were closed from 1881 to 1906 when the arrival of the T & T made reopening them economically feasible. Having purchased interests in the mines from the heirs of Osbourne and his partner, James H. Lester formed the Tecopa Consolidated Mining Company, making a sporadic profit until the arrival in 1912 of Dr. Lincoln D. Godshall as superintendent. Godshall was a phenomenon in the world of Mojave Desert mining, which was crowded with self-taught men whose heads were filled with get-rich-quick schemes. A graduate of Lafayette College in Pennsylvania, Godshall was a metallurgist and chemist who had mining and smelting experience. Finally, the mines had at their head a man who was more interested in what was happening at the three-hundred-foot level of the Noonday than in what was happening on Wall Street. Until the mines closed again in 1928 because of falling lead prices, they produced between $3 and $4 million worth of ore, mostly under Godshall's supervision.[72]

About ten years later, a Kentuckian by the name of W. Buford Davis came to Shoshone looking for mines in which to invest. With war looming in Europe, he was interested in strategic metals and minerals. Lead's principal uses were in solders, cables, lead-acid storage batteries, paint, and as an antiknock additive to gasoline. The unit price of lead had begun inching back up from a low of $70 per metric ton nationwide in 1932 to $104 in 1938.[73] Davis had extensive mining experience as a consulting engineer for the US Bureau of Mines and had been manager of the Golden Anchor Mining Co. in Idaho. He had coauthored with S. H. Lorain a paper published by the US Bureau of Mines that assessed the Golden Anchor operations, describing them as "a successful small-tonnage gold mine in one of the newer and more inaccessible mining districts of central Idaho." Located in the mountainous Marshall Lake district, the Golden Anchor was so remote that the access road was closed every fall when it began to snow, after which the mine could only be reached by dogsled.[74]

No stranger to difficult mining conditions, when Davis arrived in Shoshone, he sought out the advice of Charlie Brown, who pointed him in the direction of the Noonday mines. Brown had just been elected to the California State Senate and was concerned about the lack of jobs in the Amargosa region. The closing of the talc and lead mines in the 1920s had caused substantial economic hardship, a situation that threatened to become worse if the T & T folded, so the possibility of reopening the

Noonday mines was a bright spot in a gloomy economic picture. Davis formed the Shoshone Mining Co. with himself as president and George W. Nilsson, a lawyer who specialized in oil, gas, and mining, as secretary. Then in January 1940, he acquired quitclaim deeds from the Godshall family as well as from the widow of Godshall's partner James E. Belden.[75] Finally, he hired Ernie Huhn, a miner who lived in Shoshone, to deepen the shaft in the Noonday mine. Ernie was about sixty years old, and his nicknames were the Dutchman and Siberian Red, the first because he was born in Germany and the second because he had red hair and had prospected in Alaska and Siberia. Why he made the move from some of the coldest places on Earth to one of the hottest is not known. In his book *Loafing along Death Valley Trails*, William Caruthers writes that he was told by the woman who ran the dining room in Shoshone that there was "no place on Godamighty's earth [Huhn] hasn't been. As soon bet $1,000 as two bits on a pair of jacks." Huhn had helped Louise Grantham (one of the few female mine owners anywhere) successfully develop the Warm Spring Canyon talc mine located in Death Valley, of which he was part owner. He had also spent considerable time prospecting for gold and had an archetypal tale to tell about rich ore that he had found and then subsequently lost. He was very knowledgeable and had a reputation as a decent guy who never caused trouble, although as Caruthers makes clear, he was quite a cardplayer, being a regular at the poker table in the Mesquite Room in Shoshone, as well as in the Snake Room in Tecopa. Huhn himself told Caruthers about going into the Noonday mine for the first time for Davis, "Honest to God, I hadn't dug a foot when I turned up the prettiest vein of lead I'd ever seen."[76]

Assured that the Noonday mines still had great potential, Davis started production in 1940. Then on January 17, 1942, just forty days after Pearl Harbor, he was killed in a plane crash when the TWA DC-3 on which he was a passenger plowed into the east face of Mount Potosi at night, thirty miles southwest of Las Vegas. Besides the crew of three, also on board were fifteen US Army pilots as well as the actress Carole Lombard, the wife of Clark Gable, who was returning to Los Angeles with her mother and press agent after appearing in a war bond rally in Indiana. In all, twenty-two people were killed in the crash. Workers at the nearby Blue Diamond mine in Arden, Nevada, reported hearing a terrific explosion on the mountain and seeing the "shroud of snow suddenly lightened by the burst of flame shortly after the plane had passed over the mine."[77]

After Davis's death, the Noonday mines continued to operate during the war. In 1945, the mines were sold to the Finlay Company, the second largest lead producer in California, which then sold them to Anaconda Copper in 1947 just as the unit value of lead began to spike, rising from $179 per metric ton in 1946 to $323 per metric ton in 1947 and $398 in 1948, driven in part by the post-World War II demand for leaded gas.[78]

Harry never met Davis, who died while the Rosenbergs were living in Death Valley Junction, but he knew of his reputation as a first-rate mining engineer.

> I think one of the reasons Finlay sold the Noonday mines was that Davis had been viewed as indispensable to its operations, even though he had died three years before. He was legendary. The owners thought he was the only one who could run it. He was simply known as Davis to everyone. I'm not sure if anyone even knew his first name. I didn't. I never met the man, but those who did were in awe of him. Admiration, even adulation, was tonally present with every mention of his name. And it was not the kind of admiration that arises in beer halls where fame is often initiated by tall tales that have little substance in fact. He was not a desert character but a real mining expert. All that may have arisen simply from the miracle of finding so much pretty ore in such a barren and remote place. Davis shot craps and won that one. He surely deserves a larger place in the history books. His position was filled by Anaconda people including Frank Baby—a French name pronounced Bah-be—who was a mining engineer; Harold Hill, mining superintendent; and Charles "Chick" Joy, geologist.

As for Ernie Huhn, he retired from mining and built himself a house in Shoshone, financially comfortable from the talc mine but still dreaming of lost gold up in the mountains.

Harry's first job was in the War Eagle, mucking round after round to extend the main haulage drift into a new ore body. To get there, each morning, he drove over a rough road that turned increasingly rocky as it ascended from Tecopa, passing through sparse vegetation of creosote and desert holly. The portals to the mines were drilled into the steep mountainside and could be spotted easily from a distance because over them towered the wooden head frames. The power plant at the Columbia could also be seen for miles, jutting out from the slope just above the mine road. "That road up to the mines took out many an automobile tire, so many in fact, the Columbia mine had its own tire dump. A commuting miner, such as myself, needed to have the skills of an auto mechanic just to get to work regularly."

The ore was in mineralized seams that extended approximately two miles in a disjointed pattern. The War Eagle, the most productive of the mines, was located on the easternmost end of the mineralized zone. Lead sulfide (galena) was the principal mineral with zinc sulfide as an important accessory mineral. Lead carbonate (cerrusite) and silver and gold at near-trace levels were also present.

The operations at the Noonday mines, including the War Eagle, were more modern than at Western Talc. For one, it used what were called slushers that were a type of air-driven dredge used to scrape ore down a raise or up an inclined winze and into an ore car. As for the winze, neither Western Talc nor Gerstley had one. It was a shaft that began and ended underground. One was drilled under Davis's guidance; a second was drilled by Anaconda. Yet another difference was that instead of calcium-carbide lamps, the miners used rechargeable alkaline batteries with sealed lights that easily ran up to ten hours. To Harry, the biggest change was that the Noonday mines used electric mules to tow eight to ten ore cars at once out to the ore bins. "It was quite an improvement over Western Talc where we had to push each car out to the shaft, pull the signal bell for our level to alert the hoist-man, and then dump the ore into the skip the hoist-man lowered down."

Another advantage was that a lead mine was less prone to cave-ins and so did not need to be timbered as extensively as a talc mine. However, there was one major danger that talc did not present: lead is a neurotoxin that can be ingested or inhaled, and there were almost no safety precautions in place to mitigate the hazard. Inhalation was lessened in the mines because the exhaust from the compressors was always very moist, which kept down the dust, although in the earlier mining period under Godshall's supervision, that was not the case.

We were aware of the risks of lead poisoning in the 1940s.
The problem had existed since Roman times. But we were

*not as aware as we are now. Nor were there mine safety
rules. Basically miners were responsible for their own safety.
As a result, many a Noonday miner became "leaded" in the
local jargon. On my first day, my partner taught me how to
eat lunch underground so as to avoid becoming leaded. You
unwrapped your sandwich as you ate it, never unwrapping
it completely and never ever touching it with your hands.
From that day on, I was careful indeed not to ingest it. I may
have picked up some, but I never recognized any symptoms.
Fortunately, before too long, I was promoted to a job topside,
so in my case, the exposure was not prolonged.*

Until 1928, when the mines had closed down because of a drop in
prices, the hot springs in Tecopa had been a favorite spot for lead miners
because the water helped to relieve joint pain. Originally, the hot springs
was very small, only about eight feet in diameter and three feet deep, until
one day, two lead miners enlarged it with dynamite. Deke Lowe, who lived
in Tecopa in the 1920s and whose father worked for the T & T, remembered
the miners coming to the springs for relief: "But what would happen is, a
miner would get leaded—crippled from the lead…It was the lead, and their
joints would be bad. Or else they'd just have rheumatism. So they'd come
in, they'd pitch a tent, and they'd boil out, as they called it." Boiling out
may have helped ease the pain temporarily, but there was no cure for lead
poisoning in the long run.[79]

Risks such as hearing loss from the blasting and jackhammers were the
same as at Western Talc, as were those involved with handling dynamite.

*I knew a bit about dynamite from working in Western Talc.
And I knew that old dynamite can become unstable as some
of the nitroglycerin separates out. It has to be stored carefully
at mine temperature, about 75 degrees Fahrenheit (about
24 degrees Celsius) because as temperature increases, the
physical bonds weaken as diffusion rates increase. You don't
want to leave dynamite sitting out in the sun. One day, while
looking for a tool in an old drift, I ran across a coffee can
with a half dozen sticks of old dynamite in it. No crystals
indicative of chemical degradation were evident, but the
bottom of the can held a yellowish liquid that had separated*

from the sticks. I gingerly picked that can up and hand-carried it out to the dump where I tossed it, quickly ducking the other way, expecting a humongous explosion. I was at once chagrined and astonished that there was nothing more than a thud to be heard. I lived to tell the tale. That's not completely true. I lived, but I never told anyone—until now. It was basically a very unwise thing to do.

Because the Anaconda operations were larger and more complex than Western Talc's, they required more specialized jobs. Before long, Harry's enterprising nature came to the attention of Harold Hill, the mine superintendent, who brought him out of the War Eagle hole and put him in charge of the air compressors and doing surface repairs. Besides the obvious, a major benefit of being topside was that Harry had the chance to gain more knowledge from skilled tradesmen. He wasn't required to do so, but he was too inquisitive to let any learning opportunity go by without taking advantage of it. One of his first topside teachers was a blacksmith.

He taught me how to heat-treat picks and other tools that had to stay sharp for the miners pounding up rock. I'd learned some things from my father and grandfather. My grandfather was a heat-and-beat blacksmith who could do the obvious with hot metal using a hammer and tongs. Being self-taught, however, he never learned about the second critical steps needed to harden the articles he otherwise shaped so handily. But my new mentor, whose name was Bud, had those additional skills needed to make tools useful. His tools lasted weeks instead of mere days for my grandfather's tools. Bud went by colors. He'd command me: "Heat the entire pick to a bright orange-red. Quickly quench just the red-hot tip in water until the point is dark, and remove it quickly. While the tip is reheating, scrape the crust off on the ground and watch the tip reheat as it will from the sensible heat in the body of the still red-hot pick. When the tip turns a straw color as it reheats on its own, dip the entire pick into water." In that instant, I surpassed my grandfather. This was my first encounter with the world of physical metallurgy, and it stood me in good stead later on in my career. When I began studying at Stanford University, I realized Bud knew how to create austenite and quench only the tip of the pick in water just long enough to create hard and brittle martensite in the point. Then he allowed the sensible heat in the still red-hot massive part to reheat the tool tip to a straw color, which tempered the point by removing the brittleness. Then it was quenched again, which brought the martensite down to a very hard and tough mixture of cementite and ferrite. It was then called tempered steel and stayed sharp for a longer time in use. Bud wouldn't have used those terms, nor would he have cared theoretically about different crystal microstructures. When I got to college, my work in the real worlds of mining, mechanics, carpentry, and electricity gave me an edge academically and professionally. With respect to physical metallurgy, Stanford University gave me the why, but the mines and the other early experiences introduced me to the how.

Harry further expanded his knowledge of physical metallurgy by learning how to weld, "enough so I could get by in the rough-and-tumble world of acetylene torch and electric arc." It was a milestone for him when he realized that employers would gladly pay extra for skills if he knew how to apply them, so he immediately found another mentor, this time in electricity, a subject in which he had been interested since he had been in high school building crystal radio sets and sound amplifiers. The Anaconda Company had an electrician on staff at its Darwin mine 150 miles away who made periodic trips to the War Eagle and its mill, which were electrified by a powerhouse with diesel engines. At full power, the powerhouse was capable of approximately 500 kilowatts (or about 670 horsepower). But it rarely operated at full capacity, because at least one engine was always down for repair, requiring the electrician to be onsite more than he liked. Harry learned rapidly from him, soon becoming one of the three operators who kept the powerhouse going around the clock.

An incident on graveyard shift, about 3:00 a.m., remains indelible. I was changing oil in the diesel engines and dumping it in the designated spot outside. About 4:00 a.m., I noticed a red light flickering from the outside. When I investigated, not only was the oil dump on fire, but also some old tires looked ready to ignite. All alone and fighting panic, I imagined the entire dump of oil and old tires becoming a three-alarm fire and jumping to the powerhouse—on my shift! The nearest fire station was in Las Vegas, some ninety miles away, and there was no phone and no hydrants in any event. So I grabbed some buckets and shuttled between the water tank and dump. Water was all there was and not that much of it. It seemed like a losing game for the first three loads, when the fire finally stopped spreading. By 6:00 a.m. or so, with only a few buckets of water left, the last flames went out. Big sigh of relief. I had just enough time to fuel up the engines for the day shift. Herman Daisy, chief mechanic for Anaconda, was the first person to know. His response was a low-key, "Oh, okay." That came as a jolt, but when I thought about it, the fire was not likely to have spread and was some twenty feet from the corrugated metal powerhouse. A sober realist—that was Herman. In my life, I had seen two houses burn to the ground, and I did not take time to think that the powerhouse was quite fire-resistant. The applied lesson there was: think ahead and keep your cool.

As powerhouse operator, Harry was responsible for supplying electricity to the mill, which gave him the chance to get to know its operators, who explained the milling process as best they could, although they had little understanding of the complex chemistry involved. What the operators did know was that lead and zinc occurred together in the ore that was brought up from the earth and that the two had to be separated in a process called froth flotation. The process required a huge amount of water, the lack of which had been the undoing of many other mill operations in the Death Valley area. To solve the problem, in 1948, Anaconda put in a second very large water tank fed by a well in addition to the one Finlay had built in 1946. This water system also served the mill camp where the married miners lived.[80]

Froth flotation—my first exposure to chemical metallurgy— was a wonder. How bubbles could carry lead that is thirteen times heavier than water was beyond me at the time. I never understood it, probably because the operators didn't either. But they knew how to operate a ball mill, which is a type of grinder that grinds very finely. And they knew how to add chemicals to mysterious, stinking cells gurgling a steel-colored froth being scraped off rotating paddles into a trough called a launder. I marveled at how the mineral values went one way while the waste went another. I did not learn how the process really worked until I was at Stanford University with a Kennecott fellowship that took me in the summer of 1955 to Kennecott's copper mill near Ely, Nevada. Put simply, you use what is called a polar promoter chemical where one end of a molecule will react and attach to a metal mineral while the other end is an organic that is hydrophobic, meaning it is repelled by water. Add a bit of soap, called a frother, to a thin slurry of ground-up ore, and you have fine mineral particles attaching themselves via the promoter to soap bubbles. Blowing air into the bottom of the flotation cell creates bubbles that can be skimmed off. Modifying agents, called depressors and activators, can also be added to prevent unwanted minerals from being collected. The separation efficiency can approach 100 percent. The froth is then dewatered with the solids sent to the smelter that burns off the anions to leave crude metal.

The mill's capacity was one hundred tons of milling per day, but it usually processed seventy-five to eighty-five tons per day. It had two-cell, three-cell, and six-cell (five in all) Denver flotation machines with numerous pumps, tanks, and conveyors. The tailings were pumped into a pond while the concentrate from the froth flotation process was hauled by big eighteen-wheeler Kenworth trucks that were owned and operated by V. B. Morgan Trucking in Tecopa. Heavily loaded, the trucks lumbered slowly across the desert to the siding of the Union Pacific Railroad at Dunn. From there, the concentrate was shipped to the International Smelting and Refining Company plant at Tooele, Utah.[81]

Already a capable auto mechanic because he had to be able to fix his own car if it broke down in the desert, Harry completed a National Schools course in diesel mechanics so he could repair powerhouse diesels in addition to gasoline trucks. When one of Anaconda's regular truck drivers blew an engine coming down the steep grade from Townes Pass in the Panamint Mountains on his way back from the Darwin mine, Herman Daisy and Harry loaded a new engine into Herman's pickup with a "come along" and tripod for lifting out the old engine and laying in the new one. Townes Pass descends steeply from nearly five thousand feet to the floor of Death Valley. It is not the place to blow out an engine, nor is it a place to change one.

> *We changed that engine out in the middle of nowhere, just the two of us, and when we were done, I drove the truck back to the Noonday. We were both pretty good mechanics, but rolling stock back then was not what it is today. So after that, when they needed me to, I drove that two-ton flat bed, hauling equipment, supplies, and dynamite between Darwin and the Noonday mines.*

It was no surprise that with his range of abilities, Harry was soon promoted out of the powerhouse to work full-time for Herman Daisy with a raise to $13.20 per day—top dollar for a nonprofessional.

> *Herman was a big, husky guy, about forty years old and single. I worked for him the last two years at the Noonday. He was a superlative on-the-job handyman. He could fix absolutely anything. He taught me all sorts of things. The funny thing about Herman was that he had a dog that was passionately loyal to him. Some thought the dog was half-coyote, but I think he was at least part German shepherd. He was bigger than any coyote I ever saw. If he had a wild parent, it was more likely a wolf. That dog tolerated me. He was Herman's dog emotionally and would even go into the mines with him. I can still hear Herman talking to him. Herman spent a week in Los Angeles one time, taking the dog with him in his pickup in which he always had several boxes of tools in the back. I asked him if he took his tools inside at night. Herman said he left his dog in the pickup, and he was so fierce nothing was stolen.*

The other person whom Harry admired to the point of awe was Chick Joy, geologist and engineer for Anaconda. Harry was not the only miner who felt that way toward Joy. While it is no longer true today, in the 1940s, a mine geologist was a bit like a sorcerer and the miners a bit like his apprentices, because it was the geologist who (by dint of much college-level learning and field experience) could determine where the ore was located, its quality and quantity, and whether it was accessible enough to make mining profitable. Field maps, surveys, and diamond-drill samples were all used to figure out exactly where in the vast expanse of gravel-covered hills the miners should begin tunneling. Once ore was located, it was the job of the mining engineer to develop surface and underground operations, including the mine's physical structure (its adits, shafts, etc.) as safely and economically as possible. However, in the 1940s, the two jobs were often combined as they were at the Noonday mines. Just the fact that Joy was a thorough professional who always wore neat khakis and worked in an office at the mining camp, which was cooled by a swamp cooler, was enough to impress the miners. But more important, he was at home down below and was willing to take the time to explain to miners how and why he took samples.

In the late 1940s, using diamond-drilling, Joy located a new high-grade ore body in the War Eagle in the faulted section of the main vein at the 690-foot level. The grade ran from 20 to 40 percent lead with up to one-half ounce of silver for each percent of lead as well as some gold. Joy designed an adit approximately two thousand feet long to reach the new ore body to be tunneled from the inside of the mine outward and from the outside of the mine inward, coming from the eastern side of the mountain. Joy's job, as he described it, was to make sure the tunnels met. But when the final blast occurred, he was initially disappointed. In an interview with Susan Sorrells, the granddaughter of Charlie Brown, he described the event: "After the blast there was just a solid wall of rock. No breakthrough. So I got up on the rock pile and dug around in the dirt. I could hear some voices. I reached my hand down and found a drill hole, and I reached my hand through and someone grabbed my hand and shook it." It was cause for great celebration. "We went to Shoshone for champagne, but the champagne was beer in those days." The exactitude amazed everyone and made Joy legendary in the local mining community. Harry was very impressed with Chick's engineering: "What Chick did was to close a traverse over rough terrain, not an easy thing to do given the inaccuracy of the transits and tape measures of the day complicated by temperature variations between the surface and underground portions of the traverse. His bull's-eye only needed the lateral two of the three coordinates to be considered a bull's-eye."[82]

That particular ore body enabled Anaconda to restart its mill, which had been shut down when the vein began to play out. It kept the War Eagle profitable for several more years until in 1957 the price of lead began to fall and Anaconda closed its operations at the Noonday and Darwin mines.

> *Chick was not the mentor Lauren Wright was, but he went about his business very openly, and he freely answered my questions. Like Lauren, he was an all-around nice guy with a nice family. He inspired me by example as Lauren did. But otherwise I didn't see that much of him. What I saw was his work product and that was impressive. I was a junior at San Jose State before I learned how he matched his drill cores with the stratigraphy of the Noonday dolomite. The diamond-drill cores were kept in long, shallow wooden boxes and properly labeled. They were identified mineralogically. Chick explained to me what he saw in the drilled core samples. I was so in awe of him that I thought he knew all about everything. When I looked at Chick, I saw the man I wanted to be—a mining geologist who knew exactly what he was doing. My resolve to go to college became stronger.*

Hanging heavily over his head was the issue of how to pay for college. With his promotion, Harry was earning $1.60 more per day, just enough to pay off the grocery debt and to make a down payment on a small sixteen-foot house trailer. "It was blue-gray in color, brand-new, and really very nice. To Geri and me, it seemed spacious, even luxurious, because neither of us had ever lived in a big house. We bought it on time and moved it to the mill camp, which cut the cost of traveling each day from Tecopa. Plus, the space at the camp came with a combination laundry and bathroom. It was shared, so there was not much privacy, but it was free." Harry parked the trailer at what was called Married Man's Camp (to differentiate it from Single Man's Camp, which had its own bunkhouses, showers, and a kitchen/dining area), choosing a spot as far from the mill as possible. "The mill reeked with chemicals. You didn't want to live near it."

It was not an easy life for Geri. There wasn't much to do during the day once household chores were finished, and for a small trailer, chores didn't take long. There were no jobs open to women at the mines. Whereas Tecopa Hot Springs and Shoshone had at least some activities going on, the mining camp had nothing for diversion except the occasional board or card game, chess and pinochle being favorites.

There was also baseball—a sport that amounted to a passion in the Mojave region as exemplified by the famous 1938 Fourth of July game between the Shoshone Indians and the Death Valley Junction Giants. The difficulty was that it was nearly impossible to listen to the major league games on the radio because AM radio signals could not be received during the day. The big leagues had begun playing games under the lights in 1935, but nighttime radio reception was intermittent in the desert, so out of necessity, baseball had to be of the homegrown variety. There were both town teams and mining teams, though they often overlapped, with an informal league comprised of Shoshone, Darwin, Beatty, Baker, Death Valley Junction, and Pahrump. The competition was intense; in fact, there was a common joke that the mine executives were more interested in hiring good ballplayers than in hiring good miners, at least during the baseball season. At the Noonday mines, the Shoshone Indians got a second chance at local fame, with some of the same players in the lineup as in its glory days before World War II.

> *Our Shoshone team was very good. But the "turf" was mostly rock and gravel and the temperature was often over 120 degrees. It was at the Noonday one summer that I actually took the thermometer used on the diesel generator and measured the temperature of the sand only to find, with dismay, that it was a blistering 180 degrees! To protect myself when I played, all I did was put on an extra pair of wool socks for insulation and drink plenty of water. No one ever slid into base—you'd burn your skin if you did. I played center field and first base. Occasionally, I relieved the pitcher. My friend George Ross could play any position pretty well, including pitcher. We almost always won, even against Darwin, the big brother team in the league. In one memorable win against Darwin, both George and I homered. George went for power. I could only go with finesse. I could hit the ball where I wanted, and that is how I got my home run, barely in, down the left field line. George got*

*his in straightaway center, as I recall. We expected the local
barkeep to keep his promise of a case of beer to the first guy
to homer. But he invoked a "Darwin only" clause after the
fact. A lesson in poor sportsmanship was learned the hard
way. At least there wasn't any fight as there had been at
Shoshone in 1938.*

On the weekends, Geri and Harry hiked and prospected a little just
for something to do, although they never found anything of much value.
Harry also hunted, supplementing their food supply, often taking Herman
Daisy with him. "Daisy came from Idaho and did not know the desert. He
appreciated me taking him to hunting places only the locals knew about.
It was my way of repaying him for all the mechanics and electronics he
taught me." It was Daisy whom Harry took to Scranton tank high up in
the Funeral Mountains to the northeast of Death Valley where they found
the skull of the bighorn sheep Harry and his father had shot before leaving
the desert for Long Beach. "There it was where it had fallen from the cliff
with my bullet hole through the horn. My father's bullet had gone through
the heart. I had been only fourteen years old at the time."

Harry also was leader of a Boy Scout troop made up of boys from
Tecopa and Shoshone. Once, when he and some boys were camping, they
woke up just before dawn as the stars were beginning to fade. "Suddenly,
the sky lit up bright as day from an atomic bomb explosion up at the
Nevada test site near Yucca Flats approximately seventy miles to the north.
The Cold War had come to the Mojave, and none of us ever forgot it."

In a letter to Ethel and other family members dated April 28, 1950,
Harry joked about all the activities in which he and Geri were involved.
"Many of you have had a promise from us to visit you. Well, we ain't got
no excuse except that we're too busy dancing, scouting, picture showing,
fixing radios, etc." He mentioned that it was election season and Charlie
Brown was campaigning for state senator again and his father Harry Sr.
was running for constable. "I'm gonna run for dog catcher and run all the
communists out of Tecopa. I'm gonna handcuff all the winos and ding
bats to telephone poles. Somebody has to hold them up. There'll be some
changes made—I'm gonna domesticate all the coyotes and build a dam
across the Amargosa. Why? So I can fish for lynx-cat fish. You know it
takes a genius to write tripe like this." In a more serious vein, he wrote
that "we have it in our heads that maybe we can both go on to school."

With a little money saved, Harry had started to look for colleges, but the only one he could afford was San Jose State College. Fortunately, it offered a major in geology. His opportunity came in 1951 when the mine workers union called a strike against Anaconda at the Noonday mines. Coinciding with the start of the fall term, the strike was expected to last about three months, which meant that if Harry went to San Jose State and it didn't work out, he could return to the mines following the strike, having wasted only the cost of tuition—all of twenty-five dollars. He took the chance.

In 1916, flooding of the Mojave River caused extensive damage to the rails. The Proctor gas station was flooded in the mid-1920s.

Traveling to Crucero in 1917, the Proctors found nothing there but desert and railroad. In this photo taken in the 1930s, Elmo Proctor leans against the remains of the wagon similar to the one they used.

In 1920, Elmo (holding Mary), Alma, and May stand beside Mrs. Edwards, the teacher assigned by the State of California to teach the children in Crucero.

Harry and his brother Lloyd in front of their grandfather's gas station in the early 1930s.

Dressed up for the photographer in sailor suits and shoes, Lloyd and Harry stand with their mother by the caboose in which they lived.

Harry, fourteen months old, attempts to paint a post under the watchful eye of his father. From his earliest years, he wanted to know how everything worked.

In 1906–7, it took a workforce of approximately nine hundred men to lay track through the treacherous Amargosa Canyon. The trestle was one of their greatest achievements.

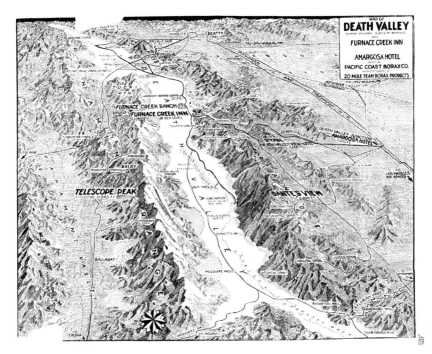

In the late 1920s, Pacific Coast Borax stopped mining in Death Valley and turned to promoting tourism instead, printing this map to show the location of the hotels.

As foreman of the bridge repair outfit, Harry Rosenberg Sr. had a reputation as a skilled builder. Here his crew works on the trestle in Amargosa Canyon.

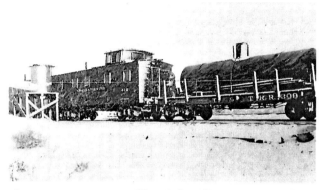

*In a rare snowstorm at Silver Lake siding, Nona Rosenberg
holds Harry between the water car and the caboose.*

*Harry Sr. was a crack shot who supplemented the family's
diet with rabbits, ducks, and bighorn sheep.*

*Harry and Lloyd play beside the caboose in 1930. Keeping
children safe was a challenge. Besides trains, there were
venomous snakes, sharp tools, and caustic chemicals.*

*Nona holds Harry as she and Harry Sr. prepare to wash clothes in a tub at
Riggs, one of the T & T's most remote sidings near the Avawatz Mountains.*

Harry plays in the sunlight in a boxcar in the autumn of 1928.

Despite its name, Silver Lake at the base of the Avawatz Mountains is a dry lakebed that can flood following heavy storms.

When Harry was three, he and his family were sleeping outside in Death Valley Junction when a lynx tried to attack him in the middle of the night. The sound of his mother's screams and the blast from his father's rifle terrified him.

On this postcard are the words "Christmas Eve in the Tecopa Snake Room," a hangout for prospectors and miners including Cross-Country Mike (standing sixth from left).

Charlie Brown was big-hearted and helpful in Shoshone, looking after miners and down-on-their-luck prospectors.

Harry Rosenberg, Carl Rook, and the boys swim in the Shoshone swimming pool, one of the few places where they could escape the heat.

The Proctor gas station was located near Cat Mountain, named after the dune on its side that looks like a sitting cat with a twitching tail.

Roads through the Mojave Desert were so terrible that automobiles and buses often got stuck in the sand.

The gas station in Cronese Cove had three manual pumps under a metal awning. Customers could come inside to buy candy and soda and look at Elmo Proctor's rock collection.

Ethel Proctor (holding Carl Rook Jr.) was Harry's aunt. Only six years older than Harry, she provided emotional support to both boys following their mother's death.

A friend of Elmo Proctor, Jim Hyten was one of the last of the prospectors in the region. At the end of his life, he survived by eating cans of dog food while still dreaming of finding gold.

Harry and Lloyd traveled an hour and a half one way on a rickety bus to attend school in Yermo. Wearing suspenders, Harry is sixth from the left in the back row and Lloyd is fourth from the left in the front row.

The artist and writer John Hilton and Mary Proctor on one of his painting trips. Hilton loved to swap tall tales and search for rocks with Elmo Proctor.

After World War II, the Rosenbergs built a motel and café near the hot springs in Tecopa using the abandoned railroad ties for lumber.

There were only two people in Harry's graduating class from Death Valley Junction High School in 1946.

*What remains of the Western Talc mine can be spotted from a great
distance because of the gleaming white dumps and exposed seams.*

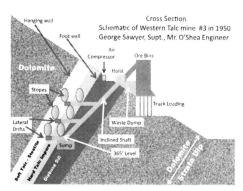

The schematic of the Western Talc mine shows the 365-foot level where Harry's partner was killed when the roof collapsed.

The Noonday lead mines opened in the 1870s. By the time Harry worked there, they had been taken over by Anaconda.

The roads were so bad, it was necessary for the Rosenbergs to be competent auto mechanics to get to work or to go hunting on Paiute Mesa.

The wooden head frame towers over the mine portal. The diesel powerhouse is to the right of the bins and head frame.

The view south from the road to the War Eagle portal. The dark jagged feature in the middle is a tributary to the Amargosa River that passes the remains of Mill Camp.

In 2011, Harry returned to the War Eagle where nothing is left but foundations, dangerous air vents, rubble-filled entries, and rusting hulks.

Harry holds his son, Keith, in 1954 on the San Jose State College campus.

INDIVIDUAL HELP to students by faculty members is plentiful in the closely knit curriculum in metallurgy at Stanford. Here a professor discusses with a student the microstructure of a casehardened gear as seen with the metallurgical microscope.

At Stanford University, Orson Cutler Shepard was a dynamic teacher who infused his love of metallurgy into his students. Here he works with William Nix who would also be influential in Harry's life.

McGill, Nevada, was a company town for Kennecott Copper.

Beginning in his laboratory in Europe and continuing at the Bureau of Mines in the United States after World War II, William Kroll opened up a new era in titanium metallurgy.

Titanium Metals Corporation of America (TIMET) began operations in 1950 on the site of an abandoned World War II magnesium factory in Henderson, Nevada.

*More than 90 percent titanium, the SR-71 Blackbird
was the most spectacular aircraft ever built.*

*Marrying Harry in 1967, Kris Rosenberg was a psychologist
who helped him come to terms with his painful past.*

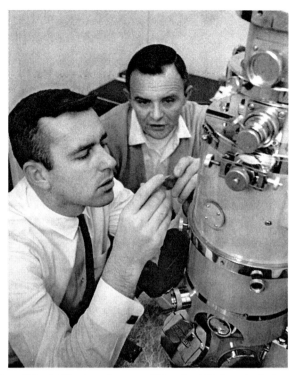

William Nix (left), then director of Stanford University's Center for Materials Research, works with a technician on an electron microscope. Nix set the bar high for Harry on the physics of plastic deformation.

Flowing on the surface as it nears Death Valley, the Amargosa looks benign, but after a storm, it can turn deadly. Harry Rosenberg Sr. drowned in the river in 1969.

The second of Harry's three sons, Neil Rosenberg was in the
US Army when he was diagnosed with a brain tumor.

Harry Rosenberg supervises the first production of high-purity titanium at the Alta Group in May 1985.

The employees of the Alta Group in the 1990s in Fombell, Pennsylvania. Harry is second from the right in the front row.

In 1996, the former British Prime Minister Margaret Thatcher cut the ribbon for the new titanium sponge plant in Utah. (L. to r.: Jack Bollick, Nigel Winters, Michael Miller, David Savage, Geoff Wild, David Davies, Margaret Thatcher, Sir Denis Thatcher, Benoit Pouliquen, Harry Rosenberg.)

In 2008, Harry and Joselyne Mivumbi visited her family in Cyangugu, Rwanda. (L. to r.: Niece Fiona, Joselyne, father, mother, Harry, and brother Victor.)

PART II
STRANGE NEW WORLD, STRANGE NEW METAL

He who drinks from the Hassayampa can
Never after tell the truth.
He who drinks from the Amargosa can
Never after tell a lie.
Between the river of lies and the river of
Truth, are many suns of scorching sands,
Confusing mountains, straying trails;
He who does not speak at all
Is a widely traveled man.

From *Rhymes of the Mighty Mohave* by Elmo Proctor

CHAPTER 8:
LEAVING THE AMARGOSA

Once the decision was made to leave the mines and go to San Jose State College, Harry and Geri hitched up their little trailer and left immediately. Engine trouble dogged them from the moment they pulled out of Married Man's Camp to the moment they sputtered into a trailer park on the edge of San Jose a day later. The trailer park was run by an Eastern European whose English was heavily accented, reminding Harry of Bohunk, his partner at the Western Talc mines, whose death four years earlier had given him the resolve to get out of the "hole." Nor were living conditions much different than in the camp, although the temperate benignity of the weather was a definite improvement. Rent was twenty-five dollars a month, the only amenities provided being a community bath, shower, lavatory, and washing machine. It was more than they could afford, but housing was at a premium in San Jose, which had started to expand after World War II, a process that would pick up steam over the next three decades as it transformed itself from the center of agricultural Santa Clara Valley to the center of technological Silicon Valley.

Geri's father, Johnny Davis, a truck driver of very modest means but with a very generous heart, gave them some money to help buy food and pay the rent, but to survive to the end of the quarter, they had to find jobs right away. In the early 1950s, one of the chief industries in San Jose was fruit packing and canning. Within a week of arrival, Harry found a night job paying ten dollars per shift at American Can Company boxing cans of locally grown cherries for market. Geri got a job working in a movie theater in downtown San Jose. When the cannery closed at the end of the growing season, Harry did odd jobs, painting and repairing, and also sold shoes—almost anything to earn a dime.

> *I rationalized that we'd take it one day at a time, although I was nervous too, not only about working nights while trying to attend classes during the day but also about making it in school academically. At twenty-three years old, I was five years beyond high school, which put me five years behind my classmates. My grades at Wilson High in Long Beach averaged C+ only because I aced athletics. My A's at Death Valley High School seemed not to count because standards were rural at best. But then there was Helen Ogston, still there in my mind, tantalizing me with the idea that I just might make it if I tried. And working into better, more skilled jobs in short order at the Western and Noonday mines had given me added confidence.*

San Jose State, then a teacher's college, accepted Harry on probation because of the unevenness of his high-school education. One of his first classes was mathematics, a subject in which his desert schooling had been well below par, there being no one at Death Valley Junction High School able to teach anything beyond basic arithmetic. To fill the void, he had taken a correspondence course run by the University of California Berkeley extension system. "No one explained anything; it was all rote learning." Harry felt keenly the lack of quality mathematical training and tried hard to make up for it at San Jose State, and if grades are any indication, he succeeded. However, throughout his career, he believed he never achieved the level of mathematical skill he thought he could have reached had he been taught properly early in his life. Years later, he wrote of his struggles with mathematics in a speech titled "Origins of an Ethos."

> *After having accomplished something new, I often cannot relate the "logic" I used, even when engineering results seem self-evident. Usually, a new idea simply appears as a picture or hunch in my mind. Translating it into mathematics can be a trial. I must have had the poorest math teachers on the planet. In grad school, I felt I was sitting on a limb about to be chopped off. So when I was at Stanford University, I audited several math courses taken several years before at San Jose State to reach a better understanding. From that experience, I can tell you, rote learning is for the birds.*

Understanding the roots comes before you can learn about the tree.[83]

Harry also took courses in English and history. Some people who have an aptitude for engineering and science chafe at studying liberal arts, but Harry did not, seeing them as a way to understand the world more broadly while eventually helping him make the transition into the tough technological world of metallurgy. He had arrived on campus with considerable skills in electronics, mechanics, surveying, carpentry, and mining, but none of his learning had been systematic or book-based; it had all been hands-on and hard knocks. "I am convinced that those who specialize too narrowly miss out. The word *consilience*, meaning a unity of knowledge, was not in wide use back then, but already in my first quarter at San Jose State, I was glimpsing its truth."[84]

About Christmastime, Harry and Geri were able to move into Spartan Village, a mix of small apartments and trailer spaces named after San Jose State's athletic teams and run by the college. With minimal facilities, it was Spartan in more than name, but it was also cheap at only ten dollars a month rental for the trailer site, power, water, shower, and laundry facilities. Harry also discovered to his relief that his freshman class was not comprised solely of recent high-school graduates who knew little of the world and who planned on becoming teachers following graduation. It was also made up of many married World War II veterans going to college on the GI bill. Because they were older, had families, and had seen the hard side of life, they offered much-needed friendship and moral support. Two of his and Geri's closest friends were Philip and Tatiana (shortened to the nickname Tawts) Anderson, who lived in a trailer next door. They were both music majors who, like Harry and Geri, had barely enough money to live on. Phil had been seriously wounded in the Philippines. "In facing problems, they were as harmonious as any couple I have ever known. Each had, and took, total latitude to be themselves—their real selves. Their bond was as strong as any I have ever seen. They also had worldviews much wider than mine, and I was fascinated."

A war mentality still lingered over the campus because while World War II had ended in 1945, the arms race between the USSR and the United States was intensifying, and the Korean War had begun. Lloyd had graduated from Death Valley Junction High School in 1948, the only other person in his class being his sister-in-law Geri Rosenberg. He had become a truck driver before being drafted into the US Army at the age of twenty and sent to Korea. He served in the artillery as a tank mechanic and took part in the Battle of Pusan in August and September 1950. Harry was very proud of Lloyd, although their lives had begun to move in different directions. Ever since the death of their mother, Harry had felt responsible for his little brother, but at the same time, he had felt guilty at being unable to shoulder that responsibility adequately. Even as an adult, he reflected back on the incident at the dam in Cronese, seeing in his mind's eye the earth collapsing behind Lloyd as they both ran for their lives. He also recalled with guilt a time at Death Valley Junction when he and his friend Tony Castillo had outpaced Lloyd on their bikes on a trip to a place they called Clay Camp, leaving him far behind in the desert. Realizing too late that he should not have allowed his brother to become separated from him, it was with a huge feeling of relief that he finally spotted Lloyd in the distance peddling resolutely across the sand. Similarly, once when Lloyd and Harry were teenagers in Long Beach, they decided to swim the length of the breakwater known as Rainbow Pier; again, Harry got too far ahead. He wrote to Lloyd years later about that incident: "Man was I ever glad you made it alone without drowning! Again I felt guilty." But now that Lloyd was grown up—even though he was in harm's way in Korea while Harry was safe at San Jose State—Harry's heavy sense of responsibility finally began to wane. In the years ahead, the brothers kept in touch via chess games played by mail one move at a time. What had been played merely for fun became a means to stay connected; just like the desert and trains, chess was embedded in their minds and always would be.

At the end of the quarter at San Jose, which coincided with the end of the strike against Anaconda at the Noonday mines, Harry was stunned to learn he had made straight A's except for a B in English and that he was invited to join the national freshman honor society, Phi Eta Sigma. "But the biggest joy was that my break from my roots was finally complete." He did not have to return to the lead mines. He and Geri could stay at San Jose State.

The second quarter, Harry found a better job working at a Union Oil service station, right across from the college library, every weekday evening and all day Saturday and Sunday.

Earning all of fifty dollars per week, our income was back
to the sustenance level. And I had just enough time to study.

I always had a book with me to read if a slow moment
arrived. Truth was I was on the edge of exhaustion all the
time and could be grumpy. Three or four times a year, we
would visit Uncle Harry and Aunt Millie Rook who owned a
poultry farm in Hollister about fifty miles away. Millie was
my mother's younger sister. Not only would they feed us, but
they would load us up with eggs and chickens. And that's
how we made it from one quarter to the next.

Academically, he began to take courses in his major, which meant he
came under the guidance of Norman Dolloff, a professor in the geology
department. A remarkable man, Dolloff was as kind as he was intelligent,
teaching Harry about the value of mentoring in addition to geology.
"Dolloff made himself available to his students in ways that encouraged
them to stretch. Right from the start, he showed me that mentoring is a
two-way street, which needs an emotional component—the element of
caring—to work." Dolloff had graduated from the Massachusetts Institute
of Technology (MIT) in 1930 and then had gone to Stanford University
earning his doctorate under Cutler Shepard, under whom Harry would
also eventually study. He had begun teaching at San Jose State College in
1946, staying there until his retirement twenty-seven years later in 1973.
Dolloff had adopted many of Shepard's teaching techniques, chief among
them being the use of the Socratic method in which students were asked
questions and encouraged to seek their own answers.

Norman was the rare friend who could laugh at himself as
easily as he laughed at me, which he never hesitated to do.
His enthusiasm was boundless, and he really could teach
with ease the most arcane topics, improvising on the Socratic
method, blending in drill and experimentation. That approach
did wonders for me because I'd always been asking questions
and seeking answers on my own. Now I learned to ask myself
the same questions he would ask in class or on a field trip.
The only straight-A quarter I ever had came after learning his
methods. You don't learn geology in the classroom. You must
get out in the field. When we went with Norman, we saw for
ourselves the grand works of nature, eroding, reprocessing,
remelting the earth into lava, eroding and depositing anew.

He honed my professional insights and taught reality—let theory catch up and explain things later; this is the way it is. He was careful in his training; every test had a vocabulary section, and he gave them every Friday and returned them without fail the next Monday with annotations.

Only once did Harry ever see Dolloff get flustered. He had taken his geology students on a field trip to a quarry in the foothills west of Santa Clara Valley to examine some fossils when the owner suddenly appeared and demanded to know what was going on. Dolloff had taken students to the quarry numerous times, and he assumed the area was in the public domain. But his explanation bore no weight with the irate owner who kicked them off his property and told them never to return. On a similar misadventure after Harry had left San Jose State, Dolloff broke a leg in making a hasty retreat from private property, but that didn't deter him from continuing to lead field trips, which he considered vital to the study of geology.

Financially, life was as tenuous as ever. For Harry it was work and study, work and study with no breaks or time off. For Geri, it was work and trying to make trailer life in Spartan Village livable. There was no money for anything but the basics, particularly not for vacations. However, being resourceful, they managed to get away occasionally.

Phil, Tawts, Geri, and I all wanted to see the Grand Canyon, but neither couple had a serviceable car. We had a 1936 Dodge pickup that was on its last wheels. Phil and Tawts drove an ancient Nash sedan that used almost as much oil as it did gasoline. So Phil bought the rings and bearings needed to fix his heap of a Nash and I overhauled the engine over a weekend. It ran perfectly the whole trip using nary a drop of oil. We hiked to the bottom of the canyon and did a three-day campout on the river just below Phantom Ranch. Aside from the fellowship and relaxation, for the first time, I began to really appreciate the immensity of geologic time exposed on the canyon walls. By then, I had learned enough geology to be able to begin interpreting what I saw. I was becoming the person I had wanted to be when I had met Lauren Wright while working for Western Talc. We drove

home through Ely, Nevada, and were about fifty miles east
of Reno when we ran out of gas about midnight. But veteran
Phil knew just what to do. He jumped out of the car and put
his thumb out. Sure enough, a car came along and picked him
up. After the lights disappeared, things got quiet indeed for
what seemed an eternity. No traffic whatsoever. A half hour
later, headlights appeared and slowed. Out jumped Phil with
enough gas in a can to get us to Reno! Much relief.

On May 6, 1954, Geri and Harry's first child, Keith, was born. It was
at the end of the quarter (the only one in which Harry had made straight
A's) and the beginning of yet another troubled time. Keith's foot was turned
inward such that his toe almost touched the inner anklebone. "We were
thrilled to have a son but dismayed at his physical problem because we
were too poor to pay for surgery. The doctor knew we had no money, so
he advised us about organizations that helped in situations such as this. He
was right. The Shriners covered Keith's medical care, including surgery, all
the time I was in school for which we were deeply grateful." The baby's
medical problems added great strain to their lives, especially for Geri. To a
degree, Harry could escape from the reality of his son's pain by studying
and working, but Geri could not. The brace Keith wore to hold his foot at
the proper angle kept him awake all night every night, and the casts that
were used to straighten his foot hurt him terribly. "He cried and cried and
kicked his foot against his crib. Casts were replaced every week or two,
but they only lasted a day or two. It was heartbreaking to see him scream
and kick his little foot. His foot straightened considerably as a result of the
casts but not enough. It took two surgeries later on to give him a decent
walking gait."

That summer, Harry took classes in photography, philosophy, history,
English composition, and psychology. Photography was memorable because
of the unique style of the professor.

The photography professor's first words to the class were
"There will be just one A in this course." His second words
were "And you will decide who gets it." We took pictures
each week that he developed. Then he would show the best
ones to the class and we would vote not knowing who took
the pictures. Weeks went by. None of my gems ever appeared,

*but I was so taken with all the things he said and the pictures
my classmates came up with, I kept trying. I was resigned to
getting a C when the final week of class arrived. The winner
that day would get the A. I was the most stunned person in
the room when one of the photos I took of our neighbor girl
reaching out to me through a gate in the picket fence at Spartan
Village won the A vote. I never seriously pursued photography,
but my sons are excellent photographers. I don't know that my
taking that course had any influence on them, but I do believe
that in some way, all things influence all others.*

Harry's philosophy professor that mind-broadening summer was also
unique. Peter A. Bertocci was from Boston College; had a high, squeaky
voice; and was idealistic in a way that was radically different from the more
practical viewpoints associated with geology and metallurgy. "I'd never
met anyone quite like him before—not in the Mojave, not in Long Beach,
and definitely not in the mines." His book *Introduction to the Philosophy
of Religion* had been published in 1951. He was at work on his next book
Free Will, Responsibility, and Grace, which would be published in 1957.
Bertocci believed strongly that while everyone may not actually be equal,
they should have equal opportunity, telling the class with deep conviction
that he would be willing to spend one day a week collecting garbage so that
he could fully appreciate the living conditions of the garbage collectors.
His concern for the working conditions of the poor, his assertion that they
had the right to aspire to a better life, and his idea of the vertical sharing of
responsibility resonated with Harry, who knew far more than the professor
about dirty, dangerous jobs; long days; and poor pay. Years afterward, first
as a senior engineer in charge of other engineers in the titanium industry
and then much later as a cofounder of a company making the highest purity
titanium in the world, Harry made a conscientious effort to practice what
his professor had preached, becoming a mentor who took the time to listen
to and learn from employees regardless of their positions. "Dr. Bertocci was
not the only influence on me, but what he said stuck with me. It took me
a while to understand the full psychological difference between a mentor
and a protégé relationship. But by instinct, I made it a two-way street from
the start. Instead of a top-down management style, I encouraged mutual
understanding and shared responsibility."

At the end of that summer while working at the gas station and preparing to start his senior year at San Jose State College, Harry got the biggest break of his life, and it came out of the blue.

> *One August day, Norman walked into the station where I worked. I wasn't too busy at the time, and he came over and said to me, "How would you like to have $2,000?" Without giving it a thought or asking what for, I said yes. That was at least ten times more money than I had ever seen before all in one place. It turned out there was a slight string attached. I had to go to Stanford University and change my major from geology, my first and continuing love, to metallurgy. It turned out that Cutler Shepard, chairman of the Department of Mining and Metallurgy at Stanford, had received a letter in his inbox while he was in the field for the summer. The letter was from Kennecott Copper Corp. offering a fellowship where the student and the university each received $2,000 a year. Having no ready candidates that late in the year for a graduate fellowship, Cutler began phoning his former students, including Norman, to see if they had any likely students at the senior level they could recommend, which was what brought Norman to the gas station to see me. The upshot was that I went for an interview. I didn't even have a decent suit. Just a tie. I took the train up to San Francisco and John C. Kinnear Jr., general manager for Kennecott operations in Nevada, took me out to dinner at the swank restaurant the Top of the Mark. A few days before the fall quarter was to begin, I was accepted at Stanford University. I was thrilled. At the same time, some of the old precollege nervousness set in. But I had gained confidence, thanks to Norman, along with a decent transcript.*

There was no question of turning down the offer. Keith's ongoing medical care put the family under great financial and emotional strain even with the enormous help of the Shriners, and the fact of the matter was Stanford University graduates could find jobs easily, whereas San Jose State College graduates had a harder time of it. What worried Harry about going to Stanford was changing majors so late in the game. "At that time, geology and metallurgy were very close, metallurgy having to do with extracting metals from their ores. But even so, there was much to learn, I was entering my senior year, and I knew nothing of the metallurgical vocabulary." The other downside was leaving Norman Dolloff with whom Harry had a rare affinity and relationship. However, the opportunity to attend Stanford was not to be missed, so saying good-bye to their friends at Spartan Village, Geri and Harry hooked up the trailer to their rickety pickup, put the baby in the middle of the front seat (cast and all), and headed for Palo Alto. They pulled into a trailer park on the Bayshore Freeway on the eastern side of town just in time for the start of the fall quarter.

> Our old '36 Dodge pickup barely made it. It was running on only five cylinders with just three operable brakes on four wheels. You had to be super careful driving it. Neither door window was operable, and the windshield was cracked. Springs poked through the driver's seat. The driver's door was missing a spring latch; you had to latch it manually. Geri refused to drive it, it was so bad. So not long after we got to Palo Alto, we bought a 1948 Ford for $150 with a $20 down payment, which I think came from Johnny Davis, Geri's father, who continued to help us financially across the hard spots. It drove like a dream in comparison to the pickup, which I promptly drove to a junkyard. It was so bad the proprietor refused to take it. Not one part was salvageable! Weeks later, a mechanic friend in business for himself took pity on me. "Park it behind my shop. I can sell the metal in it to a junky"—meaning a scrap metal dealer. But at least it had gotten us to Palo Alto.

The campus of Stanford University was magnificent with long rows of palm trees, red-tile roofs (made with the talc that came from the Western Talc mine), and buildings of carved sandstone. The entire campus was laid out on a grand plan by the famous landscape architect Frederick Law Olmstead, designer of Central Park in New York City. Opening the school in 1891, Leland and Jane Stanford had spared no expense in making it a showpiece that could stand up to its eastern academic rivals both architecturally and intellectually. But for Geri and Harry, not only did such splendor not matter, it was not even noticed. The trailer park was about survival. There was no grass, only blacktop, the trailers were squeezed together, and everyone who lived there was poor. Once they had settled in, Geri and Harry made friends with the Moss family who lived next door.

> *They were as poor as we were and shared our plight. Their younger daughter had lost her lower leg at the knee, so they understood about Keith's problems and the stress it put on us. He was an expert mechanic who owned his own little garage business, so he and I had much in common. Oh, but money was short, very short. The Kennecott scholarship was not nearly enough.*

Just as he had done in San Jose, Harry got a job at a Union Oil gas station on Middlefield Road in Menlo Park working for a man named Elmer Bocks. It was back to pumping gas, read a page, change a tire, read another page, trying to complete in one year a new major, metallurgy, on top of his old major, geology. He also distributed newspapers in the early morning.

> *I was in shock over my change in schools. Continuing those straight A's I had received at San Jose State in my last quarter was out of the question. No way was I ready for the academic load at Stanford, but I buckled down and managed one way or the other, mastering the language of metallurgy until it felt like an old friend. I even won a nomination to Sigma Xi, the scientific research society, which I accepted. What set me apart from my peers was not my knowledge but my ability to apply what we were learning. They usually beat me out grade-wise. But I already knew a lot about how things worked and that gave me an edge, especially when it came to research.*

His move to Stanford brought him into the sphere of yet another remarkable man, Orson Cutler Shepard, chairman of the Department of Mining and Metallurgy. He was known as Cutler even to his students, to whom he was deeply committed. He had a sense of humor, was humble, and was direct and honest. "Cutler believed in getting your hands dirty and to practice what you preached just as Norman Dolloff had. In fact, he spent summers practicing his craft at a mill or smelter. His voluminous practical experience set him apart from the usual department head." Shepard had graduated from Stanford's Mining and Metallurgy Department in 1925 with his specialty being extractive metallurgy. Then he had joined the research department of Anaconda Copper Mining Company processing copper ores in Montana. He had also worked for Anaconda as an assayer and assistant mill superintendent at a remote gold and silver mine in Mexico before returning to Stanford to earn an engineering degree that gave him expertise in physical metallurgy.[85] He never earned his PhD, but that lack had no effect on his academic career.

By the 1940s, Shepard realized that metallurgy was moving away from mining with which it had been connected. The field of extractive metallurgy had reached a point of maturity. Only a few metals, titanium being one, still presented challenges in winning metal from ore. Therefore, the focus was shifting to alteration of the structure and properties of materials through the application of physics and chemistry. The realization of this fundamental change led Shepard to develop new courses grounded in the scientific method. For example, in the late 1940s, he taught a course for the first time on the use of X-rays as a characterization tool in metallurgy. His own work of the period looked at the effects of environment on the creep of metals, which is the tendency of solid metals to slowly deform under the influence of stresses. He was also involved in materials problems in nuclear reactors, a radically new development.

When I knew him, Cutler was a slender man about five feet eleven inches with a big, booming voice; a large shock of gray hair; and dancing blue-gray eyes. He absolutely loved teaching. And he could inspire. Something as simple as dumping mud on a conveyor belt, then washing it on an oscillating table with water to move the light minerals off first and dropping the heavy stuff into a bin became a drama in his description. We sat on the edges of our seats to catch every word. One early exposure to his teaching skill came when he strung a piece of iron wire across room 101 in the Mining Building. He hooked a variable electric power source to each end and began to heat it. Finally, it got a little red, then redder and redder still. As it heated, it sagged of course. But then something strange happened. It stopped sagging and got suddenly shorter, reversing the sag even as it continued to get redder! We were enthralled by our introduction to the ferrite-to-austenite transformation in steel. It seems in austenite, which is the high-temperature form, that the atoms are packed more closely together than in ferrite at low temperature. That is just one lecture I shall never forget. Cutler used ordinary words to explain the complex and arcane and to make it all so real and obvious after the explanation. Years later, when I saw the Nobel Prize–winning physicist Richard Feynman on TV, he reminded me of Cutler. Feynman demonstrated for the US Congress how the rubber gaskets used in the Challenger *disaster turned brittle when dipped in ice water. This temperature effect was the cause of the disaster. Miles apart and in different fields, Cutler and Feynman, who was at Caltech, were brothers in the dramas of science and technology. They could make complex things clear by demonstration. There was no Nobel Prize for Cutler. What he had were hundreds of protégés and students to carry on his very beingness—a better word I cannot find.*

When Harry first met Shepard, both metallurgy and geology were undergoing phase changes. Geology appeared to be a field that had reached its peak, although plate tectonics and dramatic advances in geophysics would demolish that assumption in the years ahead. Then known as continental drift, plate tectonics had been around since 1915 when Alfred Wegener proposed the idea, but the majority of geologists rejected it because there was no evidence of any mechanism by which the Earth's crust could move. Not until the 1950s when the ridges and trenches of the oceans began to be mapped and geologists recognized magnetic patterns indicative of the spreading of the seafloor did the theory gain traction. By the 1960s, enough hard data had accumulated to blow the field wide open. Suddenly, there was a whole new vocabulary of terms, such as subduction zones, transform faults, and plate boundaries. What had appeared to be a rather stodgy field of study, as deep and solid as the craton under the prairies, became as dynamic as an active volcano.

Concurrently, the connection between geology and metallurgy began to thin, as did the connection between those fields and engineering. Rather like the spreading of the seafloor in which new crust was being formed in the deep ocean trenches, so metallurgy was in the process of being transformed into the new field of materials science encompassing not just metals but—as its new name implied—ceramics, polymers, and composites, moving inexorably toward solid-state physics. One of the driving factors in the 1950s was aviation, which had come up against the limitations of metals such as steel and aluminum. To build more powerful aircraft and rockets, the industry required lighter and stronger materials. But these materials did not exist. It wasn't a matter of taking a standard alloy off the shelf and tweaking it a little to get a better set of physical properties.

Harry's own educational history is exemplary of this enormous change. He started out as a geology major at San Jose State College with the dream of following in the footsteps of Lauren Wright and Chick Joy, studying the Amargosa chaos in Death Valley or drilling samples of Noonday dolomite for the mining industry in search of a new strike. Instead, he would graduate from Stanford University with a BS in extractive metallurgy and an MS in metallurgical engineering. Put simply, extractive metallurgy focuses on the separation and concentration of raw ore. Metallurgical engineering builds off of extractive metallurgy, adding a design and construction component. For example, an extractive metallurgist would study how to concentrate raw material more efficiently after it has been milled; it would then be the job of the metallurgical engineer to redesign the concentrator to achieve the goal. It was the right combination of disciplines for Harry, who liked to learn how something worked theoretically so that he could improve the process practically. However, when he returned to Stanford nine years later in 1966, having spent the interim period working in the nascent titanium industry, he would get his PhD in materials science.

To underscore the significance of the change, one of the reasons Harry decided to return to Stanford after nearly a decade away was because he felt strongly the need for a new, broader pool of knowledge applicable to the research he was doing on the development of titanium alloys. It would have been much easier for him to stay at the professional level he had reached in his metallurgical career, but the intellectual restlessness that was part of his nature goaded him on. The field of materials science was expanding so fast that the only way for him to keep up was to step out of industry, go back to academia, and then return to industry. "I needed to know more physical metallurgy so I could go toe to toe with customer engineers, such as those at Boeing, who increasingly held PhDs in materials science."

It was Shepard who had been instrumental in bringing about that change at Stanford. In 1960, he helped establish the Materials Science Department in the School of Engineering instead of in the School of Earth

Sciences, a shift indicative of the key role materials science was already playing in advanced technology. Serving as the department's first chair, he instilled in his students, including Harry, his hopes for the new field.

> *As vitally important as his vision of the future of materials science was, what stands out for me was Cutler's basic humanity. He was a good man. He found loan after loan for needy students, and via networking, he got them summer jobs. He invited them to his house—including Geri and me—knowing they would appreciate a good meal and conversation. He even played softball with us during the department picnics. In his fifties, he got all banged up sliding into second with a double, laughing his head off. I haven't touched as many people as Cutler did, but he inspired much of what I have been able to do in my life. Never could I match his deep and resonant voice. But I did catch his enthusiasm. Cutler taught me I could pursue new things, something I am still doing in the twilight years of my life.*

However, when Harry graduated with his bachelor's degree in June 1955, planning to begin work on his master's in the fall, the old orders still held in the workaday world of geologists and metallurgists: the first group continued to scoff at continental drift and the preexistence of a single landmass called Pangea; and the second group went on melting, mixing, cooling, and hammering ores just as their forbears had done. As a Kennecott Copper Fellowship holder, Harry was in that second group. He had a summer job waiting for him in the company's mill in Nevada, an appropriate assignment given that his degree was in extractive metallurgy. So he, Geri, and Keith, finally without his cumbersome cast, climbed in their '48 Ford hooked to the trailer (with a reinforced hitch Harry rigged up from scrap he had saved from his days in the Noonday mines) and headed for Ely, Nevada, about twelve miles south of McGill. But with the trailer in tow, they dared not go via the Tioga Pass, at an elevation of 9,943 feet, over the Sierra Nevada Mountains. Eventually, Harry would see the Sierra Nevadas as a magnificent example of plate tectonics, formed by the sliding and grinding of the Pacific plate under the North American plate, forcing the embedded rock skyward, but in 1955, he saw them as nothing but a nuisance, forcing him to take the less-steep southern route through

Fresno, Bakersfield, Barstow, and Tonopah. That route presented its own set of challenges. The Ford was designed to operate in ordinary temperatures, such as those of Palo Alto, not the furnace temperatures of the Great Basin region of central Nevada in the summer. It made it as far as Tonopah.

> Pulling out of Tonopah going north, our wonderful car balked, then balked some more, and we had several long pulls ahead. The balking ensued every time the radiator began to boil. Pulling off the pavement and letting the engine cool was the only solution available. Geri was patient but nervous too because we had Keith with us, who was only one year old. After pulling the first long grade a mile at a time, we found a service station just past the summit. It seems that Henry Ford who revolutionized the auto industry was a poor engineer. He placed the fuel pump on top of his fancy V-8 engine where it would overheat at the slightest provocation. Overheating turns gasoline into a vapor, which is not sufficient to keep a thirsty engine running. It was the same problem that had plagued our old school bus that had carried me and Lloyd to Yermo in the mid-1930s. If you have ever heard of vapor lock, this was it. Auto design rapidly improved in later models to the point it never happens today. But in our day, it was a nuisance at best, and at worst a disaster when an engine blew.

Fortunately, the gas station into which they pulled had a garage attached, and Harry was elated to find that the owner, having seen numerous cars in a similar state, had in stock an electric pump booster to raise the pressure on the pump to the point where the gas would not boil. Harry knew how to make the repair himself and had his own tools. "I got the job done by myself while Geri waited with the baby. The electric fuel pump made a racket whenever the key was on, but the engine never again balked." They drove to Ely without further problems.

Like Anaconda, which owned the Noonday mines, Kennecott Copper Corp. was an enormous company established by the "Copper Kings," first and foremost being the Guggenheims. Up until the late nineteenth century, it was gold and silver that attracted investors, not copper. Then Thomas Alva Edison and Nikola Tesla figured out how to harness the power of electricity and transmit it over long distances, and suddenly everything changed because enormous quantities of copper were needed for wire. Kennecott's beginning traced back to 1906 and the discovery of a mountain of copper in Alaska, but it was not until the First World War that its profits took off. Through various corporate changes and stock purchase iterations, even William Andrews Clark (William "Borax" Smith's nemesis in the race to construct the T & T) played a role via investments in Nevada mines acquired by Kennecott.[86]

By 1955, when Harry began working for them, Kennecott had become the largest copper producer in the United States. It also accounted for about 25 percent of production worldwide. In Nevada, it was the largest employer with five huge pit operations: Veteran Pit, Brooks Pit, Kimberley Pit, Morris Pit, and the Liberty Pit at Copper Flat, which was the largest of them all at a mile long, more than a half-a-mile wide, and an average depth of five hundred feet. Awed by what he was looking at, the writer of an article about Kennecott, published in 1955 in the magazine *Nevada Highways and Parks*, had this to say about Copper Flat:

> *When miners first began to work at the site in 1908, it wasn't a hole—it was actually two small hillocks about 50 feet high. Those hills had to be leveled down before the status as a hole could be started. After all those years with 5-[cubic]-yard shovels chewing away at five different places on the walls and bottom, thousands of pounds of powder blasting down hillsides, whistling locomotives pulling their hearts out to reach the rim over 14 miles of rails, with eight cars filled with 65 tons of ore, miles and miles of automobile roads switchbacking from the rim to the bottom, 500 feet down, millions of man hours of labor, hundreds of employees, and millions of dollars in working payrolls, you get the idea as to the staggering magnitude of the material removed and the size of the hole.*[87]

Harry's summer job was at Kennecott's huge mill where his assignment was to write an operating procedures manual. McGill had been chosen as the site of the mill and smelter back in 1906 because it had a stream named Duck Creek that provided plentiful water—a necessity for the milling process. Running twenty-four-hours a day, the mill processed about twenty-one thousand tons of low-grade ore daily that was processed down to about 750 tons of concentrates by separating the copper minerals from the waste material. The concentrates were sent to the 132-foot-long furnace at the nearby smelter from which they emerged as a molten substance called matte.[88] Treated in a converter to burn off the iron and sulfur, the matte yielded the end product known as blister copper that was 99.5 percent pure. Besides processing the ore from all of Kennecott's pits, the mill and smelter also processed, under contract, the ore from the mines of Consolidated Coppermines Corp. in nearby Kimberly, Nevada.

> For an extractive metallurgist, it was excellent training, because by the end, I knew the mill better than just about anyone. Ore was shipped by rail from the pits to the mill, a distance of about twenty miles. At the mill, each car was turned upside down to dump some one hundred tons of ore at a time into the throat of a jaw crusher big enough to crush a house. Watching that event was awe-inspiring for a guy who had been a pick-and-shovel miner. After additional crushing, the ore was ground in a row of twenty ball mills with classifiers separating coarse particles for regrinding. The finer particles that were suspended in the water were laundered (troughed) to the flotation cells. I'd learned some of this when I worked at the War Eagle, but at Kennecott, my education went much further.

That summer, there were two streams of ore coming into the mill, one from the Kennecott pits and the other from Consolidated Coppermines. Keeping track of the respective ore streams was part of the operating procedures on which Harry worked, giving him exposure to quality control concepts. "Quality control was not formal, nor was it explained well. Basically the department head knew what should be done and tried to do it. My job was to figure it out and formalize it." Like so many other experiences in Harry's life, such as learning to harden steel back at the Noonday mines, his first encounter with quality control was of great value. "By the end of the summer, I had learned many things that would be of use when I started my own company years later."

For Geri and the baby, Ely and nearby McGill were pleasant locations for spending the summer because both were essentially company towns where Kennecott had built playgrounds, swimming pools, libraries, and several other amenities. As was her habit, Geri made friends quickly with the neighbors, one of whom had a husband in the US Army stationed in South Korea, whose long absence had not put a crimp in her love life, adding spice to the gossip. Then there were serious bridge games on the weekends. Michael Speer, another Stanford graduate student who was at McGill that summer, was a regular at the card table. "He continuously tried to control who played what out of their hands. As a result, he and whoever was his partner usually lost."[89] Life at Ely and McGill was more relaxed and more fun. Money was still short, tempers still flared, Harry still worked long days, but living in a company town designed to meet the daily needs of workers and their families gave the Rosenbergs a break from the constant stress of Palo Alto.

One evening, Harry was invited to dinner at the home of Annan Cook, Kennecott's chief geologist, to whom he had been introduced in the mill laboratory. Cook was as charismatic as he was knowledgeable, possessing a sweeping view of geology. "To listen to him that evening was like listening to the real world talking, and I could only sit up and pay attention." Harry came away with a new appreciation of how copper deposits were formed not just at Eli and Butte but in Chile and Rhodesia where Cook had been born and raised before leaving the country to earn his geology degree in South Africa. He had then gone to Oxford as a Rhodes scholar. He and his family had immigrated to the United States from South Africa only six years before in 1949 when he began working for Kennecott. "Part of Cook's job was to check out new finds by prospectors too poor to start operations alone. Like Shepard's lectures, his description of how he assessed hydrothermal deposits kept me on the edge of my seat that evening. I had the feeling that here was a man I could follow to the ends of the earth." While Harry had already made the shift from geology to metallurgy, which he did not regret, Cook renewed his interest in the subject.

As the summer wound down and Harry and Geri prepared to head back to Stanford, they had one special visitor. Harry's father, who rarely traveled and never took a vacation, had purchased a small camper for his pickup truck, closed the Tecopa Hot Springs Resort for the summer (there being few tourists at that time of the year because of the extreme heat), and headed to cooler Idaho to do some fishing, a sport he enjoyed though he lacked the skill he had in hunting. On his return in late August, he stopped at Ely to meet his fifteen-month-old grandson Keith for the first time. "The minute he saw Keith, I saw a new side to him. Women commonly ooh and aah over a baby. Men don't. But he did. Here was this hard-nosed boss of a bridge gang in tears. I shall never forget that moment. He had a big heart, but I didn't realize it for years." By this time, Harry Sr.'s life had settled down from a marital and business standpoint. He had married a woman named Gladys in February, 1949, after Grace's death from cirrhosis. Of all Harry Sr.'s wives up until then—Nona; Audrey, who used marijuana; and Grace, who was an alcoholic—Gladys was the most sophisticated and independent. "She was a good person, and she had a great relationship with my father. She was the only one in the bunch who had a business head on her. They lived in an old railroad wooden house my father moved onto the motel property. Unfortunately, Gladys ended up dying of cancer and my father would marry yet one more woman, Beaulah, a retired schoolteacher in the region, but for a while in the 1950s, life was good for him."

Not long after his father left to reopen the Tecopa Hot Springs Resort, Harry, Geri, and the baby returned to Stanford, delayed by yet more car trouble. The valves had been fried by the engine overheating on the trip to Ely at the beginning of the summer. "For the last time in my life I had to overhaul an engine before attempting a trip, but we got back to the trailer park in Palo Alto on time for me to start graduate work."

During that year, word came that Johnny Davis had been killed in a terrible accident when he had driven his semitruck in front of a train near Boron, California. It was an immense blow to Geri, who, as his only child, had to take care of all the funeral details. Johnny had done the best he could raising Geri alone after he had divorced her abusive mother. Not a wealthy or a worldly man by any means, he had made an effort to help the Rosenbergs out when their financial situation became dire. His death was a blow to Harry as well. "In the list of men I admire, including Norman Dolloff and Cutler Shepard, I also put Johnny Davis. He was a simple man, but by his humanity, he was an important presence in our lives."

By the time their second son, Neil, was born (uneventfully and without physical problems) on June 21, 1956, the Rosenbergs had purchased a small house in Palo Alto, the down payment made possible by Johnny Davis's life insurance and the sale of their house trailer. It was the first time in almost ten years that they lived in a "stuck-in" house, as Harry had called it as a child, meaning a house without wheels. The two-bedroom home on Bryant Street south of downtown was not much to look at, but it was a vast improvement over the trailer. Because of the erosion of a gully to the south, a crack had developed in the floor that made the southwest corner of the house sag slightly. But on the positive side, it had a fenced-in backyard, teenagers in the neighborhood to babysit, and friendly neighbors. In addition, the location was safe and conveniently located. Though Harry and Geri's relationship was still troubled (because of their different temperaments but similar tempers), for the first time in their lives, they had some financial stability, and with Harry's degree in hand, the future was beginning to look hopeful.

With a toddler, a new baby, a home, and (finally) no trailer, Geri was unable to go with Harry to Kennecott during the summer of 1956. Geri's small inheritance included her father's 1949 four-door Ford, a considerable design improvement over the 1948 model that Harry had driven with so much difficulty to Ely the summer before with trailer in tow. So driving the 1949 Ford, Harry went by himself, living for the summer in an apartment building for single men that Kennecott maintained in McGill near the smelter. Harry's job was to troubleshoot the mill, an assignment that had a large engineering component. "The mill had a basic problem in its grinding and flotation section. So the summer's goal was to improve grinding practice so that the ore particles could be broken from the host rocks in a process called parting and be more available for flotation." He and Howard Cox, another Stanford student working at the mill, tested various reagents, but they did not have enough time to solve the problem by the end of the summer. Fortunately, Kennecott granted them a research assignment to be completed in the fall back at the Stanford laboratory, which was equipped with a mill that had never been used. Harry and Howard revised its configuration to match that at McGill and started it up. They were able to show the effects of grinding degree on flotation efficiency, but it was small. "In any event, we both learned a lot, and that may have been the point."[90]

Harry taught a mineral dressing laboratory that year, and he also held a part-time technical position at Stanford Research Institute (SRI), which had been established by Stanford University as a nonprofit organization dedicated to regional economic development through technological research. One of his projects was for Hills Brothers and involved the study of coffee decaffeination via a solvent-extraction process. Another project was the development of a new copper extraction process. After much work and some success, this project was canceled by Harry's boss who decided the approach Harry was taking would not be cost-effective. Harry was deeply disappointed because he was convinced he was on the right track.

"It was at that point, totally exhausted by all my work and study, that I decided it was time to find a job in the metals extraction industry."

After earning his master's and completing an additional year toward a PhD, Harry started interviewing for a job. He hoped to work for Kennecott, but when he applied, the company was slow in replying. So he took the first offer he received, which was from a new company called Titanium Metals Corporation of America (TMCA) in Henderson, Nevada. Ironically, after working so hard to sever his ties to the desert, he was going back, because Henderson was in the Mojave approximately 160 miles east of Death Valley. Hardly had he accepted the offer from TMCA when Kennecott came through with an offer, but Harry had made a commitment and felt he could not go back on it.

> It was hard to turn down my friends at Kennecott, but I had to. Howard Cox ended up taking the Kennecott offer. A second disappointment soon followed. The position I wanted most was a teaching job at South Dakota School of Mines that would enable me to get my PhD. They had already replied to my first application that while they were interested, they had a better candidate. I agonized big-time when they told me a month too late that their better candidate had changed his mind. But having accepted the offer from TMCA, I turned them down as well. I didn't like being short of a PhD, but I was exhausted after six years of making do while going ever more deeply into debt that by then included a student loan from the women's auxiliary of the Berkeley chapter of AIME, the metallurgical society. About that loan: I received the nicest letter from the chairperson after we paid it off in 1958; it seems I was the only student who had ever repaid a loan they handed out. It had been a hard and long haul for Geri too. So instead of entering academia, which I really wanted, I opted for industry. I did so against the advice of some of my interviewers, who considered the new metal titanium, the so-called wonder metal, to be a flash in the pan. They warned me of its failures in applications and the metal's outrageous cost, but when I went for an interview in Henderson, where TMCA had a facility, I was mesmerized, though I really didn't know just why. Perhaps it was the

challenge, or a return to be near my roots in the Mojave Desert. Was it both or something else? However, as my life unfolded, I achieved results beyond my expectations at the time, for myself, my family, and even for humanity. But I cannot help but wonder how an academic career would have worked out.

CHAPTER 9:
THE WONDER METAL TITANIUM

In the 1950s, titanium was the new metal on the block—and it was a real troublemaker. It was like a delinquent boy who shattered windows, started fights, and broke hearts, but who had enormous potential if someone could make him behave. Titanium was as strong as steel but 45 percent lighter. It was twice as strong as aluminum but only 60 percent heavier, making it an ideal candidate for aircraft where strength-to-density ratio was all-important.[91] It was also an ideal candidate for the hulls of ships and submarines because it did not corrode in seawater. But like the delinquent boy with the hair-trigger temper, titanium was highly reactive. If not handled with extreme care, there was no telling what might happen, including fire and explosion.

Titanium was discovered in 1791 by William Gregor, an English clergyman and mineralogist. However, it took until 1938 to find a process to make an almost pure form that could be made in quantity. The metal had been produced in laboratories in very small amounts since the 1880s, but every effort to produce it in large amounts had failed miserably, even dangerously, to the frustration of generations of metallurgists. As a result, prior to World War II, its main industrial purpose was as a brightening additive (TiO_2) for paint, but this use was absurdly below its potential as a structural metal.[92] Ore was plentiful, so that was not the problem. Titanium is the ninth most common element on earth, occurring as ilmenite in igneous rock and as rutile in black sand in vast mineral-sand deposits, some of the largest being in Australia and Africa. The problem with the metal was its extreme reactivity at higher temperatures, readily combining with other elements. It cannot be cheaply electrolyzed, like aluminum. Carbon will not by itself remove the oxygen from titanium as it does with steel. That is why it is classed as a reactive metal. For example, if titanium is melted by the graphite-induction method, it will react with the carbon in the graphite, making the metal that is produced very brittle and, therefore, unusable.

A far more dramatic example of reactivity occurs when titanium that is heated above its melting temperature comes accidentally into contact with water (H_2O); it bonds with the single oxygen atom and releases the two hydrogen atoms, leading to a high risk of explosion. A fireman who attempts to douse a titanium fire with water might as well pour gasoline on it.[93] Aware of the danger, metallurgists tried to obtain the metal by doing chemical reductions inside thick-walled steel bomb casings. Although the use of casings was safer, it was still very risky besides being inefficient.

The man responsible for taming titanium (in so far as it was possible to tame it) was a brilliant metallurgist named William Kroll, who developed the process in the 1930s in his private laboratory in Luxembourg.[94] He also had begun his research by using bomb casings, but when some exploded, he decided to try a new approach, using the inert gas argon to control the velocity of the reaction inside the casing. Argon turned out to be the key. Kroll wrote: "If it looked like the whole thing was about to blow up, more argon could be admitted." In 1940, on the eve of Germany marching into Luxembourg, he sought asylum in the United States because he knew the importance of his work and did not want it to fall into the hands of the Nazis. During the war, he served as a consultant for Union Carbide; then in January 1945, he began to work for the US Bureau of Mines in Albany, Oregon. At that time, the purview of the Bureau of Mines had broadened beyond mine safety; it was also involved in the development of strategic metals, including titanium and zirconium, which are in the same group on the periodic table and, therefore, have similar properties. Under Kroll's guidance, both metals were produced successfully and in quantity in the late 1940s, opening the way for their broad use in military and commercial applications.

The precursor steps to the production of titanium begin with the mining of the impure ore, either the mineral-sand rutile (TiO_2) or ilmenite ($FeTiO_3$). Because of the iron (Fe), ilmenite begins with the production of pig iron in a steel blast furnace; the slag is essentially rutile (known as synthetic rutile). No matter whether it comes from mineral sands or slag, the rutile is reacted with carbon and chlorine at high temperature to make titanium tetrachloride ($TiCl_4$), a volatile and corrosive gas that condenses to liquid at 136 degrees Celsius. Carbon must be present to carry away the oxygen in order to make the chlorination process work. These steps were well-known before Kroll's time. What was unknown was the next step: how to separate the titanium from the chlorine safely and in quantity to yield a pure metal. Simplified, the process Kroll developed is the reduction of titanium tetrachloride by molten magnesium (or sodium) in an inert atmosphere of argon. The use of argon is critical because it eliminates the problem of titanium binding with oxygen. The chemical reaction is $2\text{ Mg} + \text{TiCl}_4 \rightarrow 2\text{ MgCl}_2 + \text{Ti}$, showing that magnesium combines with chlorine, breaking its bond to titanium. The next step is to remove the magnesium chloride and excess magnesium metal by means of vacuum distillation or acid leaching. What remains is titanium, called at this point *sponge* solely because of its rough, porous appearance. The sponge is then sheared and crushed prior to being melted into an ingot using either an inert atmosphere or a vacuum. The ingot can then be forged into billet or formed into other mill products.

The making of sponge is not a continuous process as is the making of steel; it is a batch process. Because it must be made one batch at a time, titanium production is slow and requires large amounts of energy and human supervision, increasing its cost. Great care is necessary throughout the process for both safety and quality control so that the metal is not contaminated, which can lead to catastrophic metal failure, for example, the fracture of a critical airplane component while in flight.

Harry never had the chance to meet Kroll who was already a legend (at least among metallurgists) at the time Harry entered the industry.

> *I admired greatly what Kroll did in his own laboratory from scratch and then later at the Bureau of Mines in Oregon. His problems were mostly in the materials and design area. His original cell was far more complex than it needed to be, but he covered all the bases well and had good reasons to proceed as he did. He had the perseverance and creativity to do what no one before him had. Years later, when I was one of the founders of the Alta Group manufacturing high-purity titanium, the work at the Bureau of Mines on electrorefining was of great importance.*

Even after Kroll had developed his process, there were many complex production problems that had to be solved, leading to great metallurgical frustration. In the book *Black Sand: The History of Titanium*, Kathleen L. Housley writes that "in the early days of titanium research, the metal was derisively called the *street-walker* metal because it picked up everything. It was also called the *mañana metal* because its promises were always for tomorrow, and *the wonder metal*, not only in reference to its wonderful properties but because it made metallurgists and engineers wonder about their sanity in choosing to work with it."[95]

Given the difficulties involved, the question must be asked why titanium was worth all the effort. The answer is found in the arms race between the United States and the USSR, which began even before the ink had dried on World War II peace treaties and accelerated in the late 1940s as both countries tested powerful nuclear bombs. With the outbreak of the Korean War in 1950, the US Air Force needed aircraft that could outperform Soviet aircraft. However, that could only be achieved if there existed a light and strong metal to replace full reliance on steel, especially in the engine, the heaviest part of a plane. At a Senate hearing in 1953, General Kern Metzger, head of Wright-Patterson Air Force Base, explained why titanium was so important: "A pound of weight eliminated in basic design will permit six to ten pounds reduction in weight of the total aircraft. The reduction in weight could be absorbed in greater fuel carrying capacity and therefore longer range. It could result in higher speeds, or a smaller aircraft to accomplish the same mission."[96] Among the contractors with which the US Air Force was working were the engine makers Pratt & Whitney, Westinghouse, and Curtiss-Wright and the airframe makers Bell, Boeing, Convair, Douglas Aircraft, Lockheed, North American Aviation, and Northrop.

Recognizing that titanium could give America a critical military edge over the Soviet Union at a time when the threat of all-out nuclear war was increasing sharply, the US government made the decision in the early 1950s to pour huge amounts of money into unlocking the metal's secrets and funding the construction of an entire industry to produce it. No other project except the Manhattan Project in developing the atomic bomb had received so much funding or so much high-level attention. The new companies were usually partnerships between chemical companies that had the knowledge to make sponge and steel companies that had the expertise to roll hard metals, such as stainless steel. One of the first to be formed was a partnership between Allegheny Ludlum, a steel manufacturer, and National Lead, a chemical company that manufactured paint. Named

Titanium Metals Corporation of America (known at first as TMCA, then later on as TIMET), it began operations in 1950.[97] To make sponge, TMCA took over part of a cavernous empty factory in Henderson, Nevada, that had produced magnesium during World War II for use in incendiary bombs, flares, and tracer bullets. Before closing at the end of the war, the plant had employed thirteen thousand people on a remote two-thousand-acre site in the Mojave Desert about fifteen miles southeast of Las Vegas. The facility was perfect for making titanium sponge for two reasons: it was at a safe distance from human habitation (chlorine release and explosions were risks), and the cells that had been used for magnesium chloride and chlorine gas could be used for titanium. There was also plentiful electric power from nearby Boulder Dam. The only thing lacking in the area was rutile, which had to be shipped in from Australia.

The first major challenge the US military, the research institutions, and all the new companies had to face was the development of alloys because commercially pure (CP) titanium had some properties that made it unsuitable for high-temperature aerospace applications where great strength and the ability to withstand fatigue, fracture, and creep at high stress are required. As its name implies, creep does not occur suddenly. It is a permanent deformation of metal that happens over time as the metal is subjected to a constant stress or load, which is often the case with aerospace applications, particularly in the jet engines. Fortunately, the properties of CP titanium, which is 99.7 percent pure, could be improved by alloying in which the addition of small amounts of usually two (binary) or three (ternary) or even four or five elements make an enormous difference. A good alloy is like a decathlon athlete who performs well in ten track-and-field events but does not excel in any one of them. It is exactly that overall goodness, but not singular greatness, that wins gold medals for a decathlon athlete. Likewise in metallurgy, if an alloy excels at one characteristic, it will probably be lacking in another, such as being strong but with little ability to bend plastically. For titanium to succeed, metallurgists needed to find the equivalent of the decathlon athlete—the all-around good alloy.

There are a number of ways by which a metal can be strengthened, toughened, softened, or made resistant to failure during cyclic loading at stresses well below the fracture stress, all of which are affected by alloying and subsequent processing. Harry compares it to cooking, with each metal having its own set of recipes. Metallurgists are like chefs who determine how much of an alloying element to add, how long to hot-work or cold-work and heat-treat so that the final product has the right set of properties. "But like cooks who specialize in specific foods, such as French, Mexican, or Cantonese, metallurgists typically specialize in a particular metal system, or, a bit more broadly, by the crystal system."

As a solid, titanium has two principal crystalline phases that are like geometric lattices in which the atoms bind to each other. The shape of the lattices affects the properties of the metal and is temperature-dependent. The alpha phase, which exists at room temperature, is hexagonal and the atoms are packed closely together. As titanium is heated to approximately 1621 degrees Fahrenheit (depending on several factors), the hexagonal alpha phase changes to what is called a body-centered cubic phase known as beta. That critical temperature is known as the beta transus. The process is two-directional, so as the beta phase cools, its crystalline lattice changes to alpha.[98] This is where alloying elements become important because they act as stabilizers of one or the other phase. It was already known that the most important alloying elements for titanium were aluminum (Al) and vanadium (V), which, in combination, gave the metal excellent strength, ductility (the ability to undergo deformation without fracture), and heat-treatment characteristics. Aluminum is an alpha stabilizer (transus increaser), and vanadium is a beta stabilizer (transus decreaser). What was unknown was the all-important percentage of each phase that would enable the optimum amount of beta phase to persist at low temperatures. In the early 1950s, metallurgists from the US Army's Watertown Arsenal in Massachusetts and two renowned research institutes, Battelle Memorial Institute in Columbus, Ohio, and Armour Research Foundation in Chicago, Illinois, raced against each other to determine the most efficacious percentages of aluminum and vanadium to add to titanium. The answer turned out to be 6 percent aluminum and 4 percent vanadium. The 6 percent aluminum was critical because if the percentage was pushed too high, embrittlement could occur, leading to sudden metal failure. The alloy Ti-6Al-4V (90 percent titanium, 6 percent aluminum, and 4 percent vanadium) is neither all alpha phase or all beta phase, but both, with a unique microstructure of plates and planes. It was the metallurgical equivalent of the gold-medal decathlon athlete doing many things well.

In 1954, just three years before Harry joined the company, TIMET was the first to melt a two-thousand-pound production heat of Ti-6Al-4V successfully. From then on, it became the most common alloy in the industry, a position it still holds. However, by no means was it appropriate for all applications. It was essential to develop other alloys, which meant that very challenging metallurgical research remained to be done.

The second major challenge for the nascent industry was how to handle the vast swings in military spending. Because the production of titanium was tied to military use, if the military needed it, business was good. If not, business was bad to the point of being nonexistent. Eventually, commercial uses for titanium, particularly in aerospace and the chemical industry, helped level out the peaks and valleys of military spending, but that would take decades. The cyclicality problem first surfaced in 1957, immediately after Harry joined TIMET, and brought the infant industry to its knees. Until then, titanium was being produced as fast as possible. The solving of production problems, such as the use of vacuum annealing to prevent embrittlement of the metal caused by hydrogen, the rolling of titanium alloy sheet, and hot-extrusion techniques, led to the building of additional facilities and the hiring of more employees. Every economic indicator pointed to the sustained growth of the titanium industry. No one anticipated the plunge that was caused by a sharp and sudden cutback in the number of orders by the US Air Force of the long-range bomber the B-52 Stratofortress. Built by Boeing, the behemoth aircraft was powered by Pratt & Whitney's gas turbine engine, the J-57, which used large amounts of titanium. The Stratofortress was meant to be the US military's answer to what they were convinced was a "bomber gap" with Russia. Driven by the fear that the Soviets had the capability to drop atomic bombs on America's heartland, the US Air Force had ordered the building of more B-52s. But then in 1956, a U-2 spy-plane flight over the USSR revealed the Soviets had far fewer long-range bombers than the United States had thought. That being the case, there was no need to expand bomber capacity; instead, intercontinental ballistic missiles appeared to be the future of warfare. The launch of *Sputnik* on October 4, 1957, seemed to provide confirmation. Because missiles did not use much, if any, titanium, the metal went into free fall.

When Harry joined TIMET, he was totally unaware of the crisis that was about to hit:

> *I flew in on a Lockheed Constellation, landing at the Las Vegas airport, which was nothing but a single runway and an adobe building with three rooms. Someone from TIMET picked me up and we drove the dusty road to Henderson. It was very bleak with World War II prefab cracker-box*

houses. But TIMET was growing. It had just constructed an office building and research labs. Its melt shop was in one of the Basic Magnesium buildings. So I started to work as a control engineer in July 1957 in the titanium tetrachloride department. Then in August, there was the first big layoff. Within four months of my starting to work for TIMET, after another layoff, there were two process/control engineers left in Henderson, and I was one of them. The two of us were sitting in a room with thirty-two empty desks. Approximately 80 percent of the entire staff was cut although they kept on the research and development people. TIMET was making about forty tons of sponge a day when I arrived. The cutback reduced that to four tons a day. That was the minimum they could produce and keep the place running. In 1958, TIMET was barely treading water.[99]

It was at this point that Harry got a telephone call from Kenneth Schellinger, who was on Cutler Shepard's staff at Stanford University. He was planning to leave Stanford and asked if Harry would be interested in taking his place.

Talk about being torn! Self-doubt played a role, I am sad to say, in my saying no. Tenure at Stanford was simply beyond my ability to think of as a career. But a sense of responsibility also played a role: to TIMET that had kept me on when so many others were laid off, perhaps because I was a natural to the tough stuff—the overbearing desert heat, ill-tempered people, and frustration; and to my family who were just settling down in Henderson after so many hard years. Add to that the fact that Geri was pregnant again and would give birth to our third son in December 1958. Reluctantly, I said no even though my job at TIMET was none too secure.

Even with the B-52 cutback, there was still a need for titanium. Commercial aircraft including the DC-7C Seven Seas used titanium wing tanks. The decrease in weight enabled the DC-7C to increase its range, thereby opening up routes across the Atlantic and the Pacific. Titanium was also used in the first turboprop, the Lockheed Electra, and the turbo-jet-powered DC-8. Because it did not corrode in salty environments, it was a good choice for chemical processing and in heat-exchangers for desalination plants. Other commercial applications were under development, so if the titanium companies could hold on, things were bound to improve. It helped that some of the partners behind those companies, including P. R. Mallory, Sharon Steel, Allegheny Ludlum, and National Lead, were profitable in their main businesses, so they could infuse cash into their titanium subsidiaries. But some companies went out of existence even though they had big corporate brothers, including Cremet, a partnership between Crane and Republic Steel, and Electromet, a subsidiary of Union Carbide.

To keep Harry and the other engineer busy during the downturn, TIMET arranged for them to take a month of classes in industrial statistics. What Harry learned proved to be extremely useful throughout the rest of his career; in fact, he eventually became an expert statistician who stressed to his employees the importance of using advanced statistical methodologies to reduce both defects and variability in manufacturing.[100] Harry would not have sought out a course in statistics on his own, seeing no need, but when given the opportunity, he was grateful.

> *In statistics, I discovered a whole new world—a world that embraced not just one discipline or industry but one that describes the universe. Instead of guessing, I could calculate the likelihood for events, or rather lack of them, for statistics can never prove anything. Learning the formulae was the easy part; knowing when to use which one was the hard part. But I had the good fortune to work with two men at TIMET, Max Parris and Al Hatch, who each had firm grasps of when to use what formula and why.*

In the late 1950s, the slide-rule was still king. There were no computers or hand calculators available for research at TIMET, although its labs were among the best equipped in the industry. Only the accounting department had an IBM computer with 8K of memory. The saving grace for statistics was the Monroe desk calculator that could give decimal points to slide-rule calculations and could also accumulate sums and sums of squares. To ensure against entry errors, every critical data point was entered twice. Grace Guyette, a TIMET laboratory technician, became the resident resource for these calculations by being both accurate and fast. Her sums and sums of squares were used to test data reliability. "The only audit trails were our notebooks and laboratory orders. So checking and rechecking calculations was important to getting it right the first time. Grace was great at it."

As a process engineer at TIMET, Harry combined his newly acquired training in statistics with his knowledge of chemical metallurgy to increase the efficiency of sponge production because the Kroll process still presented several major problems in terms of automation.

> By the summer of 1959, Bill Olds, Walt Long, and I had completed a year of shift work operating a full-size, but experimental, sponge reduction station. Working ten days straight, then four off, on a rotating shift basis, we had all gotten tired of graveyard, as we called the midnight shift. That routine brought back memories of being a powerhouse operator at the Noonday. Even though we were proud that we had been able to increase productivity, I was never satisfied with our yield, which was usually about 86 percent or above. One run actually got as far as 98 percent, but we never figured out why. However, we did figure out the reaction kinetics and in a general way why yields will never be 100 percent.

Two of the ongoing manufacturing problems that would take a long while to solve were high-density inclusions (HDI) and low-density inclusions (LDI)—defects that can cause catastrophic metal failure. HDIs were linked to the use of recycled titanium scrap and included such things as residual bits of tungsten welding rods or tungsten carbide cutting tool bits that accidentally got into titanium during melting into ingot but did not melt. The problem of HDIs was basically one of quality control and was solvable, albeit with much work. But the same could not be said of LDIs, which presented a much more severe and long-lasting problem. LDIs are primarily titanium nitrides that typically derive from small titanium sponge fires. With a very high melting point, nitrides do not dissolve easily during melting. While their existence was recognized, being in the sponge stream, there was no efficacious way to eliminate them. It would be many years before dramatic improvement would be achieved by means of changes in the reduction process and more sensitive and careful defect analysis.

What was known when I started was that titanium alloys had two broad sets of problems: the first set was intrinsic to the particular alloy; for example, fatigue fracture. Like people, metals can get tired, not literally of course, but it amounts to the same thing. Like the breaking of a hip of an older human, a repeatedly stressed metal can break at only a fraction of its strength. The second set of problems was related to incidents during their manufacture. There was still much to learn, and some of that learning was experiential, indeed tragic. The crash of a United Airlines DC-10 in Sioux City, Iowa, in 1989 was due to a low-density inclusion that remained below the sensing ability of inspection methods at the time. The problem is now solved, but it took over a decade to do so. Suffice it to say that working as an engineer in the manufacture of titanium, especially at the beginning, was to be on a steep learning curve with no one knowing exactly what had to be learned.

Then in 1959, with business at TIMET only slightly improved, Harry was called into the office of Carl Blake, manager of process engineering, and asked if he had ever taken a course in the use of X-rays to analyze metals while at Stanford University. His affirmative answer led to a turning point in his career, transforming him into a metallurgical research engineer working in physical metallurgy. Donald Cooper, who would become Harry's boss, remembered his promotion well: "Harry always preferred in his thinking the science of extractive metallurgy—getting the ore out of the ground. That was his focus. We transplanted him from the factory into physical metallurgy because he was so smart. He was a fish-out-of-water, but research turned out to be no problem at all for him. He was the kind of researcher who follows his nose."[101]

The transition into the lab had me swimming at first. Physical metallurgy was not my focus in graduate school. Extractive and process metallurgy were. People who are unfamiliar with metallurgy think of it as a single cohesive field of study, but it actually has several subfields, each quite different from the other. I had never heard of an edge or a screw dislocation, which are defects in a metal's crystal structure, nor had I ever seen a micrograph, which is a photo of a metal surface at high magnification taken under a microscope. Nor could I have told you clearly what the difference is between alpha and beta titanium. I owe debts of gratitude to Liz Bondurant, who taught this neophyte how to create great micrographs, as well as to Karl Snow, who aided greatly in my understanding of the phase rule. I may have had degrees from Stanford, but at TIMET, I had much to learn, and fortunately, there were some great people there, especially Max Parris, Al Hatch, and Gil Lenning, to teach me the physical metallurgy I needed. What I did have was a knack for efficient experimentation and analyzing the results supported by my new knowledge of inferential statistics. I also had a deep appreciation for hard data, what I like to call the "data sez" approach, meaning that a "fact" has to have a small error bar of known origin—say as measurements that are necessarily limited in their precision and accuracy—before the fact is a fact. This appreciation has affected both the professional and private sides of my life because with understanding comes control whether dealing with inert material or biology.

His first projects in the laboratory involved creep-resistant alloys, attempting to track the slow elongations metals go through under stress at high temperature. Although lacking laboratory equipment of sufficient sensitivity to accurately measure his results, he nevertheless was able to conclude that beta alloys showed no promise, so he shifted to the study of alpha alloys. Two alloys were already under development for engine high compressor applications running at 1,000 degrees Fahrenheit or higher, so he set out to characterize both alloys in depth to understand where the project stood. His work both succeeded and failed: It failed in that neither alloy made the grade at 1,000 degrees. It succeeded in that Harry gained an understanding of how to test titanium alloys for high-temperature service, plotting results on a map of compositions.

By then, Harry's work on high-strength alloys had led to his promotion to senior engineer. Along with Al Hatch, who was an expert in mechanical metallurgy, Harry worked under Warren "Max" Parris, the laboratory supervisor. Then one day, out of the blue, Don Cooper, manager of the Henderson laboratory, called Harry into his office and said, "We want you and Max to trade places." Incredulous, Harry asked why. It turned out that Max was averse to all the travel the job required and had personally requested the specific switch. "Like before, I was not ready. And like before, I jumped into it headlong. In the space of a minute, Max transitioned to being my most valued senior engineer, who mentored me, his supervisor."

However, neither Max nor anyone else could keep Harry from occasionally getting into hot water. "My knack for analysis could, and did, get me into serious trouble. Truth is I very nearly lost my job once, not because I was wrong—I turned out to be right—but because I was naive and was not politic in the way I went about pointing out a serious problem with an alloy we were working on." The problem had to do with a promising alloy that was being considered for use in both the airframe and engine of a new supersonic transport (SST) then in the early design stages. The SST was to be the most spectacular commercial aircraft ever built, keeping the United States at the forefront of international aviation. On June 5, 1963, President John F. Kennedy addressed the graduating class at the US Air Force Academy, using the opportunity to state that "it is my judgment that this Government should immediately commence a new program in partnership with private industry to develop at the earliest practical date the prototype of a commercially successful supersonic transport superior to that being built in any other country of the world." Concluding that such a plane could be designed and built by the end of the decade, he said that it was essential "to a strong and forward-looking Nation, and indicates the future of the manned aircraft as we move into a missile age as well."[102]

As valuable as the SST may have been in keeping the United States at the forefront of commercial aerospace, reaching "all corners of the globe" as Kennedy enthusiastically stated, in fact, it was also a way to keep the foundering aerospace industry alive. By 1960, employment had been cut 25 percent from the 1957 levels.[103] Conceived in a time not of panic but of desperation, the SST was a lifeline. Forecasting a need for hundreds of SSTs, Douglas Aircraft, in a 1961 design study, envisioned a jet with the ability to cruise at seventy-one thousand feet at Mach 3, over three times the speed of subsonic aircraft. Boeing's SST model 2707 (for which it was awarded a contract for two prototypes in December 1966) was to have a range of approximately four thousand miles carrying a maximum load of 350 passengers. Boeing estimated that sales would be between seven hundred and a thousand aircraft.[104]

It all sounded too good to be true. The reality was that it was impossible to build such a jet without lessening the weight by a very large factor, which is why Boeing, North American Aviation, Lockheed, and the engine makers General Electric and Pratt & Whitney (all of whom were vying for large government contracts) invested heavily in seeking ways to use titanium. A lighter titanium aircraft would need less fuel to fly at supersonic speeds. The other reason to use titanium was that certain titanium alloys could handle the structural temperature an SST would reach at cruising speed whereas aluminum could not. Aerodynamic friction could increase skin temperature to as high as 420 degrees Fahrenheit, with some NASA simulations indicating even higher temperatures.

Weight reduction and stiffness (the ability to resist elastic deformation) at temperature were the reasons Boeing was extremely interested in the new alloy Ti-8Al-1Mo-1V (known as 8-1-1) for the "skin" on the airframe, among other uses. The word *skin* is a bit of a misnomer, implying a very thin covering spread over internal structural supports, harkening back to an earlier aeronautical time when cloth, wood, and aluminum were used for that purpose. But by the late 1950s, the word referred to the outer component of the airframe that supports structural load. Skin required totally different alloy properties than did engine components, including the ability to be rolled into sheet.

The alloy 8-1-1 is a near-alpha alloy, meaning that some of the beta phase is stabilized down to room temperature in a matrix of 95+ percent alpha phase. The addition of molybdenum (Mo) helped to raise the melting point of the alloy as well as make it more weldable. What was critical about 8-1-1 was not the molybdenum or the lower amount of vanadium (V) but the higher percentage of aluminum that increased strength and stiffness while reducing density. Besides its potential use for skin, 8-1-1 was being considered for the front end of the turbine jet engine that typically has three temperature regions ranging from low to high. Alloy selection for the various engine stages was partially based on one simple rule: achieving the highest creep strength to density at maximum operating temperatures.

The patent for 8-1-1 was held by Allegheny Ludlum, and the alloy was being developed by TIMET at its production laboratory in Toronto, Ohio, under the able direction of Harold (Hal) Kessler. According to Kessler, "it was a really good alloy but the problem was the high aluminum, which could cause embrittlement."[105] In 1954, Kessler had come to TIMET's Henderson laboratory from the Armour Institute in Chicago, where he had been instrumental in researching Ti-6Al-4V under contract to the US

Army's Watertown Arsenal, although the patent on that alloy had been awarded in a bruising patent war to the Battelle Institute in Columbus, Ohio. Transferred to TIMET's production laboratory in Toronto, Kessler had been working with 8-1-1 and was upfront in stating in his reports that there appeared to be a problem with surface oxidation at elevated temperatures. Before checking for brittleness in his test samples, Kessler either used a surface treatment called pickling that removes impurities by means of an acid, or he milled off the surface. It was the peculiarity of the oxidation problem that goaded Harry into investigating further on his own.

Hal assumed a fix would be found to the problem of surface oxidation at 1,000 degrees Fahrenheit and that the alloy 8-1-1 would pass muster and would be used in aircraft. He was always careful in his reports to mention that the alloy surfaces were pickled or milled off before testing. Nothing was hidden. But unfortunately, the sales and technical services people either agreed with him that a fix would eventually be found, or they ignored the problem altogether. In any event, I doubt that they read his reports with care in the context of supersonic jets with engine high compressors running at 1,000 degrees Fahrenheit. Since the lab was abuzz with 8-1-1 because it appeared to be a beautiful alloy, I began to study it intensively to see what made it tick, rather like the way I had studied the fire ants in the Mojave Desert as a little boy. I discovered to my dismay that it did not tick for engine compressor applications where its high stiffness and low density combined to make it the most efficient material available. It would not remain ductile for the thousands of hours above about 800 degrees Fahrenheit it was expected to survive in commercial airline service. That realization was a powerful intuitive aha moment for me because even before running the tests needed to prove it definitively, I shouted out after reading Hal's report, "But you are going to have to pickle the airplane engine after every flight!" Of course that is impossible. I had perceived the essence of the problem visually right at the start before I had any data to prove it. I worked out how to simulate the long-term flight service environment by short-term laboratory tests. Hundreds of tests later, I was sure. What happens is that titanium and aluminum atoms like each other so much that when they meet by diffusion within the metal at high temperatures, they stick together and grow into small submicroscopic clusters of Ti₃Al—a brittle compound. Above 7 percent by weight aluminum, the clusters become numerous and close together so that if one cluster cracks under stress, its neighbors will too, in zipper fashion. Fracture toughness decreases to dangerous levels after even moderate times at embrittling temperatures. But this is only half the story. The other half is oxygen. Like aluminum, oxygen alloys with titanium but with ten times the embrittling effect. Oxidation of the metal surface at elevated temperatures thus embrittles the surfaces of test specimens even more than the interiors. The details only became abundantly clear when I completed my thesis later on.

From his voluminous test data, Harry constructed a c-curve map that included the length of time a jet was in service at a range of temperatures and the ductility of the titanium. The map was striking and troubling because it revealed that the embrittlement region was intrinsic and could not be prevented. Embrittlement occurred between 900 and 1,300 degrees Fahrenheit. At approximately 1,050 degrees Fahrenheit, it was rapid, taking only an hour or two to occur. This was where Harry made his mistake by not alerting his bosses and the marketing department about the insolvability of the problem. Instead, during a routine visit to General Electric, Harry showed their engineers the map and explained what was going on. They peppered him with questions as to how he had figured it out. What intrigued them was that instead of approaching the research by the normal route of the weight percent of alloy additions, Harry had used atomic percent instead, considering it much more meaningful even though it required complex calculations. "Formulating new alloys using weight percents is unambiguous and minimizes the potential for error, but it fails to lend sufficient insight as to how alloy additions affect properties." By choosing instead to study the ratios of atoms, Harry was able to comprehend the embrittlement problem with 8-1-1.

Boeing was on the call schedule the next day. I showed them the map too, and their eyes popped out. They questioned me closely and tried to pin me down. How did I do it? What was the time at which embrittlement occurred? So I answered them honestly and went home that night without giving it another thought. But when I got back to TIMET the next day, all hell broke loose. As soon as I walked in, I received a call from a friend in marketing. "What the hell did you tell those people yesterday?" he demanded to know. "What people?" I naively asked. "Boeing!" It turns out I had killed the alloy for use in the SST engine compressors running at high temperature, although the ultimate blow for skin applications would come not from high-temperature instability but from aqueous stress corrosion—a different problem altogether. The airframe would see this environment. He rightfully blamed it on me. I hadn't meant to hurt anyone or undermine Hal Kessler, not to mention TIMET, but that is what I had done, and boy, was I in trouble! At the same time, my boss and his boss got calls from their counterparts in marketing, equally livid. The next day, Schuyler Herres, my boss three levels up, flew in from New York City. He called me to his hotel room and chewed me out unmercifully for two hours. I wondered why, if what I had done was so wrong, he didn't just fire me. That answer came as he dismissed me. He said, "It will be all right—if you are right." I felt humiliated and mad at the same time. "Schuy, I'm right," I said nervously, aware of the stakes involved. I think that my emotional reaction was fraught with a residue from my childhood beating by my father. Herres never brought it up again because within a short time, both General Electric and Boeing had confirmed the high-temperature brittleness with their own simulations—and neither could find a fix. It was a blow to TIMET temporarily but nowhere near the blow it would have been had the problem been discovered later after the alloy was further along in development. I relaxed, but I also learned that a person can be right and also wrong. Marketing, not to mention my bosses, had been taken by surprise and they were all justifiably upset. In the end, my work had very little impact on the program; it just didn't seem so at the time. As sometimes happens, however, there

were both corporate and career upsides; henceforth TIMET
had faith in me and my emphasis on solid data, and so did
our customers and suppliers. And I was left with a valuable
lesson in being politic. In a more positive vein, I believe
TIMET earned respect for its technical integrity.

Despite Harry's findings, 8-1-1 was not ruled out for use as the skin, and the airframe makers continued to carry on research. The writer of an article in *Life* magazine, published in October 1966 just before Boeing was awarded the contract, stated that the SST was expected to get so hot in flight that it would expand one foot in length. "Yet engineers have developed such precise techniques for simulating this environment on the ground they are convinced the SST will be as safe as today's airplanes. In tests, the titanium skin is tortured by massive shaking, heating and stretching. In 28 seconds one titanium sample can be subjected to the stresses of a whole SST flight." At least one titanium mockup of the SST fuselage was built with 8-1-1 for the skin and 6-4 for the structural members.[106]

According to Rodney Boyer, who joined the SST project at Boeing in 1965, "The alloy 8-1-1 seemed like the right decision at the beginning because it had the higher stiffness and lower density, but it also had a stress corrosion cracking problem. We figured we couldn't live with that, so we switched. We utilized Ti-6Al-4V for all kinds of applications." The stress corrosion cracking problem had been discovered by the US Naval Research Laboratory. Under stress in a corrosive environment, such as hot salt, the alloy under load can react with the salt in a humid atmosphere and can develop cracks that propagate rapidly leading to sudden failure. Further research done in Harry's laboratory showed that the problem may have been less critical in actual service than first thought.[107] However, in the long run, it didn't make any difference, because in 1971 the SST project came to an ignominious end when the US Congress cut off all funding because of serious environmental concerns about damage to the ozone layer and sonic booms, as well as huge cost overruns and projected high fuel use. It was a severe blow to the aerospace and titanium industries. Subsequently, France and the United Kingdom jointly built the Concorde and the USSR built the Tupolev Tu-144, both aluminum-based, but the United States never built a supersonic transport.

The demise of the SST was by no means the end of 8-1-1. Its low density made it excellent for use in the first stage of compressor engines where inlet temperature reached to approximately 800 degrees Fahrenheit, well below the embrittlement region. "It was used successfully in blades and disks in jet engines," said Kessler. "Because of its creep resistance, high tensile modulus and low density, 8-1-1 was a good alloy once we had learned how to control it."[108]

It is impossible to understand the issues surrounding the SST without considering a top-secret project that was beginning to reinvigorate the depressed titanium industry. It was a new CIA spy plane intended to travel at or above Mach 3, eventually known as the Blackbird for its heat-dissipating color. In the late 1950s, it was being designed by Lockheed's research facility with the peculiar name of the Skunk Works, under the guidance of a brilliant powerhouse of an aeronautical engineer named Clarence "Kelly" Johnson. To use titanium as the skin, Johnson needed an alloy that was formable into complex shapes that were age-hardenable, meaning they could be heat-treated over a period of time to increase strength. No alpha, near-alpha, or alpha-beta alloy came close to meeting Johnson's specifications. Only a beta alloy, with its age-hardenable cubic structure, could possibly fill the bill. But beta alloys were notoriously difficult to manufacture and handle, and high temperature was an issue. At that time, there were very few beta alloys even under development, the principal one being produced in very small quantity by Crucible. The cost of $Ti–13V–11Cr–3Al$, known as 13-11-3 (aka B 120 VCA), was astronomical. It required long aging times, but if the manufacturer was not extremely careful, it could be overaged during heat treatment causing embrittlement due to the high chromium (Cr). However, Johnson was adamant about using it, telling a colleague "any material that can cut our gross weight nearly in half is damned tempting even if it will drive us nuts in the bargain."[109]

The only company that had the manufacturing capacity to make 13-11-3 was TIMET, although it had no better idea of how to do it than did Crucible. Absolutely everything had to be researched and equipment reconfigured to manufacture 13-11-3, and for a long while an 80 percent to 90 percent rejection rate was common. Hal Kessler was one of the few who had top-secret clearance: "I remember well our first beta ingot, which we hot-rolled at Allegheny Ludlum. It came through as a coil all right, but as it sat there [cooling], the coil exploded and shot metal all over the place. Fortunately no one was injured."[110] The problem was surface oxygen contamination again, as it had been with 8-1-1, requiring descaling and pickling to get down to metal that was ductile. Then it had to be quenched, followed by putting it in a very large mill, called a four-high mill, to be straightened, and then annealed and pickled yet again—and that was just to get the metal to the point that it could be cold-rolled.

Harry did not work on the Blackbird directly, not having top-secret clearance, although he had figured out that the customer was Lockheed. However, because 13-11-3 affected his research, he studied it closely and realized a new approach was needed.

> *Because the beta alloy 13-11-3 was high in chromium, it was not well suited for what they wanted it for. I said to the other metallurgists at TIMET, "It doesn't look like a good fit. I think we can do better by producing a new alloy with less chromium." But I was told, "You're not going to change Kelly Johnson. He's going with this material. He started with it; he'll stay with it." With the alloy 13-11-3, we would ship about 10 percent of what we melted and Kelly would throw about half of that away. He would nick each piece that came into the shop, and if he could break it, he threw it away. It was rudimentary. I'm sure there were more sophisticated metallurgy tests, but what we sent had to work in Kelly's environment. So I got metal shears, and I would nick the new alloy compositions that we were studying. That's how we finally figured out it was primarily the chromium level that was causing the problem. We stayed away from high chromium levels in all subsequent beta-alloy development.*[111]

Despite the problems with 13-11-3, it ultimately worked extremely well in the Blackbird. The existence of the jet was made public by President Lyndon Johnson in 1964, with the A-12 single-pilot model becoming operational in 1965. In 1968, it was replaced by the double-cockpit SR-71. Even the alloy 8-1-1 played a part, being used by Pratt & Whitney in the first stage of the Blackbird's compressors. With more than 90 percent titanium in both its engine compressors and airframe, the Blackbird became the most spectacular aircraft ever built. In the book *Black Sand*, Kathleen Housley writes that once the plane's existence was made public by President Johnson, "It immediately streaked into mythology becoming the plane of superlatives. At a speed of 33 miles per minute, it moved faster than the sun. It could travel from New York to London in one hour and fifty-five minutes. On July 28, 1976, an SR-71 broke both speed and altitude records flying at 2,193 miles an hour at 85,069 feet in sustained flight."[112] The plane was retired in 1990 as part of a cost-cutting measure. It has never been surpassed.

Harry developed the beta alloy Ti-8Mo-8V-2Fe-3Al (known as 8-8-2-3) as an attempt to solve the problems attending 13-11-3, but it never caught on in part because Johnson's design philosophy for the skin of the Blackbird did not carry over to commercial aerospace. No other aerospace project had such immense top-secret funding or such dictatorial control. The SST, on the other hand, was a bureaucratic nightmare with fierce political interference and corporate battles. "Being strip-rollable, 8-8-2-3 was much more economical to produce than if it had to be flat-rolled on a handmill, which was what 13-11-3 required. If it had been used for the Blackbird, I estimate that yields would have been closer to 50 percent instead of the 5 to 10 percent Johnson got with 13-11-3. If used to its fullest dimensions, it would have reduced cost dramatically."

Developing cost-effective beta alloys with improved cold formability would take up a good part of Harry's research career, and he would have several major successes. However, timing matters in the introduction of an alloy, and the timing for 8-8-2-3 was wrong. TIMET sold only a single ingot of 8-8-2-3 to Dynamet (now part of Carpenter Technology) in Pittsburgh, Pennsylvania. "There is no substitute for knowing the real needs of your direct customers and your product end-users if you want your timing to be right. More times than not, my timing on alloy development was good, meaning it was anticipatory instead of just responsive to a need. But with 8-8-2-3 that was not the case." One good lesson to come from it was that Harry learned how to listen to his customers.

> At a metals society meeting, Lou Jahnke, materials manager
> of the jet engine group at General Electric, teased me that I
> was not listening to him about the next generation of alloys
> he needed. I wasn't, because he was asking for properties
> that I did not believe were needed in a deep hardenable
> engine alloy. When he had explained to me what GE was
> looking for, I had responded in a very lukewarm way, saying,
> "Okay, but that will take a lot of beta eutectic addition."
> I thought to myself that chromium might do the trick, but
> I knew the problems it presented with 13-11-3 in terms of

forming brittle compounds. So I did not pursue his request seriously. A few weeks later, I received a purchase order to melt some sample alloys for him to his specifications. I did. You guessed it—one of his formulations with chromium became the next new alloy to be qualified on jet engines. Had I listened, my group would have worked in that direction and he would have left the development to us. Never mind that his alloy was almost impossible to make profitably on the industrial scale. He got the patent and the product he wanted while I got the headache of taking his alloy out of the lab and learning how to make it commercially. That experience made me eat humble pie. I only saw this man two or three times in my life, but he left me with an indelible imprint and a lesson in listening.[113]

Along with his work on 8-1-1, Harry and fellow engineer Roger Peebles worked together to develop a new alpha-beta alloy to be used in engines, Ti-6Al-2Sn-4Zr-2Mo-0-0.25 Si (known as 6-2-4-2, Sn being tin, Zr being zirconium, and Si being silicon), which had good tensile creep and fatigue properties. Silicon enhances creep resistance over 900 degrees Fahrenheit. It was a challenge working beyond the normal ternary alloy form in which there are only three elements. "I was plotting alloy behaviors like mad, playing around with the Hume-Rothery rules, which pertain to the conditions under which an element, such as molybdenum, dissolves in a metal." Roger and Harry had a great deal of research freedom at TIMET along with the equipment to test out their ideas.

One day, Don Wruck from TIMET's Technical Service Department in New York City walked into my office in Henderson unannounced and sat down. After the usual chitchat, he addressed the purpose of his visit. The jet engine folks badly needed something more creep resistant than the alloy Ti-6Al-4V, an alloy that would run in jet engine compressors. Not knowing that Roger and I had been working on just such an alloy, he was a bit stunned when I replied, "You want 6-2-4-2. It fits their needs exactly. On all counts except modulus and density, it beats out 8-1-1 and is stable against embrittlement for at least ten thousand hours." Don went straight back to New York and got to work; within weeks, potential customers were testing the alloy for themselves. Pratt & Whitney loved it, and so did General Electric. Literally thousands of tests were run as the industry searched in vain for an Achilles' heel, such as the embrittlement problem with 8-1-1. But none was ever found. It became one of the most commonly used high-temperature alloys in jet engine compressors and airframe structures.

The patent for 6-2-4-2 was filed under Roger Peebles's name because his notebook entries were complete and the date on the first entry was earlier than Harry's. "Roger was issued a patent on what was our mutual concept, but it was of no real consequence then or now. Patents are legal documents and must be unassailable in court, and TIMET's patent agent was a stickler, which he needed to be for legal reasons. He just wasn't up to the strategies of writing strong claims." Further work to enhance 6-2-4-2 by the addition of a critical amount of silicon was carried out at Reactive Metals Inc. (RMI, formerly Mallory-Sharon) in order to better meet Pratt & Whitney's design needs. The alloy as modified was patented by Stanley Seagle and Howard Bomberger.

Patents arising from research are central to corporate profitability.[114] An alloy or a process (such as a better method to roll sheet) is developed, and if it is sufficiently different from other alloys or processes, it is patentable. In a corporate laboratory, the researcher who is awarded the patent (in this case Peebles) assigns the patent to the corporation, which then has the rights to make that alloy, sell the patent, or to allow other companies to make or process the alloy via contract. In metallurgy, the surest way to gain status is to hold patents, especially of worthwhile alloys. It is like an athlete earning a gold medal; its value is related to the significance of the event. In the course of his career, Harry would be issued thirteen patents on titanium and five relating to tantalum.

Of value to Harry in regard to 6-2-4-2 was that his research led him to a critically important formula: $Al + 1/3(\% \ Sn) + 1/6(\% \ Zr) + 10 \ (\% \ O_2) < 9$. Derived from maps Harry drew of the stable and unstable regions of various compositions, the formula defines by weight percent the safe range for nonembrittling, creep-resistant alloys. For example, it would take three times as much tin (Sn) in weight percent to induce the embrittling effect observed by adding 1 percent aluminum (Al). "In the overall scheme of things, the formula was more important than my eventual insights into the Larson-Miller parameter and more important than who held the patent on 6-2-4-2. The formula became popular among metallurgists, but it is not generally known otherwise. To my knowledge, it was never challenged."

In his investigation into the problems with the alloy 8-1-1, Harry had used the Larson-Miller (L-M) parameter, which is a predictive tool in metallurgy. However, he had found it to be inadequate. In fact, his dissatisfaction was so great it would be one of the spurs to his return to Stanford University to complete the work for his PhD.

> *The L-M parameter nagged and nagged at me. It was supposed to predict long-time performance from short-time data and was widely used for that purpose. Moreover, it had a rigorous foundation on the Boltzmann equation in thermodynamics, then and now a cornerstone of chemistry and physics. But it just did not work well enough in titanium alloys to suit me. Beyond about a thousand hours, alloy performance departed significantly from predictions. How could we possibly invent new alloys without being able to project accurately. This question had no definitive answer for another half century. We did, however, add a factor to the parameter that produced acceptable accuracy for alloy selection.*

Harry also wanted to understand more fully why alloys behaved as they did so he could present the facts clearly in scientific terms to TIMET's customers. The field of materials science had come into existence since he received his master's degree. TIMET customers, including Boeing and General Electric, were hiring PhDs in that specialty.

> *As supervisor of the Metallurgical Research Division, I was doing well, but I did not understand sufficiently the science of metal behavior and I was concerned that it detracted from our credibility. I wanted to have a better theoretical grasp of such topics as the difference between a screw dislocation and an edge dislocation, stacking faults, and all the deformation mechanisms that make metals ductile in the first place. Thus far in my career, I had been lucky on the strength of my ability to experiment and conservatively interpret how our*

alloys would perform in service, but I was still a long way from being a finished metallurgist. So one day in casual conversation, I mentioned my concerns to my boss Don Cooper, telling him that I felt I was in over my head, because I was doing physical metallurgy with only an extractive background. I needed to get my PhD.

Cooper agreed with Harry and immediately took up his cause, convincing his superiors at TIMET not only to pay Harry's tuition at Stanford but also his full salary for three years. "The reason we sent him back to Stanford was that we felt isolated at TIMET," explained Cooper. "We wanted to hire some PhDs, but the ones we did manage to hire did not work out, so we decided that we would create our own by sending Harry for his PhD in materials science."[115]

In 1966, at age thirty-eight, Harry returned to Palo Alto. "I went with the intent of making the L-M parameter ambiguity my primary research objective. I had no clue at the time just how difficult that would prove to be."

CHAPTER 10:
IN SEARCH OF DEEPER UNDERSTANDING

The year 1966 marked a major turning point in Harry's life not only because he returned to Stanford University for his doctorate but also because his marriage to Geri finally disintegrated after being on the verge for several years. They had started dating when they were teenagers, seeing no other choice for their lives but to get married in Las Vegas and settle down in the Mojave Desert, with Geri (still in high school) becoming a housewife and Harry a miner. This inauspicious start had been followed by the difficult years living in mining camps and run-down trailer parks when there was barely enough money to buy milk and pay the rent. Meanwhile, class by class, Harry's horizons had broadened. His job at TIMET after graduation from Stanford increased the divide between them because it involved more travel, bringing him into closer contact with engineers and scientists across the country from Boeing in Seattle, Washington, to Pratt & Whitney in East Hartford, Connecticut, as well as in Europe.

> *Slowly, I began to realize Geri and I were not only different people; we were so different in basic temperament and worldview there could be no bridge between us worth the building. Basically, we shared only character. That realization took several years to play out. It ended in an amicable divorce with joint custody. We each wanted the best we could manage for our boys. But they suffered grievously, each in his own way.*

Before the divorce, Harry had met a woman named Kris Ellison, who lived in Boulder City, Nevada, with her husband and four daughters:

Bonnie, Robin, Joy, and Aleta. She had given a sermon at the Community Church in Henderson where the Rosenbergs were active members, with Harry serving as moderator as well as singing in the choir. It was during a period when the church was searching for a permanent minister and was relying on guest speakers to fill in on Sunday mornings. Tall and good-looking with honey-blond hair, Kris had been tapped for the assignment that hot August day because she was the director of a Sunday school at a Methodist church in the area. She was also taking classes at the University of Nevada at Las Vegas. As a result of her complicated life, she had a unique down-to-earth approach to Christian theology that grabbed everyone's attention, including Harry's:

> *Never in my life had I heard such a sermon. I was mesmerized. And so was everyone else. I had never known such stage presence, such lucid explanations of why we need moral directives—not in biblical terms, but in language we all understood. No references to this or that passage in the Bible; just straight talk. At the end of the service, the congregation slowly filed out, thanking our pinch-hitter and her family. I was among the last. I clasped her hands and said she would be welcome back any time. I meant every word. She must have picked up on that because two days later, I received a note in the mail that began: "I feel that I know you." She went on to explain why, mentioning the way I had handled the church business before her sermon. I was not, and still am not, the social type. But I realized her note required an answer. I didn't remember how I phrased things or even what I wrote, but I was complimentary. Before the week was out, the phone rang. It was Kris. I swallowed hard. Anyway, with just another week before departing for Stanford, we made a pact to stay in touch. It turned out that she was in a worse marriage than I was. I came home over the Christmas holidays and was able to see Kris briefly. Telephone wires had been burning up daily with messages and conversations. Along about March, we notified our respective spouses that we were moving out: me to a room with a friend, Kris and the kids to her parents, Bob and Maxine Christian, who lived in Boulder City. Maxine had an outsized fit of hysterics when*

> *I was presented to her, but I won her over. Bob and Kris's*
> *brother, also named Bob, were supportive. Her youngest sister*
> *Jan, who was barely a teenager, didn't get into it. Divorces*
> *were filed for and granted. Everything looked and felt bright*
> *and rosy. We married in a private ceremony conducted by*
> *her Methodist minister. We expected that the kids would love*
> *each other as we loved each other. Everyone would be on our*
> *side. But it was not to be.*

At the time of the divorce in 1967, Keith was thirteen, Neil eleven, and Eric eight—vulnerable ages when emotional damage can be great and healing difficult. Kris's daughters were also jolted by the divorce and the fact that they suddenly had three stepbrothers, close in age but different in temperament. "Only Neil and Bonnie, Kris's oldest, ever cared much for each other. The only time we had them all together, it did not work out. I felt a deep sorrow and regret that we did not foresee all the many difficulties of trying to merge families."

Three years younger than Harry, Kris had returned to college in 1965 to study English, but she soon changed to psychology, finding in that field a direction for her life. After she married Harry, she finished her undergraduate work and went on to earn her master's degree writing a thesis on the Guilford-Zimmerman Temperament Survey (GZTS), her study cohort being people who assembled nuclear weapons at Lake Mead Base (now Nellis Air Force Base) north of Las Vegas.[116] She worked as a school psychologist with a small private practice on the side until she and Harry moved to Pittsburgh in 1976, at which point she taught college and had a larger private practice.

By default, Harry was Kris's longest-term client. Over their years together, she helped him comprehend what the death of his mother and the frequent periods of separation from his father had meant. Up until their marriage, Harry's life had been so difficult that working hard all the time had been more than a financial necessity; it had been a way to hold back the darkness of his early life. Kris gave him the chance to understand.

> *Kris introduced me to myself—warts and all. She taught me*
> *how the psyche can be distorted to the detriment of its owner.*
> *In the context of her unconditional regard and acceptance*
> *of my being, I was able to realize how I had hang-ups that*

were self-defeating even though they were a healthy means
of coping at the beginning. No man could have had a better
life-mate. Her fearless revealing of her inner-self encouraged
reciprocity and closeness.

Kris had problems of her own, both physical and emotional: she had been stricken with polio at age twenty-six while pregnant, losing the baby as a result and developing chronic right-side muscle weakness in her back and torso that worsened as she grew older; she had been in an abusive marriage that left emotional scars on her and her daughters; and her marriage to Harry unsettled her daughters even more although Harry adopted them and tried to provide stability. However, Kris had the ability to look honestly at her problems, learn from them, and then turn around and in her counseling practice help others similarly afflicted. Her relationship with Harry was not always easy for the simple reason that she was as intense as he—her focus being on understanding the human condition and Harry's being on understanding metals, although with her encouragement, his interests broadened to include psychology and the nature of conflicts between cultures. Nor did the negative dynamics of trying to raise seven children in separate families help. Yet, Harry came to realize that "the pluses in our relationship far outweighed the minuses for each of us. In a very real way, Kris altered my inner personhood for the better, and that was priceless to me and indirectly, to others as well."

Just as Harry's personal life was tumultuous, so also was his return to Stanford, the upheaval being caused by the enormous changes in metallurgy that had occurred since he had earned his master's degree in 1956, only ten years before. "I had gotten my master's in metallurgical engineering, which was principally focused on chemical metallurgy, but that field was no longer even offered. The academic turf had moved on in my absence and quite properly so. It was now materials science. But that meant I had a whole lot of catching up to do."

According to William Nix, who was director of Stanford's Center for Materials Research at the time of Harry's return, the organization and course offerings of engineering schools and departments prior to 1960 matched the metallurgical industries served, including steel, aluminum, copper, and brass. "Then the threat of Sputnik and the increasing role of government funding pushed universities to broaden their outlook on advanced materials and to focus on the basic principles that apply to all classes of materials," explained Nix. "At the same time, fewer and fewer of our students were taking jobs with the primary metals producers, and more and more were heading toward aerospace and, later, electronics."[117]

As the largest titanium sponge maker in the world at the time, TIMET was a primary metals producer, albeit much smaller than Anaconda or Kennecott. Therefore, Harry's employment in their research laboratory put him squarely in the earlier era that Nix mentions. However, his trajectory was already toward the development of alloys for use in aerospace and high-purity titanium for use in electronics. As a refresher, Harry opted to take some physical metallurgy and mathematics courses at the undergraduate level while also taking graduate courses. Mary Sunseri, one of Stanford's legendary mathematics professors, kindly let him audit a few of her classes to reinforce his calculus. "Mary was inspiring not only to me but to generations of Stanford students because she brought math to life. John Shyne was another professor who helped me get back on the academic track by teaching me about tensors, enabling me to fulfill the PhD requirements in electromagnetics." Tensors are a way to describe mathematically the physical laws that operate in crystalline lattices. To become a capable metallurgist, a person needs to have a basic understanding of tensor properties; but to become a metallurgist who can advance the science, a person needs to have an extensive understanding coupled with a degree of restlessness about all that is not yet understood.

Just as Harry began to make headway in these complex subjects, he was abruptly called back to TIMET because of serious personnel problems that had developed in the research laboratory. He didn't return to Stanford for a year. "I ended up cramming my graduate work into two years instead of the normal three. It was absolutely grueling. Then I had to do all my thesis work back at TIMET while I was simultaneously supervising the laboratory."

Mitigating the struggle somewhat was his association with Nix, a brilliant academician in the mold of Norman Dolloff and Cutler Shepard. Nix was several years younger than Harry and, like him, had attended San Jose State College, graduating with his bachelor's degree in metallurgical engineering before going to Stanford where he earned his master's and PhD in metallurgical engineering and materials science.

What Norman and Cutler did for me emotionally,
encouraging me when I needed it, and opening doors for me

when every door seemed shut, Bill did for me intellectually, really sharpening my analytical abilities. He taught the tough stuff. The miracle was not just his teaching but his insistence on getting all the tiny details right; accuracy was imperative. I had to learn that lesson again and again. Fortunately, patience is one of Bill's long suits, though I am sure I tried him sorely at times.

That Nix taught "the tough stuff," as Harry recalls, is confirmed by Nix himself. "Looking back now at some of the courses I was teaching and he was taking, we did get rather deep into the physics of plastic deformation of alloys," Nix said. "I still have the notes from a course in dislocation dynamics that I taught that are far more sophisticated than the courses I teach now. I suspect that Harry, with his practical orientation, must have wondered what I was raving about. But it must have stuck. Indeed, in his dissertation he made quite a bit of use of thermodynamic principles to analyze the basic controlling mechanisms of deformation in Ti-Al alloys."[118]

The operant word in Nix's statement is *physics*, because in making the shift to materials science, metallurgy had moved into applied physics as well as applied chemistry, a shift that had begun at Stanford under the leadership of Shepard. Back in time, blacksmiths would never have used the word *thermodynamics* to describe their work. In fact, the word didn't exist until Lord Kelvin used it for the first time in 1849 in regard to steam engines. The only things the blacksmiths knew were that careful heating followed by rapid cooling (quenching) of iron, after hammering it just so on an anvil, could change the properties of everything from a pickax to a sword. Unbeknownst to the blacksmiths, they were inducing defects and second phases in the crystalline structure of the metal to their advantage, which is exactly what materials scientists do now. All this Harry had learned from the blacksmith at the Noonday mine who had commanded him to begin sharpening a pick by heating the entire pick to a bright red-orange and then to quench "just the red-hot tip in water until the point is dark and remove it quickly." Throughout the process, the blacksmith relied on color to determine the metal's readiness for the next step. Done right, the final result was a pick with a tip that was hard and would not break. Done wrong, the final result was a pick that quickly became dull, or worse, shattered when a miner swung it against a rock face.

Other metallurgical terms that the blacksmith did not know but that played a large role in his success or failure are *deformation*, *dislocation*, and *defect*. *Elastic* deformation is the change in shape of a body under stress that is recovered when the stress is released. For example, if a paper clip is used to hold several pages together, it will return to its original shape when removed. *Plastic* deformation is the change in shape of a body under stress that is not recovered when the stress is released. If a paper clip is bent around a pencil, it stays bent. One simple tensile test performed in the metallurgical laboratory is to stretch (deform) a small cylindrical metal specimen in a machine designed to record both the applied stress and the resulting stretch (strain). As the load is applied, the metal first stretches elastically. Then, when the load is released, the metal returns to its original length. However, beyond some characteristic combination of load and stretch for the particular metal being tested, it deforms plastically and will not return to its original length. At the atomic level, this increase in hardness is due to the successive movement of imperfections in the crystal lattice known as dislocations, which are like linear mismatches that add strength, sometimes dramatically. Depending on the metal, when the stress reaches a maximum (a point known as the ultimate tensile strength), the specimen develops what is called a neck, analogous to a human neck. This narrow place is where fracture (rupture) occurs.

There are many kinds of defects that make it harder for dislocations to move through the lattice, essentially putting up barriers that lock them in place, further strengthening the metal. One defect is substitutional atoms in which some foreign atoms take the place of some of the host atoms. For example, in the case of copper, the substitution of zinc atoms (foreign) for copper atoms (host) in the crystal lattice makes brass, and the substitution of tin atoms makes bronze, both of which are stronger than copper alone. Again, this was a process used by ancient metalworkers to make swords, shields, drinking chalices, and farm implements, although they had no idea why it worked. The ability to make bronze was of such enormous cultural importance an entire epoch was named for it—the Bronze Age. Just as zinc and tin are substitutional in copper, so in a titanium alloy, such as Ti-6Al-4V, aluminum and vanadium are substitutional, making it stronger.

Another useful defect is interstitial atoms that reside in the space between the host atoms, a location that is usually vacant. Because of their small atomic radii, oxygen, nitrogen, and carbon are interstitial in a titanium alloy. But no matter the defect, it is quite possible to have too much of a good thing. For example, too much of an interstitial element, such as oxygen, can make a titanium alloy brittle; too much of a substitutional element, such as aluminum, can do the same. The result could be a titanium airplane part that fractures under the stress of one too many takeoffs. It is the job of the materials scientist to determine, on the basis of the ultimate application of the alloy, the level at which defects are either efficacious or deleterious. None of this was understood until the twentieth century when X-rays, first created and detected by Wilhelm Conrad Röntgen, led to the knowledge that metals are crystalline by nature. That eventually led to the field of crystal dislocations, which would play a role in Harry's doctoral work on the deformation behavior of aluminum and titanium alloys.

Harry's practical orientation, his ability to ask both process and theoretical questions, and his ten years of experience in the titanium industry set him apart at Stanford as did his age. "Harry was no greenhorn," said Nix. "He had a big storehouse of knowledge that most students don't have. Realizing what his background was when he came back, he got really deep into the mathematical weeds of how to understand the microscopic processes that control things in materials. A lot of people in industry get so far away from the theoretical that they just can't get back to it. They go through the motions when they return to graduate school, but they don't get deep into the underlying physics and mathematics. Harry did, and it was remarkable."

The other aspect that set Harry apart as a doctoral student was his expertise in inferential statistics, a branch of statistics that draws conclusions from data generated when looking for the effect of some variable, such as an alloy addition, that is subject to random measurement. One very important use of inferential statistics is to answer the question of what should be done next in selecting and developing a new alloy for specific applications.

> *Rather than try to memorize formulas, I tried to make part of my thinking the deep ideas and concepts behind the formulas. I could always look up a formula and plug in the numbers, but to do so would be to miss what the world is all about. I always needed to think about the usefulness of whatever I was learning and how it could be applied. My understanding of statistics and how it can actually guide research was a big part of that, but to this day, statistics*

*is rarely a requirement in materials science departments.
Professors I have queried have replied that it is a theoretical
subject for the mathematics department. They haven't made
the connection. So they are turning out PhDs who do not
know how to design experiments or analyze data. Its use
extends beyond research and setting limits to measurements
in general, including production process control, food quality,
drug approvals, and almost any event that can be counted
or given magnitude.*

Nix is in agreement with Harry regarding the use of statistics: "It is something we don't do well in academia. They have to use it in industry because they have mounds and mounds of data from which they have to nurse out what the heck they have to do. But in the university you don't have that many data points and you don't rely on it in the same way. The importance of statistical analysis to Harry is apparent in his dissertation that includes an appendix on the subject. Virtually no graduate student thinks like that." Indeed, his introduction in the appendix pertaining to the fundamental use of statistical analysis is clear and unarguable:

*Statistical analyses have two fundamental uses. The first
is to define experimental scatter for use in assigning proper
levels of significance to results or expected correlations.
The second is even more important. In this case, one can
systematically search for effects and interactions not self-
evident from the data. Experimental designs can be quite
efficient when amenable to statistical techniques. Although
this second application may raise more questions than it
answers, that is the essence of science and the requisite of
progress.*[119]

Harry hoped to address the Larson-Miller parameter, but many problems stood in his way. In 1968, he was taking a class from Oleg D. Sherby, who had just published with Peter Burke a well-received paper in *Progress in Materials Science* that focused on the factors influencing the deformation of polycrystalline materials. In metallurgy, there are two very important ways to approach plastic deformation: the first pertains to the pristine volumes of the single crystal; the second pertains to polycrystals.

As ingots cool and solidify, many crystals nucleate and grow into masses of polycrystals. They have the same crystal structure, but they do not have the same orientation and often lie at high angles relative to each other. The very thin contiguous region between them is called a grain boundary. Although only a few atoms wide, it is stronger than the grain itself. Another factor affecting deformation is that several different deformation mechanisms can occur simultaneously, acting in tandem or in parallel.

The work of Sherby and his colleagues was not on titanium per se but on the influence of high stresses and temperatures on diffusional-creep, which occurs as low-strain rates in the direction of stress. To understand what was being studied, it is helpful to envision a small metal strut that is being elongated extremely slowly by a heavy weight hanging on it. According to Harry, "Their work was akin to the flow of molasses where all atoms move by diffusion, while my work with titanium was more like cards in a deck gliding over one another, where only the dislocations move. Diffusion follows a power law and glide follows an exponential law, but there is a gray area where they overlap." The Larson-Miller parameter is a means to predict the time for the small metal strut to rupture. The problem is that it uses an empirical constant that is an approximation, working better for some metals than for others. Frequently, this means that the further out in time that a metallurgist needs to estimate, the poorer that estimate gets. This is particularly troublesome in aerospace applications, where instant repairs in event of failure are rarely, if ever, possible.

Actually, the Larson-Miller parameter had less to do with Sherby's work on high-temperature alloys than with Harry's work on titanium and aluminum. What goaded Harry was not so much Sherby's research as his presumption that a solution was virtually impossible a word that was not in Harry's vocabulary. In retrospect, Harry admits that his natural curiosity going back to his epic battle with the fire ants in the Mojave Desert when he was a child just wouldn't let him leave the problem alone, no matter how intractable. For decades, he would return to it again and again, occasionally publishing papers.

> *Sherby was well aware of the Larson-Miller problem and was a self-styled "enlightened empiricist" like the rest of us working on high-temperature alloys. One day in class, I said to him that I wanted to resolve the Larson-Miller parameter issue. His reply: "That will take fifty years." Being already*

forty, my chances looked dim. Sherby was an enthusiastic promoter and defender of his own ideas and a lively teacher who could be demanding, even picky. I never went to sleep in one of his classes, and I learned a lot from him. It was only later that I understood what I needed to know to take issue with some of his ideas. At the time, the deformation problem was well-known, but many academicians thought it was of secondary, not primary, structural importance. I think most suspected that might not be true, but no one seemed to have tackled the problem head-on. I was more than a little naive to think I could fix that situation straight away. Dogma dies hard sometimes, even for otherwise accomplished researchers.

Behind Harry's fascination with the Larson-Miller problem was his previous experience with problems concerning the alloy Ti-8Al-1Mo-1V (8-1-1) that was to be used on Boeing's SST. Aerospace alloy development is most effective when an alloy is ready at the time a new aircraft is being designed; otherwise, the alloy may have to wait until the next plane is conceived, which can be years later. This reality is captured in a favorite expression of Harry's: "Be in line at design time, or catch the next plane." That is why an accurate prediction of long-time behavior from short-time test results can be critical in aerospace. This is the crux of the Larson-Miller parameter. To some materials scientists, it might have appeared that Harry was tilting at windmills, like a metallurgical Don Quixote, but that was not the case. His past as a miner, blacksmith, and mechanic meant that he never lost sight of the centrality of practical application, and thus he saw problems in a different light than some of his peers.

To solve the Larson-Miller problem meant two things to me: It would add to the scientific understanding of structural-metal—polycrystals—deformation. But, more important, it would enable more precise and effective selection of alloys for use at temperatures at "red heats" for extended times. The Larson-Miller parameter misses by miles when guessing where an alloy will be after ten years of service from a one-thousand-hour (forty-two-day) test. Ten years works out to about eighty-five thousand hours. We had to do better and

> did. The constant of twenty that Larson and Miller selected
> was for convenience; each metal has its own constant that
> is not always "constant." Typically, they range from about
> ten to thirty or so.

Buttressing his technical and intellectual skills was Harry's unshakeable optimism, no matter how hard the work and uncertain the outcome. His optimism was contagious. Being older by approximately fifteen years than the other graduate students and with significant industrial experience, he was respected. "Harry had the ability to close out the world and focus on his work," said Nix. "He was a little apart, but if someone asked him a question, he would always cup his ear to make an effort to hear and to help in a brotherly way. But he had no time for goofing off, such as playing ball or drinking." Harry recalls that he became a kind of mentor to other doctoral students who were struggling.

> Like all things learned, the real mechanics of the mentor/
> protégé relationship came slowly at first. One day, I
> accidentally walked in on a fellow student telling a professor
> he was quitting. When I left, my fellow student followed
> me out and continued talking in his quitting vein. I asked
> questions of the why-not-try variety. By the time we reached
> the library, he was asking some questions. We stood on the
> steps talking for the better part of an hour. Upon leaving, he
> said, "I am enthused." In retrospect, his impact on me was
> as great as mine on him. Why else would I remember his
> exact words and the tenor of his voice? This young man took
> his PhD just a year later with a transcript much superior
> to mine. But I had realized the value of being a mentor even
> outside the workplace. It was a lesson that would bear fruit
> many times in the future. It was only with Kris's help later on
> that I came to understand that the highest form of mentoring
> is a two-way street, which was the kind that Cutler Shepard
> and Bill Nix practiced.

But all the optimism in the world would not make a dent in metal deformation. Ultimately, Harry's doctoral thesis, carried out at TIMET, was on alloys of titanium and aluminum. While not giving up on researching the Larson-Miller parameter, he put it off. "It kept bothering me, but when I was working on my doctorate, it was one of those things that was beyond my reach." For his part, Nix remembers Harry's struggle: "At the time I thought he was being overly ambitious in setting his research goals, but he always surprised me with what he could accomplish. His dissertation was a masterpiece of completeness that has rarely been matched by my other students. Often, dissertations will pick up on one little thing. They won't be systematic or complete, but Harry's dissertation was exhaustive. He was trying hard to understand very hard problems. To this day, we still don't fully understand what causes all the property changes that he was seeing." Harry himself describes his 1971 dissertation, titled "Deformation Mechanics of Alpha Titanium Alloys," as "sort of a descriptive bible" of the effects of alloying titanium with aluminum. Don Cooper, Harry's boss at TIMET who had championed his return for his PhD, concurs with the description of his thesis as a bible. "It was read and reread by graduate students and engineers studying titanium for a long time afterwards. It was impressive."[120]

Despite the fact that his thesis did not deal with the Larson-Miller parameter, it hinted at potential lines of attack. "Professor Sherby was kind enough during my orals not to remind me of our earlier conversation on my solving the problem with the Larson-Miller parameter. Even so, he was very tough on me during the orals, criticizing me for the many typos, and his handshake afterward was of the dead-fish variety." Nix believes the differences between Sherby and Harry were more a matter of style than substance. "Sherby was always a pure phenomenologist," said Nix. "He was a person who would form a picture of what was happening, not necessarily in a physics-based way. Sherby was apt to say things like 'It smells right.' Harry was a practical person who would think about the underlying mechanistic physics of things."

Beyond personality differences, which were really of little consequence, there was the fact that the Larson-Miller parameter worked well enough for most applications relying on short-time data, so although it was poorly understood from the standpoint of physics, there seemed to be no compelling reason to pursue a better understanding at Stanford.

The Larson-Miller parameter accounts for something called the activation enthalpy that arises intrinsically from the acting deformation mechanism, and that theory

*was well-known as the Boltzmann equation in the field
of thermodynamics. What right does a mere blacksmith
who had worked in talc and lead mines have in tinkering
with such well-known science? For an event to occur on the
atomic scale requires an activation energy supplied by heat.
This fundamental concept envisions a bar whose height
is the activation energy. The first high jumper to clear a
bar at seven feet knows all about activation energy! Who
dared question that? Something in our experiments had to
be wrong!*

The part of his dissertation that ultimately led to a deeper understanding
had to do with edge and screw dislocations, which are terms for geometric
irregularities (linear defects) in the crystal lattice. Harry had spent
countless hours in the lab bent over a transmission electron microscope
searching for the reason that aluminum strengthened titanium steadily
(linearly) with each addition. All he could see were straight dislocations in
screw orientation, no edge dislocations or complete loops common in other
metals. "No one could explain it. Then out of the blue came one of my aha
moments: edge dislocations are the ones that encounter the barriers that
require a thermal assist to get through. But an edge dislocation can be any
length, even one atom long! Of course!" The morning before his orals, he
presented his research to the materials-science student body and some of
the faculty. When he began to discuss one-atom edge dislocations (edge
kinks in the jargon of metallurgy), an alert grad student in the back row
interrupted him and asked how he had come to that realization. "I didn't
have a ready answer, but managed to say something like: 'It just came to
me.' As to figuring out the constant, that came much later."[121]

Harry's research had put him in a better position to tackle metal
deformation and his enhanced mathematical ability had given him the
requisite skills. Don Cooper, as impressed as he was by Harry's thesis,
was even more impressed by the improvement in his math. "When he left
Henderson to go to Palo Alto, Harry was okay in math. Sometimes he made
mistakes in his calculations and I had to correct him. When he came back,
he was brilliant in math, way ahead, a real pleasure to work with."[122] But
for years, the Larson-Miller parameter acted like a pebble in Harry's shoe,
even though with the wisdom that comes from hindsight, Harry realized
Sherby had done him a favor by discouraging him at the time.

Decades passed before I realized that, all along, I had been framing the question wrong. Boltzmann was right. What was wrong was that Boltzmann's equation does not apply to polycrystalline metal deformation. Only if properly oriented single crystals are used does it work well enough. But except in certain electronic applications, single crystals are rarely used; polycrystalline metals provide the backbone of modern metallurgy. There is much more to it than this, and, of course, this realization did not come to me at Stanford. Only over the past decade or so have I come to a more definitive rendition of the constant. And I had to do nothing less than jettison Boltzmann as the basis and reframe the question from first principles that included the structural issues arising from polycrystals. That was conceptually hard, for Boltzmann was all about temperature effects. What else was needed? Such thinking required abandoning a lifetime, and lifeline, of belief. It was difficult both intellectually and emotionally. In short, what I had come to was virtually a reformulation of deformation mechanics in polycrystalline alloys and metals at elevated temperatures that included modulus effects on the effective stress seen by moving dislocations. Sherby had said it would take me fifty years. It took me forty. But without my discovery of the "kink effect" it might never have happened.

Harry's personal life continued to be unsettled. On February 27, 1969, at 1:00 a.m., he was awakened by a phone call from Stella Proctor Rook, his aunt who lived in Shoshone. His father, Harry Sr., had been swept away in a flood on the Amargosa River. "When I was told that the water had knocked him down, I knew it would keep him down. His body was found around noon the next day about a mile and a half south of Shoshone, just a few hours before Kris and I flew in from Stanford."

A series of heavy storms flowing north out of the tropics had begun the month before in January, causing severe flooding and landslides all over Southern California and bringing both the Amargosa and the Mojave Rivers to the surface. In severity, the January flood was similar to the great floods of 1916 and 1938 that had filled the playa lakes and destroyed miles of railroad track and numerous bridges, keeping Harry Sr. and his crew busy for months repairing the damage. At the beginning of February, there had been a brief respite in the rain, but in the middle of the month, a second series of storms swept in from the Pacific inundating the same areas. Precipitation for the period from February 22 through 25 ranged from five to fifteen inches in lowland areas of California, with almost thirty inches recorded at Lake Arrowhead in San Bernardino National Forest. In the Death Valley region, the flooding was made worse by the thawing of snow in the mountains. Badwater Basin in Death Valley, the terminus of the Amargosa River, flooded to between two and three feet at its lowest point.[123]

The last day of rainfall was February 26—the day that Harry Sr. drowned. At dusk on that day, Harry Sr. and his fifth wife, Beaulah, were returning on Route 178 from Las Vegas where they had gone to stock up on supplies. Near Shoshone, the valley through which the Amargosa flows is narrow, bordered to the east by badlands that rise abruptly, forming a formidable wall, while to the west, it rises toward the steep gravel hills that form the western border of the town. Route 178 crosses the Amargosa River from east to west at what is usually a dry gulch. But that day, the rains had brought the river to furious life. As the Rosenbergs approached on Route 178, the river was bullying its way south past the town. A water-over-road warning sign had already been posted in Pahrump, Nevada, through which they had passed on their way home from Las Vegas, but Harry Sr. was unconcerned. "I doubt my father thought the sign was meant for him. After all, he had the river mastered, having walked on its waters many times." Beaulah was driving when they reached a barricade that had been set in place to keep vehicles out of the floodwaters, but Harry urged her to drive around it, assuring her they could make it across. As she stepped on the gas, the road collapsed beneath the pickup truck, and the front of the cab nosed down, killing the engine.

> *My father, of course, tried to do something about it. At seventy-four, he was still a powerful man—in some ways larger-than-life, though he was much frailer than he had been. But I doubt he was completely sober, which was probably why Beaulah was driving. He got out on the upriver-side and went to the back of the pickup to get out of the water and to signal for help. While he was trying to open the tailgate, it let go all of a sudden, pitching him into the flood. Beaulah saw him just once trying to stand up. Then he was gone.*

Beaulah managed to climb out the window into the back of the pickup where she lit pieces of paper with matches she had in her purse, waving the paper in the air to signal for help. Looking out the window of her house in Shoshone, Stella Rook saw the flames in the darkness and alerted her son-in-law Luvon Messer that someone was in trouble down by the river. Messer, who worked for the county repairing roads, immediately got the large road grader, drove it into the floodwaters, and nosed it up against the truck, rescuing Beaulah.

Harry Sr. was not the only person to lose his life during the floods; two people drowned north of Shoshone when their vehicle was swept away near what had been the Evelyn siding of the T & T. In total, the flooding in January and February took sixty lives and caused an estimated $400 million in property damage in Southern California. In the Death Valley region, Badwater Basin remained flooded for several months, providing visitors with the strange spectacle of a large lake spread out at the foot of the Panamint Mountains.

When he was alive, Harry Sr. had requested that when he died he be "planted" near his good friend Bill Greer in Tecopa. "My brother Lloyd and I planted him as close to Bill as we could. My father had always been able to beat the odds, always able to master the river. Such irony—in the end, the river mastered him."

Six weeks later, on April 11, another death rocked the family. Kris Rosenberg's brother Robert M. Christian Jr., known as Bobby, a second lieutenant in the US Marine Corps, was killed in a firefight in the Vietnam War. He was twenty-three years old.

> *It was a real blow to Kris and her family. Her parents, especially her mother, never really recovered. There was such turmoil over Vietnam then. It was the hated war. Bobby's death brought it home. More than thirty years later, Kris and I started a website named Road to Peace (roadtopeace.org) dedicated to understanding the root origins of violence and making a difference in a world of violence. The immediate impetus was the destruction of the World Trade Center and the attack on the Pentagon on September 11, 2001, but its roots stretched all the way back to that day in April when we got the phone call about Bobby.*[124]

CHAPTER 11:
A TURBULENT TIME

In the spring of 1971, two real estate agents put up a billboard near the Seattle airport. It showed a lightbulb dangling by a wire with the words, "Will the last person leaving Seattle—Turn out the lights." The message was apt because Boeing, the largest employer in the area, was on the verge of bankruptcy. Funding for Boeing's SST—which would have used prodigious amounts of titanium—was cut off on May 20, 1971, by a highly contentious vote of 215 to 204 in the House of Representatives. Driving the negative vote was a major concern about damage caused by sonic booms that would crack plaster, shatter windows, and, more seriously, harm human and animal health. Another concern was that the large volume of water vapor produced by the SST might result in depletion of the ozone layer. While there was disagreement from a scientific standpoint about how major these threats were, there was no disagreement that the cost overruns on the project were astronomical. There was also an underlying uneasiness with government funding of a commercial venture of this size. An overwhelming majority of Americans were opposed, partially because the SST was seen as a plane for wealthy jetsetters who wanted to get to Europe faster. The ever-lengthening production timeline only served to fuel that negativity. In his speech at the US Air Force Academy, John F. Kennedy had predicted that the SST would fly by the end of the 1960s, but in 1971, when the program came to an end, not even the two prototypes Boeing had promised had been completed.

At the time of the cancellation, Don Cooper (who as Harry's boss had championed his return to Stanford) was manager of TIMET's production laboratory in Toronto, Ohio. He was attending a meeting at Boeing when the announcement came over the loudspeakers.

> *We were discussing the problem of preparing the titanium*
> *plate for the SST and getting the structures the way Boeing*
> *wanted them. Right in the middle of the meeting, Richard*
> *Nixon's words were broadcast over the public address system.*
> *He apologized to the Boeing people, saying he would not be*
> *able to support the SST effort anymore because Congress*
> *would not give him any more money. His statement was*
> *followed by an announcement that meetings were to take*
> *place immediately throughout the company at which people*
> *would find out who would lose their jobs and who would stay.*
> *So people got up and left our meeting right then, and when*
> *they returned, some of them folded up their briefcases and*
> *without saying a word left the room. That was the end of our*
> *meeting. As we were leaving, people were being instructed*
> *over the loudspeaker to empty out their desk drawers and to*
> *dump the contents into trashcans placed in the hallways. It*
> *was unbelievable.*[125]

Similar stories abound with the common themes being shock and devastation. Donald Goehler, who worked at Boeing, remembers that it took about a day to get all the pink slips out to all the employees who were being laid off. He had already laid off seventeen of the eighteen people in his group when he himself was called to a meeting at which he expected 250 managers to be in attendance. Instead, there were only twenty-five in the conference room. "We were told that we were the only ones left!"[126] Within months, the housing market collapsed in the Seattle area because unemployed workers could no longer pay their mortgages. Everyone was trying to sell, and no one was buying. Automobiles were sold at half their value. About the only statistics that soared were the number of people receiving food stamps and the suicide rate. A gallows humor became the norm among the remaining Boeing employees, who joked that an optimist was someone who brought a lunch to work; a pessimist kept his automobile running while he went inside.

It wasn't just the cancellation of the SST that brought about the severe downturn in aerospace and the recession in the national economy. Orders for military aircraft had dropped because of the winding down of the Vietnam War. So also had orders for commercial airplanes, nearing zero in 1970, because some of the airlines had overbought in the late 1960s only to find themselves with more seats than passengers. During the same period, a few airline companies began to put heavy pressure on the airframe builders to design bigger and faster planes, the heaviest pressure coming from Pan Am, which wanted to expand its overseas routes. Trying to comply, airframe builders had borrowed money and when that ran out, had borrowed more.

Part of the problem was a major technological disjunction between the airframe manufacturers who were developing larger passenger aircraft (e.g., Boeing's 747, Lockheed's L-1011 TriStar, and McDonnell Douglas's DC-10) and the engine makers, none of whom had adequate engines sitting on the shelf waiting for insertion in a wide-body airframe. Much more powerful engines with optimum fly-weight to achieve greater fuel efficiently were required, but this was easier said than done. Overexpectation of what the engine makers could deliver led to foolhardiness as exemplified by Rolls-Royce in Great Britain, which went into receivership in February 1971. Rolls-Royce had made a misguided attempt to further decrease the weight of its new turbofan engine, the RB.211, by using a carbon-fiber laminate called Hyfil, instead of titanium. When a Hyfil fan blade shattered during a routine FAA test in which a four-pound chicken carcass was fired at the engine to mimic the impact of a collision with a bird in flight, confidence in Rolls-Royce's ability to deliver the RB.211 evaporated. This, in turn, spelled trouble for Lockheed because of its large contracts for the RB.211 to power its new L-1011 TriStar, and Lockheed was already in trouble because of fierce competition with McDonnell Douglas, which was building the DC-10.[127]

Complex technical problems added to Boeing's woes as well. The company's new wide-bodied 747, the world's first jumbo jet, was in dire straits, causing nail-biting anxiety for Boeing's engineers and executives. The 747 was to be powered by four JT9D engines, the first of the high-bypass-ratio turbofans built by Pratt & Whitney. In flight, the generation of engine thrust must be transmitted to the airframe in such a way that the engine is not distorted, even under maximum power at takeoff. Being the first engine of its kind, previous experience was not always an accurate guide as to how the JT9D would perform in service. For these reasons, problems arose during final engine qualifications under the conditions imposed by the pylon that transmitted asymmetric thrust to the wing and airframe. A process called ovalization occurred in the engine casing at maximum thrust, causing the rotor blades to rub against their stator counterpoints.[128] The result was total destruction of the engine, an all-too-common occurrence during testing.

Meanwhile, the 747 airframes kept rolling off Boeing's production line. In September 1969, *Time* magazine reported, "On the apron outside Boeing's plant in Everett, Wash., 15 enormous 747 jets stand high and silent, harbingers of a new era in aviation. They are painted in the colors of several international airlines: TWA, Pan Am, Lufthansa, Air France. For the moment, however, the planes are the world's largest gliders—because they have no engines." Without the stabilizing weight of the engines, the planes were in danger of tipping over, so workers hung cement blocks on the wings for balance—an incongruous reminder that technological advance is never a straight line.[129]

Back at Pratt & Whitney, everyone was scrambling, studying all possible culprits, from the position of the engine on the wing to the materials of the case. It took sophisticated analysis to find a solution. It turned out to be transferring thrust to the pylon at the rear of the engine by means of a Y-shaped frame made of titanium that extended from the compressor to the rear turbine case mount. It was a fairly simple solution that did not add too much weight and that had applications to other engines as well. Once the titanium frames were installed, Pratt & Whitney began to deliver the JT9Ds to Boeing at which point the 747 quite literally took off, becoming the most successful passenger jumbo jet ever built, indeed, an icon of the air. However, from 1969 to 1971, it wasn't clear whether the 747 would fly at all, even though both Boeing and Pratt & Whitney had bet their respective stores that it would.

Before solutions were found to all these problems, the economic fallout was substantial. According to T. A. Heppenheimer in his book *The Space Shuttle Decision: NASA's Search for a Reusable Space Vehicle*: "Total aerospace employment reached a peak of over 1.4 million in 1967. It then slid downhill very rapidly, dropping to 900,000 in mid-1971. Employment of production workers fell by nearly 50 percent, from nearly 800,000 to just over 400,000. It was nearly as bad for scientists and engineers, as their ranks dwindled from 235,000 in 1968 to 145,000 four years later."[130]

The titanium industry was in financial trouble well before the SST was canceled. Companies had built up their facilities to produce the amount of titanium that would eventually be needed, but delay after delay had kept them from getting a return on their investments. TIMET expanded its production facilities constructing a huge vacuum annealing line capable of handling thirty-six-inch sheet. So also RMI in Niles, Ohio, built a large-plate rolling mill to handle the expected demand. Hal Kessler, who had left TIMET in 1964 to join RMI, remembers the ramp-up and then the shock of hearing the news of the SST cancellation while sitting in the office of an executive at Pratt & Whitney. "Up until then, business for RMI was looking very good. Then suddenly the SST folded—and everything folded." The problems with the 747 only added to the mess.[131]

The shock wave that went through aerospace had long-term consequences for the titanium industry. In response to a steep decline in orders, TIMET went through a severe layoff as a result of which Harry's research laboratory dropped from twenty-six engineers and technicians to only six. "I had to handle the layoffs in the laboratory, and it was rough—necessary—but rough. I hated to lay off longtime good and loyal friends who ably did everything they could to make TIMET a success." However, there were even more serious troubles brewing, although it would not become public knowledge until the federal government filed a civil complaint in 1978. TIMET, RMI, Crucible, Lawrence Aviation Industries Inc., and Martin Marietta Aluminum fixed the prices on titanium plate, sheet, strip, billet, and bar, for which they eventually pleaded no-contest. The height of the scandal was in 1975 and 1976, but the government charged that the price-fixing had begun in 1970.[132]

Harry did not learn about the price-fixing scandal until the civil complaint in 1978, by which time he had moved to TIMET's corporate headquarters in Pittsburgh, Pennsylvania. All he knew in 1971 was that there seemed to be nothing but problems everywhere, the exception being in research where that year he made his first entry in his notebook for a new alloy that would fill yet another niche in the aerospace market. It combined high strength in large sections with high fracture toughness and crack-growth resistance. Its chemical formula was Ti-10V-2Fe-3Al, known as 10-2-3. It was the first titanium alloy to be used in commercial aircraft without first being qualified in military applications. Harry and Max Parris received a patent for it three years later in 1974 at which point the industry and the economy were beginning to improve again.[133]

At the aerospace giants, several new planes were being designed, including the B-1 bomber built by Rockwell International (for which 10-2-3 was originally intended as plate), the F-15 Eagle built by McDonnell-Douglas, and the F-14 Tomcat built by Grumman.[134] Boeing was working on the 757, its twin-engine medium-range jetliner that would take to the air in 1982. In every case, the need to reduce the weight of the aircraft was the major driving force behind the increased use of titanium and the search for new alloys. The benchmark titanium alloy against which all new alloys were measured in terms of both cost and properties continued to be Ti-6Al-4V, the workhorse alloy of the whole aerospace industry. The alloy 10-2-3 was superior to Ti-6Al-4V in strength and had superior fracture toughness at high ultimate tensile strength (UTS), but it was troublesome to produce and fabricate, hence it was more costly, so its worthiness had to be proved. Boeing was the first airframe maker to use 10-2-3 in its 757 for the forgings of the slat tracks, which extend the surface of the wing during takeoff and landing. Over all, the 757 contained approximately 6 percent titanium in various alloys. However, it would not be until twenty years after the patent was awarded that 10-2-3 would finally come of age when it was used for a critical component, the main landing gear beam of Boeing's 777. This forged piece weighed close to a ton.[135] A critical component is defined as one that if it fails results in the loss of the plane. With its first flight in 1994, the 777 became one of Boeing's best-selling models. Approximately 9 percent of the 777's structural weight was titanium, up from approximately 6 percent in the 757. But the use of 10-2-3 was not a foregone conclusion during the design stages of either aircraft.

> *Of all the near-beta alloys, 10-2-3 was the most forgeable. Eventually, the forgers loved it because they could get near-net shape with just one heat. It was tricky, but they learned fast. Boeing liked it because it had the highest combination of strength and toughness of any material out there, which was very important for the 777. But 10-2-3 had a really rough birth. The problem at the metal producers arose during the melting of the sponge into ingot. If you broke the center portion of a large ingot in two, you'd find bright, shiny spots that were high in iron, which meant there was micro-segregation going on. We called them beta-flecks, and they became the bane of manufacturing. Beta-flecking refers to overly large regions of stabilized beta phase free of alpha phase that embrittle during aging. It's a serious problem. Again, I went into emergency mode as I had done for 8-1-1, working to figure it out.*

The problem arose when melting was too rapid, causing some material to stay liquid below the solidification temperature, resulting in high local concentrations of iron in small volumes of pure beta phase with poor ductility after heat treatment. This made the alloy useless. Iron was needed for toughness, but its percentage had to be just right. A serendipitous mistake made by Edward Gubler, one of Harry's laboratory technicians who had responsibility for heat-treating experimental alloys, led to a fuller understanding of how the property balance can be affected by heat-treating. There was an atmosphere of honesty and respect in the lab, so Gubler immediately hunted Harry down and told him what had happened. "I really valued his honesty because it gave us part of the key we needed. He had heat-treated a specimen using time and temperatures different from the work request, but the tensile strength had come out better than expected while the high toughness remained." Because the alloy was still in the research stage, Harry and his team decreased the iron from 2 percent to 1.6 percent and modified melting procedures so that the thermal gradient within the ingot stayed above a certain level determined by the total alloy composition.[136]

Rodney Boyer, whose career at Boeing had begun in 1965 at the time of the SST project and would continue until his retirement thirty-seven years later, remembers working closely with Harry on 10-2-3. "TIMET had developed 10-2-3, but nobody was using it, it sat on the shelf. I was looking for a high-strength forging alloy. I looked at several alloys and ended up choosing it, but I knew we had to work out the forging process. With 10-2-3, the problem was that you had to melt it right. Then you had to forge it right. It was a wonderful alloy if you did everything right, but if you didn't, you screwed up." According to Boyer, forging took finesse. "Basically you had to do the primary forging above the beta transus. Then you had to forge below the beta transus in a narrow temperature range with about 15 percent deformation. It was also important to do just the right amount. If you did too much, you ended up with good ductility but poor fracture toughness. If you did too little, you ended up with poor ductility but good fracture toughness. Harry helped determine the critical parameters required to obtain the combination of properties I was looking for."[137]

The promise of 10-2-3 was one of the main reasons Harry accepted the position of manager of market development at TIMET's home office in Pittsburgh, Pennsylvania. The problem with beta-flecking in the ingots had been solved, but not the problems with forging. In fact, the alloy in long and thick sections was so difficult for the forgers to handle that they needed someone with a substantial technical background to work with them. Otherwise, 10-2-3 was not going to succeed, becoming one of the unfortunate alloys that despite its promise was too difficult to handle and so would be shelved. While the forgers liked the ease with which it filled dies to near-net shape during finish forging, it was the stringent requirements on forging temperature control and heat treatment, unlike any other titanium alloy, that made it tougher than usual to meet the specified properties. "The alloy 10-2-3 was a hot potato at the forgers, and they badly needed help. So I saw my calling as working closely with the folks at Alcoa and Wyman-Gordon as well as smaller forgers around the country." In some ways, working with the forgers took Harry back to his days working in the mines, then at Kennecott's vast copper mill, and finally at TIMET's sponge plant—all jobs that had a heavy dose of the practical instead of the theoretical. His new position also included product and market development, forecasting market consumption, chairing the patent committee, and administrative duties. It required travel throughout the United States and Europe. "One of the reasons I said yes to the job, leaving research after so many years, was that my awareness of self was widening. I realized that true creativity requires more than an idea, however wild. It requires solid follow-through to something people will use and pay good money for." So in 1976, Harry and Kris packed up and moved from Henderson to Pittsburgh, leaving the Mojave Desert behind, a move that made Kris feel as if she had been torn out by her roots. Learning how to drive in snow was particularly frightening for her as was the feeling of being a stranger in a strange land. Not until she began to teach at LaRoche College did she regain a sense of place and begin to feel at home.[138]

Except for Eric, who was eighteen years old and living with his mother while attending high school in San Jose, Harry's sons Keith and Neil were young adults who were beginning to build successful lives of their own, which included studying, working, and getting married. Of Kris's daughters, only Aleta, who was still in high school, made the move to Pittsburgh.

The change in environment was significant for us personally. We arrived when the weather was warm and bought a California-style house in a suburb north of Pittsburgh, not knowing any better. It had single-pane glass windows and three sliding doors—all airy and light-filled—really nice in the summer. Unbeknownst to us, our new home had gone through some four owners in a brief period of time after being built. That first winter, we found out why. About December, the weather turned cold, and then it turned really cold, well below zero for about three weeks. Not only was the furnace underpowered, but the house was drafty and the single-pane windows could become icy. Even the electrical outlets leaked frigid air when the wind blew. I tried to eliminate the drafts, patching up what I could and plugging the fireplace chimneys, but the whole house needed to be winterized and that had to wait until warm weather. So we wrapped ourselves in blankets, wore coats and sweaters, and thought about hibernation. The next winter was equally bad, not so cold, but it brought a huge amount of snow. I walked out of the house once after a storm to find our VW Bug totally buried beneath a snowdrift where it remained for a couple of weeks. It was the kind of weather that should have sent two desert rats scurrying back to the warmth of the Mojave, but we both liked what we were doing, so there was no question of going back. For me, where I lived was much less important than my work. It had always been that way, whether in San Jose, Palo Alto, or Henderson. I was always focused on the metallurgy. At times, I hardly noticed where I was or what was happening out in the world. So whether we were in Nevada or Pennsylvania didn't matter all that much to me. Plus Kris liked her new career and the opportunities for intellectual growth that it brought. She really came into her own in Pittsburgh, teaching psychology at LaRoche College, becoming good friends with the nuns there, and starting her private practice. So despite snow and cold, we became Easterners and never lived in the desert again.

It was while Harry was in Pittsburgh that the price-fixing scandal broke wide open. No one at TIMET went to jail because TIMET was the company that tipped off the government to what was going on, but it did so only when it became clear that a customer was about to blow the whistle. Harry recalls that it was a dark time in which all his research notebooks were confiscated by lawyers, never to be returned, and all the executives had to attend annual antitrust classes supervised by TIMET's outside law firm. In response to the price-fixing scandal, top management was changed and a new president, Joe Byrne, took over. His background was engineering and managing metal processing, not research and development, which meant he and Harry saw things differently, particularly regarding 10-2-3.

A while after Joe Byrne became president of TIMET, he chewed me out for developing 10-2-3 without permission. He was an authoritarian to the core and never missed an opportunity to let you know it. One day, Joe stopped me in the hall and without any warning shouted at me, "No one told you to invent 10-2-3!" I was speechless because inventing just such alloys was in my job description. It was what I did. He ranted on and on. It was similar to my being chewed out for discovering the embrittlement problem with 8-1-1 that was to be used for the SST. Byrne was under pressure from his manufacturing people at TIMET, who didn't like the tight manufacturing controls that 10-2-3 required. He was angry that I had committed the corporation to an entrepreneurial development that he did not like—an aerospace alloy that was hard to cast into ingot but which forged like butter and had the best suite of properties available for airframe forgings in its time. The latter feature allowed new shapes, the key to new markets, applications, volume, and profits. Byrne was also acting in what he perceived to be good faith for the good of the corporation. Equipment maintenance was costly when certain control margins were exceeded. Although I knew an application breakthrough was quite probable, what neither Joe nor I knew while he was yelling at me in the hallway was that Boeing would soon select that alloy for the main landing-gear beam and other parts on their 777. The alloy 10-2-3 would become highly successful, although the solution to some of its problems would come after I left TIMET. Covered by a strong patent, it became a decades-long standard against which other alloys were measured. Eventually, I was able to enjoy the irony, as well as the luck, in being able to find a target and hit the bull's-eye at

the same time. But I also learned that even if you have a
smashing success, not all of your cohorts may be pleased.[139]

All these factors began to weigh on Harry, leading him finally to a complete change in course. Another significant factor was his disgruntlement with the direction of research in general. "It wasn't just my run-in with Joe Byrne over 10-2-3. The atmosphere at the company had changed. TIMET was reducing their R and D efforts. One problem was that it cost more and more to develop less and less. We'd have to go through a hundred or more compositions before we found a new one that would have enough potential advantage over other alloys to find a niche in a market."

Deep down, Harry missed research. He had always been a tinkerer, a person who liked to be left alone in his nearly silent world to figure things out. The two attributes that had sustained him throughout his career were his intelligence and his ability to do an inordinate amount of mental and physical work. But the job in Pittsburgh, rife with office politics, required a different set of attributes. He still contacted customers, but his heart was no longer in it. Something was wrong, and for the first time in his life, he felt intimidated by the seeming lack of confidence management had in him. The crisis spilled over into his personal life, negatively affecting his relationship with Kris, who, having found her calling at LaRoche College, was shaken by the upheaval. When he was asked to move from Pittsburgh back to Henderson, he refused, the upshot being he ended up supervising both the Henderson and Toronto labs from a distance, commuting back and forth.

> *It was awful. For good research to be done, a person needs*
> *vital daily interactions. You have to be there constantly. You*
> *cannot do research remotely. Kris and I were also undergoing*
> *a trial separation at the time. We eventually worked through*
> *our problems, but it took a while. Even so, it was Kris who*
> *helped me think it all through, provided me with critical*
> *insights into my antagonists and into myself, and galvanized*
> *my readiness to pursue anything entrepreneurial.*

One thing that stayed the same was Harry's singular ability to concentrate on a technical issue and come up with a sophisticated response, pulling it instantaneously out of the air, or so it seemed to astonished observers. Edward Cawley, who was with TIMET's sales department at the time, recalls attending a high-level meeting with Harry at Electric Boat in Groton, Connecticut, concerning the US Navy's use of titanium in submarines. "Harry and I sat in a room behind secure doors to review various complex technical issues. The day was long, the meeting long, and the participants long-winded. At one point, I looked at Harry and he was asleep; at least I thought he was asleep. But when the team leader went around the room looking for suggestions and input, Harry perked up and had the best answer for the technical issue. I was never sure how he did it, or if he knew the answer early on and then was bored. I never forgot that."[140]

In 1984, in yet another downturn, Allegheny Ludlum, one of TIMET's parent companies, was facing bankruptcy. One day, Harry received notice of an attempt by management to try for an employee buyout. "In view of the pressures I was under, I was stunned to see my name among the twenty-two or so key employees that would own the company. But I just could not stomach the thought of finishing my career constantly having to defend not only my technology but my personhood as well. The ends of these threads came when I, along with two others from TIMET, Mike Popper and Mark Kelly, left to start our own company, the Alta Group."[141]

The other major event that helped change the direction of Harry's life was the death of his twenty-six-year-old son Neil in 1984. It shook him deeply, forcing him to reassess his past and what he wanted to do in the future. By then, all three sons had careers; Keith was in computer technology and systems management; he and his wife, Cathy, had three children. Neil was in the US Army, and he and his wife, Sang Ju, had two children with a third on the way.[142] Eric was single and worked for the Santa Clara Transit District; in his spare time, he pursued his interest in photography, an interest he shared with his father and Keith. Harry was proud of their accomplishments. Yet looking back at their childhood, Harry regretted that he had not given them enough attention. "They thought my career came first, and, to be honest, it often did. I realized in retrospect I was too immersed either in titanium or education, or both, to give them time at critical points." Neil's death was galvanizing. Harry wrote of the experience many years later:

> *A call came in from Texas. I was in Henderson at the time,*
> *just back from my daily workout, an easy five-mile jog in*
> *thirty-eight minutes. It was springtime on the desert. Wild*

flowers were abundant, the air was sweet. I immersed myself in the joy of the sunset. The black hills, usually somber in repose, flanked my route on the right in a new shade of purple. This was one thing about the desert I loved. It never looks the same twice at sundown. Today there was dust high in the air, turning the entire sky a wonderful shade of orange. When I answered the phone, it was Neil on the line. He wanted to know about my lifelong tendency to cough. Was it asthma? Was it hereditary? After some discussion, I realized he was suffering from a bad and persistent cough. I told him everything I knew about my own condition and that many physical tendencies can be inherited. We went on a bit about his family, who had recently joined him at his army base at Killeen. He had a degree in geology but found it too uncomfortable to be away from home as much as his new job called for. So he had reenlisted in the army where his family could at least follow him. I was only a bit concerned but thought he might be faced with a future like mine—occasional spells of uncontrollable coughing. Of my three biological boys, he was built most like me, tall and slender—while getting his brown eyes from his mother. We were also great friends, sharing other traits as well, such as an explosive temper.

Six weeks or so later, I got another phone call. Neil was getting worse. June came with still more serious news. That very day, he had stopped driving. It seems he could not lift his right foot to brake the car. He complained to his superiors, but they and the base doctor did not believe that he was losing his ability to move. This denial in the army hierarchy had gone on for over two weeks. I booked the next flight out. It was already dark when I finally arrived at his home in Killeen, but Neil was not there. Just hours before, he had been evacuated by helicopter to the army medical center in Houston.

Neil had met his wife, Sang Ju, at Fort Lewis in Washington State. Sang Ju was Korean and had spent much of the Korean War hiding out in the hills with her parents and siblings. Their children, Charlie and Marie, were born before Neil enlisted. Jeane was on the way. Sang Ju's mother had joined the family, and what a lifesaver she was. She looked after the kids while Sang Ju and I began our drive to the army medical center in Houston, some four hours away by car. The hospital reception desk could not locate Neil immediately. It was well after midnight before we were directed to the neurological ward. After a bit of a search, we found him huddled in a corner on the phone trying to report in at home. I shall never forget his look of relief when he saw us. He was simply overcome with joy. I was not only aghast at his physical condition but angry too. Why did the Army take so long to realize this man really was sick? But his condition didn't show in his spirit.

I took extra time off so I could be with him during his exploratory surgery. It revealed advanced astrocytoma— commonly called a star tumor because of the shape of its cells under a microscope—in the left temporal lobe of his brain.[143] I immediately began working the Carnegie and medical libraries every weekend. Although Neil's surgeon had reported the severity as two to three—four being the most aggressive and one the least on the grade scale established by the World Health Organization—what I found sank me deep into a pit. First, all the evidence I found pointed toward two basic extremes: one typically fatal in a few months, the other survivable on occasion for five or more years. Neil's surgeon had reported his chances were good. Perhaps he said that to save my feelings, but I had seen his report of the surgery. Second, I realized that aggressive astrocytoma is characterized by quick onset, while the onset of the slower type can be over a period of two years or more. Neil's case was obviously the former: it had been a bare three or four months from his first symptoms to hospital time. Still I hung on to hope—hoping for that miracle. Third, being trained in science and technology and in how to interpret data I found in the literature, I came to the unsettling conclusion that medical practitioners, as good as they are treating the most common diseases, are sometimes like children in the wilderness when it comes to designing and interpreting research. Fourth, in looking at the geographical occurrence of star tumors, I noticed an oddity. Some states, Nevada, for example, had significantly low rates. As it happened, about the time Eric was born, our neighborhood florist died of a star tumor. Then it hit me. Nevada is low in star tumor incidence for a simple reason: good doctors with adequate resources are scarce in the ramparts and those who do practice there are less successful at making correct diagnoses of very rare medical events, especially those that hardly ever present the same set of symptoms, which is the typical case for star tumors. Such patients are often forced to seek diagnosis and treatment elsewhere, as was the case with the florist. In defense of the good doctors, star tumor incidence is on the order of three to four cases per one hundred thousand people per year. That means for a typical career with a caseload of one thousand, a doctor might see just one random case every thirty years or so. Nevada physicians really are well advised to focus on the more common ailments. While most enlightening, I found nothing in the literature to settle my nerves. Nevertheless, I followed the medical literature several more months, to no avail, finding the very terminology, even among researchers, to be inconsistent.

Later that summer, I visited Neil in San Antonio and admired how well he was holding up as a near-total invalid. I wanted to take him on an outing, to the Alamo perhaps. But he would have none of it. He had a disease to beat and saw no purpose in deviating from that course. By summer's end, Sang Ju felt, justifiably, that the family should return to their home in Federal Way, Washington. Her mother was a huge help with the family move. We arranged for me to accompany Neil on the army hospital airplane reserved for that purpose. As he was unable to communicate for himself, it is good that I went. His trip would have been a disaster in comfort otherwise. The army nurses were capable and motivated, but they could not understand him. We were parked on the tarmac in Montana when he said something very touching. I repeated his single word to be sure we were on track. What he said was very simple: "Thanks." In reply,

I said: "You would do it for me." His nod and smile captured exactly how it was between this father and son. Of course, my response to either Keith or Eric would have been the same had fate selected one of them instead of Neil.

Neil went into a coma that deepened gradually but steadily. I visited him several more times, first at the hospital, then at home where his coma became a permanent state. Along about Thanksgiving, I visited one more time. This visit had a bright side. Late one evening, I had the honor of driving Sang Ju to the hospital where Jeane was born the next morning. About a year after his illness began, I received a call from Sang Ju. Neil had been on life support for some months and now had pneumonia. "It is time to let him rest," she said simply. Only after we hung up did I realize she had just broken her cultural tradition where the eldest male in the family is asked to make important decisions, especially those involving marriage, life, and death. For the last time, I booked the next flight out. Death waited some days and came slowly. His entire family gathered around as the end became imminent. Sang Ju was on his left; I was on his right. Sang Ju's mother, Charlie, Marie, and the baby Jeane were all at his bedside. Twice, he stopped breathing. Once, his great heart summoned enough strength for a few more gasps of air. The second time, his heart failed. In a moment, his color drained away in an awful finality. Neil was gone. Briefly scenes from his life consumed me. Where is the justice? It took some days before I could rally my thoughts and fly home. Watching an active, lively person close to you die slowly and inexorably has to be emotional torture of the worst kind. Unbelievably, two decades later, astrocytoma would also take my wife Kris. The full import of watching two loved ones die little by little each day is hitting me again as I write this.

CHAPTER 12:
HIGH-PURITY TITANIUM AND THE ALTA GROUP

In his *Fourth Book of Physics*, Aristotle wrote that nature abhors a vacuum; so also do entrepreneurs, Harry being a case in point. "New technologies create vacuums that other new technologies fill on both the supply and demand side. Such was the case with the formation of the Alta Group (now a Honeywell company) that makes the highest purity titanium on Earth. I think that IBM, Apple, and Microsoft all came about in similar ways."

In 1984, when Harry was considering leaving TIMET and founding a company with three other men, few people realized that high-purity titanium might have a major role to play in the semiconductor industry. Large titanium companies were not interested in manufacturing it because the process was too difficult and costly, producing too little for too few customers.

> *The electronics market was still a gleam in the eyes of chipmakers. The dream would take another three or four long years to become a reality. But the promise of a high-purity market was sufficient to give me confidence. I knew once the metal became available in volume, the likes of Andy Grove and Steve Jobs—with help from Bill Gates filling yet another vacuum—would find a niche for it. Demand would grow. But none of us knew for sure how much.*

As it turned out, were it not for high-purity titanium, computers would either cost more or be less efficient. Chips are made by a lithographic process similar to photography in which instead of film, silicon is used to capture the functional elements as an image. Titanium acts as an antireflective coating to control the amount of light hitting photoresist layers during manufacture of the chip. It is also used for electricity-conducting diffusion barriers and interconnects, which are like tiny household wires carrying electricity between rooms, in this case, the rooms being transistors, capacitors, and resisters. Finally, titanium is an excellent glue for bonding other metals together because of its reactivity with anything with a valence between three and seven in the periodic table. Harry could not have anticipated any of these developments, the actual market in 1984 being for research into electronic applications, not the applications themselves.

When he began to contemplate the possibility of starting a company, Harry first turned to statistics, as was his custom, to gauge both the actual and the potential markets, bringing to his analysis the same laser focus he brought to metallurgical research.

The seeding event that eventually got me going was a dinner meeting in the early 1980s of the top TIMET staff in Pittsburgh. Two questions arose that no one present could answer. One was simple and pertained to the national economy: where does the money supply come from? The second question was: what is the price elasticity of titanium? It surprised me that none of the smart people in that room knew the answers. In such august company, I wondered how that could be, because these were fundamental questions. Among my responsibilities in Pittsburgh was the preparation of a quarterly consumption forecast. Now, I pushed it a little, going beyond the simple procedures for adding up expected consumption, supplier by supplier. First, I looked at metal markets in general in the United States. Massaging the data, I realized that these materials do not follow a linear pattern but follow the basic power law of supply and demand as it applied to structural and nonstructural materials. Here was the answer to the price elasticity question posed at the dinner meeting. The Internet was not available then. Neither were desktop computers. TIMET didn't even have a mainframe computer. Fortunately, I had a remote terminal that I could use to access the mainframe at Allegheny Ludlum and I knew enough Pascal to make good use of it.[144]

Harry deduced that cutting the price of titanium in half would quadruple the market. Then, he reversed the question, asking at what price could a start-up operation making high-purity titanium become economically viable. The answer was one of Harry's aha moments because he realized that such an operation could easily support the small group of people who would be involved in its formation. His consumption forecast showed a total world market for medium-high-purity metal of less than $200,000 a year in laboratory quantities, most of it for research, but the law of supply and demand showed a far greater market if the product became readily available in industrial quantities even at much higher prices.

> *I was using actual data, not someone's guesstimate of the size of the market. Nothing is certain in statistics, but the data gave me, Mark Kelly, and Michael Popper, who were also from TIMET, and Bill Boyd who joined us, confidence that a high-purity business could support the four of us. Quantification and market assessment are more effective when contemplating starting a company than simply charging ahead on emotion and exuberance. In our case, I had a 95 percent error bar. On the low side, it was about $2 million in sales. The upside was about five times as much—a figure that would ultimately be multiples low considering the total worldwide market.*

TIMET had made small quantities of high-purity titanium in its research and development laboratory in Henderson. Although it sold some of it to customers, the company was not interested in expanding into what it thought was a specialty market with limited growth potential. It also had difficulty controlling for iron and other impurities that can cause pitting on the nanometer scale. The problems were exacerbated by the requirements of the companies making computer chips that, according to Harry, "asked for the moon" because they were uncertain about the effects of impurities. These factors played a part in TIMET's unwillingness to increase production. Edward Cawley, who was with the sales department at TIMET and who joined Alta in 1986, remembers the frustration of trying to get TIMET to pursue the manufacture of high-purity titanium. "Some of my clients needed high purity and were pressuring us for it. Up until then, I could sell some of it that was produced in TIMET's research and development department, but that wasn't enough. Then one day there was a big meeting at which one of my clients who wanted a steady supply of high-purity met with the president of TIMET and tried to convince him. He had no success. The president did not want to go in that direction. So Harry, Mark Kelly, and Mike Popper decided to take the risk themselves, leaving TIMET, mortgaging their own homes, and hocking their souls to get the funding."[145]

They were joined by William Boyd, a successful financier who had been treasurer and director of Consolidated Gas Supply before retiring in 1980 to pursue entrepreneurial interests and venture capitalism. Boyd had been a pilot during World War II assigned to the China-Burma-India Theater, flying Douglas C-47s (known as the DC-3 commercially) over the "hump," as the dangerous eastern end of the Himalayas was called, providing supplies to the British troops fighting under the command of General William Slim in Burma. Boyd came out of the war with two Distinguished Flying Crosses, three Air Medals, and four Major Battle Stars. He told Harry about an incident in which Japanese Zeros had shot down several planes ahead of him, but for some reason, when a Zero took aim at him, nothing happened. The Zero pulled up next to Bill's lumbering C-47, and the Japanese pilot indicated by sign language that he was out of ammunition. "Bill told me that the pilot grinned at him and peeled off. Bill lived to fly another day. Good thing for us." Though his combat experience had taken place forty years before the start of the Alta Group, Boyd had never lost the thrill of flying on the edge, which is why taking the risk of manufacturing high-purity titanium was to his liking. Between the four men, there was substantial experience in marketing, sales, manufacturing, research, quality assurance, and finance.

> The chemistry was such that we jelled at once. Mark, Mike, and I knew the business turf, in most ways better than the competition, and Bill Boyd gave us an equally strong presence with the local financial community. In a start-up, you can never know too much, but you can certainly know too little. For example, as prepared as I thought we all were, we had some hard lessons to learn in the years ahead about patent law. Those lessons were taught by big international companies with large legal staffs ready to trounce on a small start-up. A second huge lesson had to do with hiring effective

staff, something none of us knew much about. But all in all, the four of us had the bases covered better than most entrepreneurs do, and we were willing to work hard. Bill Boyd ran through over two dozen pro formas on profits before we broke ground with a model that fit the real world, one that provided guidance as well as pointing out pitfalls.

Ed Cawley was impressed by the synergy among the men, especially among Harry, Mike Popper, and Bill Boyd, considering it to be a major factor in the venture's success. "I don't think the risk would have paid off were it not for their combined skills. Mike Popper's basic approach was—build it, get it done. He would say, 'You need a valve? Get a valve.' Then Harry would say, 'But we need it to ten to the minus ninth Torr.' Finally, Bill would say, 'Don't spend more than a dollar.'"

Initially, when the men got together to discuss forming a company, they considered manufacturing nitinol instead of high-purity titanium, which Harry had researched extensively before moving to corporate headquarters in Pittsburgh. Nitinol is an unusual nickel-titanium material (Ti-54Ni weight percent) that has super-elasticity and shape-memory enabling it to return to a predetermined shape. Its unique properties were first discovered in 1962 by Naval researchers who were studying it for use in missile nose cones. In fact, its name is an acronym for Nickel-Titanium-Naval Ordnance Laboratory. Despite its vast potential, it presented severe metallurgical problems related to transition temperatures.

Nitinol was all the rage at places like Grumman, the builder of the US Navy's F-14, because it was ductile and had a ferocious memory. Wrap a wire of nitinol a foot or so long around a pencil, and it forms a nice, tight little coil spring, just like aluminum, copper, iron, and nickel wires do. Ho-Hum. But drop all five wires into a cup of hot coffee and the nitinol instantly uncoils itself and shoots to the ceiling! The others, being docile animals, stay in their place, boiling in the cup. Think of the possibilities. Only problem was its behavior was unpredictable, a problem now solved, though one company went out of business trying. And there was another problem: for the four of us to build an entry-level high-purity electrolysis plant would cost about $50,000, but

> *to build an entry-level nitinol plant, with less certain promise,*
> *would cost $5 million! Bill Boyd choked over that price tag.*[146]

Nowadays, nitinol is used in consumer items, such as bendable eyeglass frames, and in medical devices including stents. It is even being considered for structures, such as bridges and highway overpasses, that must remain functional after being twisted by earthquakes. However, in 1985, nitinol required far more research and, obviously, far more money than was available. On the other hand, an electrorefining process for high-purity titanium had been proven feasible by the Bureau of Mines in the 1950s. So the decision was made to go that route.

There had always been two great battles waged in the titanium wars: the first was how to *win* it from its ore; the second was how to *refine* it to a higher level of purity. While the second battle was reliant on the outcome of the first, in fact, they were fought at the same time in different ways. Essentially, it was a quantity-versus-quality issue: those processes that could make enough titanium didn't reach high enough purity. Those processes that reached high purity didn't make enough titanium. That was the problem with the iodide process that was first used in the 1920s by three scientists at the Philips Glow Works in Eindhoven, the Netherlands, who were searching for a better material for lightbulb filaments.[147] Although they failed to improve the lightbulb, they succeeded in reaching a higher level of purity, but unfortunately, the amount they produced was minuscule. In the late 1930s, the US Bureau of Mines began to experiment with the iodide process not for refining titanium but to win it from its ore. The research was done under the leadership of Dr. Reginald S. Dean and Frank S. "Pinky" Wartman at the bureau's laboratory in Salt Lake City, Utah. Unfortunately, by 1944, the two men had become convinced it could not be scaled up to make metal in quantity. That realization led to the hiring of William Kroll, who joined the bureau at its site in Albany, Oregon, in 1945. His sponge process quickly became dominant, enabling the establishment of the titanium industry. Besides the Kroll process, there was the Hunter process, named for Matthew Hunter, a scientist at Rensselaer Polytechnic Institute. Using sodium instead of magnesium, the Hunter process could reach higher purity, but it was more expensive.

With the first battle won of making titanium sponge in quantity, the Bureau of Mines turned its attention to the second battle: refining titanium. The iodide process was effective in removing impurities of oxygen and nitrogen as well as most, but not all, metals. However, it was inefficient with inherently low productivity. So the bureau worked on a process known as electrorefining in which titanium is electrolyzed off of an anode (where current flows in, electrons flow out) and goes into solution as anions that are then deposited on a cathode (where current flows out and electrons flow in to satisfy the thirsty anions looking for electrons that will turn them back into metal). They attempted to increase scale, but their cell, which was designed for high current and productivity, was plagued by structural problems. Some of those problems were as valuable to Harry as the bureau's successes because they showed him what not to do at Alta.

> *Behind everything we did at Alta were a half-dozen warriors at the Bureau of Mines who left us a blueprint for high-purity titanium. Of course, we still had to read it and figure out how to use it and how to sell the product. I knew from the Bureau of Mines that ultra-purity at 99.9995 percent was possible via fused salt electrolysis. Bureau work had also demonstrated that a much higher productivity was possible than what TIMET was achieving in its lab in the 1980s. The TIMET cell took seventeen days to produce a mere forty pounds of metal. From my calculations, I figured we could make much more in much less time. And so it turned out. Alta's first commercial cells, 1 and 2, were lifted directly out of a bureau report on deep-bath electrolysis. Those two cells remained in operation until they were replaced by third-generation models in about 1989.*

At an early dinner gathering of the founders and their wives, Kris Rosenberg came up with the company name to convey an impression of ultra and altitude. It was simple and memorable. The word *group* was tacked on in an attempt to make it seem as if Alta was already a well-established entity. The paperwork for incorporation was completed, and Harry was the last to sign off on March 8, 1985. Within a month, they rented six thousand square feet of space in a warehouse-type building in Evans City near Cranberry.

> *Alta was in business—well, not quite—we had a factory to build. Specifications were being written at light speed;*

that meant off the cuff, sometimes on a scrap of paper, if we had paper. By April, a blue tank for holding chemicals arrived. Alta owned its first piece of equipment. What seems incredible now is the fact that we began electrolysis (making metal) on May 30, in something like eighty-four days flat. I remember well the tension as I reached for the green button that first time. Of course, I knew the power supply would turn on, that there was no short in the system and that the cathode was in the hot soup ready to make titanium. Everything had to be okay. I had checked it only a dozen times. Still, I paused to take a deep breath. I had come to respect this substance so aptly named after the early Greek god Titan, but in my prior twenty-eight years, every time I thought I had this metal tamed, it managed to bite me. After what seemed like an eternity, I realized my case of nerves related to the symbolic break I was about to make from my past, from a comfortable corporate posting to penniless entrepreneur. I pushed the button. The power supply roared to life, making the highest purity titanium in the world. Then just five days after power was turned on, a tornado ripped through Evans City and took out our main power distribution system, froze our cells, killed the phone, left the roll-up doors locked open, and shut us down for four days. A bigger problem was that the semiconductor industry was falling into recession. Nevertheless, we sold our first fifteen-pound bag of high-purity titanium crystals on June 21. No more sales for two long months. We gave away a few samples, but even that was sometimes hard to do. Then some small orders began to trickle in. It was very much touch and go. Every time we faced up to the idea of maybe having to shut down, another order would arrive. Bill Boyd, our treasurer, did most of the praying. The rest of us, who didn't know how, could only ignore the clouds of mounting debt and slave away, doing the things we each knew how to do well. But there was no looking back.

Not until February 1986 did sales exceed direct out-of-pocket expenses for the month—by a few dollars. After that, orders became more frequent, and within a year and a half, much more space was needed for manufacturing. In seeking a new location, the men had to consider the environment carefully because of the need for uncontaminated air. One location that seemed to meet all the requirements was rejected because there was too much dust that would lower the purity of the titanium being produced. The goal was to make a product that contained between one and five parts per million total metallic impurities, so that meant there had to be little ambient dust. Finally, they bought an empty steel fabrication facility in Fombell, Pennsylvania. It had big bays and office space and, more important, room for expansion. The founders had to go way out on a financial limb to buy that facility, but it was the right decision.

The area had been hit hard by the closure of the steel mills in Pittsburgh, but this turned out to be an advantage because there was a large reservoir of unemployed tool-and-die people living there who were capable and motivated to learn new skills. Joseph Green, who joined Alta in 1991 as quality control manager, explained, "The ultra-pure titanium business being what it is, you didn't have many of the skill sets for what we did. You didn't have electron beam operators. You had to *make* electron beam operators. You didn't have refining operators. You had to *make* refining operators. We have had many new people since then, and the training remains just as important and fundamental as it was in the company's early days."[148]

According to Ed Cawley, Harry hired Allison Scott, a waitress at a local restaurant. He had only been in the place once before, but when he came in a second time, she remembered what he had ordered the first time several weeks prior. She turned out to be an excellent employee. She was a fast study, capable of mastering all the lab and quality techniques. Eventually, she handled the inside sales position. He hired Dr. Maria Fest, a nun who taught chemistry at LaRoche College in Pittsburgh but who never had done hands-on chemical work. She wasn't sure she could do it in industry, but she did well, helping to lay the groundwork for the quality program. He hired farmers. He hired a guy with tattoos and a rough-around-the-edges personality, but he was reliable, always showed up on time, was very careful, and ended up making Alta his career. "People were a very important resource for Harry," said Ed. "He treated people with respect, paid well, and as a result, the employees got good. He always encouraged employees to give input and participate in the decision process. Once, a shipment of scrap metal came in and the guys were separating it by hand,

and one guy picked up a piece and said, 'This isn't titanium.' He was right. We had to reject the entire load." Ed also remembers Harry finding employment for Mike Mester, an electrical technician hired to install the control system on the electron beam furnace. When the project was nearing completion, Mike was in a quandary about what to do, so he went to talk to Harry about it. Harry took the time to review the issues surrounding Alta's future and made an effort to encourage him to stay. Mike is still with the company in a supervisory position, having added a bachelor's degree in electrical engineering to his résumé. Harry looks back on all these employees with a fair amount of pride. "Only a few people were not up to snuff, but they were counterbalanced by the able and reliable assistance from all those who were."[149]

The only area in which there was an unfillable lack was in metal analysis because no commercial laboratory in the Pittsburgh area (or for that matter, anywhere in the country) was up to the task in regard to high-purity titanium, which should contain not more than one to five parts per million (ppm) total metallic impurities with less than about one hundred parts per million total gases, including hydrogen, carbon, nitrogen, and oxygen. All the necessary talent and instrumentation had to be built up in-house, which took a few years to achieve. "Our product was so pure that we had difficulty analyzing it with accuracy and precision; no one else could either. It was a problem the US Bureau of Mines had also experienced in their pioneering work. It took us time to solve it. In the process, we developed a well-equipped lab and a strong analytical chemistry group that needed hardly any external support."

Ed Cawley recalls that at the beginning everyone did whatever needed to be done to keep the fledgling company going. Alta was reliant on outside suppliers and contractors, not yet having developed in-house capacity. "Once, I was sent to pick up a chrome ingot at a company near Boston. The ingot had just been hot-isostatically pressed, which is a manufacturing process that uses high heat and pressure to improve the properties of a metal. It was cold outside when I showed up first thing in the morning, and the guy said to me incredulously, 'I can't put it in your car; it will catch fire.' So we went out for a two-hour breakfast to let the ingot cool a little more; then we went back and he put it in the back of my station wagon. I drove it to another contractor in Niagara Falls, all the way across Massachusetts and New York State, with the windows rolled down to dissipate the heat!"

Acquiring equipment was another area of making do with what was available. For years, Don Golden, who was the first permanent employee and the first to draw a paycheck (the founders having decided to forego paychecks until the company made a profit), rolled high-purity plate on an antiquated rolling mill that Bill Boyd had bought cheap from Crucible Steel in Pittsburgh when they closed down one of their plants.

> *From a distance, you could hear that old dog of a rolling mill clanging away. Bill was a true gentleman and a pleasure to work with. No financier I ever heard of would stand with you and put his wallet on the line like Bill did—unless you needed a piece of equipment! What we could not get secondhand or at auction, we designed and built ourselves including our first electron-beam melting furnace. Alta was a true bootstrap operation. Anyone who cares to try and emulate what we did had better be prepared for latrine duty and toilet paper runs. Our first winter in Fombell was a fight to keep the furnace from freezing and the operators, myself and Gene Metts, from getting frostbite.*

Harry believed in hiring optimistic and creative people and then providing them with an environment in which creativity and personal responsibility could bloom. But it didn't always go as planned. In fact, the first materials science PhD he hired turned out to be psychologically unstable, wanting to dominate everyone, instead of working cooperatively— not the personality type that is an asset to a new venture. The man had presented a paper that impressed Harry because it had application to the making of a thin-film of titanium that would be impervious to electricity.

> *He was easily the smartest guy I ever hired. But the last week he worked at Alta, I sensed that a crisis might be imminent. He made it easy for me. Without saying a word, he passed me a handwritten note on Friday that said he wouldn't be in on Monday or ever again. The next morning, I went into work to find that the laboratory entrance had been shot up with a gun. He came in on Monday to collect his pay and personal effects, and he said, "I hope you don't think I did this." I didn't even open my mouth.*

After that incident, Harry talked to Kris about instituting a program to evaluate people more accurately before hiring them so as to avoid the high cost in both capital and morale that goes with employee turnover. She suggested using the Guilford-Zimmerman Temperament Survey (GZTS), on which she had done her master's thesis and for which she was certified to do evaluations.[150]

While the survey helped a great deal, "weeding out some foul balls who looked good on the surface," it didn't tell Harry anything about a person's capabilities on the factory floor or in the laboratory. Furthermore, there were candidates who were capable of manipulating the survey to their advantage, even though it included strong and weak falsification scales. "I remember one such candidate whose answers led us astray. After we turned him down on other grounds, I asked him how he did so well on the GZTS. He said, 'I just imagine that Mother Theresa will be one judge while a second judge will be looking for good old American apple pie.'"

To get around that problem, Harry developed an interview on paper. If someone's résumé looked good, he would call the person on the phone and ask if he or she was agreeable to a written interview before coming in for a face-to-face interview that would include a temperament survey. Several questions were general, such as: What constitutes effective communication? What makes teamwork work? How do you handle mistakes? But one question had to do with activation energy in a metallurgical process and required the use of statistics.

Candidates were on their own at home and free to use any and all resources they could find or muster. I only got one answer correct from the three hundred or so candidates who took it and that was from Joe Green, who held a bachelor's degree in math. None of the several PhDs who took it even knew how the problem had to be approached. It indicated to me that something was wrong with our educational system when PhDs were not capable of analyzing data, discerning whether it was real and what the error bar was. Not only did Joe get the nominal answer correct, but he also found an interaction, a secondary indirect effect, that I had hidden in the data to separate the men from the boys. Little did I know there would only be one man and no boys. Joe was a guy who had come from a family business in coal. Like me, he had wondered about things, and he became the best quality manager I ever hired—or ever knew. If we had quality problems, he would almost invariably beat me to the answer. I never had that experience before. He is still with the company.

Joe Green, now quality systems manager, remembers the test well. "I was a mathematics major in college. Statistics was a significant part of my education, and I enjoyed it. That was the one subject where Harry and I really related. Statistics excited us both. But for his test, I had to dust off my statistics books. It was probably eighteen years since I had done any statistics. The test was long, something like twenty pages. There were a lot of business-type questions, but at the end, there was a math question. Because of my statistics background, I was able to answer it correctly. I didn't have a computer at that time and had to do all the summations with a handheld calculator. I guess I was the only one to answer it correctly. But that wasn't the end of the test. As part of the interview process, I had to write and discuss my results with Harry. I think he enjoyed that."

Harry credits Ed Cawley with developing new markets that kept the fledgling company alive during the early years. "Ed deserves a special place in Alta history for that singular achievement and for responding to Mike Popper's vision of a greater Alta. By the time Ed came on board in 1986, the red ink was drying up, but only in the sense of covering direct costs—huge facility investments lay ahead." One of the new markets was made-to-order experimental titanium alloys for companies working on the National Aerospace Plane (NASP). Being developed by Rockwell International, NASP was an attempt by the United States to create a viable single-stage-to-orbit spacecraft. The project was canceled in 1993 but not before significant research had been done. Another new market was making high-purity metals other than titanium. For example, Alta began to make high-purity nickel for IBM, which up until that point had been losing at least $100,000 a month in the production of wafers because the less-pure nickel it had been using would spit when the coating was put down. Alta also diversified into magnetic materials and sputter targets used for making thin-films. Yet another market involved alloy development for a producer of prosthetic implants. All these small specialty markets gave the company the ability to survive and then to expand.

Another smart decision the founders made was to hire a marketing consultant who specialized in electronic materials. He taught them about how computer chips were fabricated, their market dynamics, and how new developments coming down the line could affect Alta's technology and its business. As a result, Alta positioned itself correctly during the time when computer manufacturers were making rapid advances on computer-chip technology and personal computers.

> *By 1988, high-purity titanium was ready to take off. We had refined the process so much that the time from harvesting one batch of metal to starting another batch had been reduced from fourteen hours to only two, and our average quality had improved an order of magnitude. The race was on against other titanium suppliers with the financial power and technical know-how to stomp us out of existence in a blink. As it turned out, they never realized they were in a race, or maybe it wasn't their cup of tea. Their bookings for electronic-grade material had remained at low historic levels, so they saw no reason to get excited. Alta had gotten all the new research and development work. As the shift to titanium in computer chips began, Alta was already a qualified supplier, delivering metal in commercial quantity at purity levels unheard of at the time. Our high-purity titanium had proved good enough to use in making computer chips, and the chipmakers of the world had taken notice.*

Alta's production electrolysis process was an obvious engineering extension of experience gained by the US Bureau of Mines decades earlier, so the company did not patent any of the novel aspects of the production unit. But 1989 brought the first act of a big and terrible patent surprise.

> *As the year drew to a close, Stan Seagle, a friend of mine at RMI, called me and asked if I had seen the new patent on titanium. I hadn't, but from the tone of his voice, a vague nervousness set in. He sent me a copy, and I realized his full concern. I was looking at a patent covering the process we were using to refine titanium just issued to a third party. Never mind that we were practicing art indistinguishable from what the US Bureau of Mines had published decades*

before. We were stunned. Stan said he believed the patent was invalid. We thought so too, since we were selling our product before the patent's application date and could prove it. We relaxed, chalking this one up to a mistake by the patent office. That proved to be true. Later, we realized some sleight of hand. In wording their specification, they used new terms to describe old art. Since only those sophisticated in the technology would realize that, it went over the examiner's head. Nevertheless, months later, a divisional patent (based on the same application) issued covering the product of our process. Again, Stan assured us that this patent too was invalid. After some study, I agreed; we had made and sold metal of the purity claimed just days before the statutory date allowing exemption-from-royalties because of prior sale. The Bureau of Mines also anticipated not only the process but the product as well. What our nemesis claimed was also inherent. Our practice and product were commercial before the patent was applied for, so we could not be sued for infringement. You can probably guess what happened next. A third, then a fourth, etc., began issuing all over the world where patent requirements vary substantially from in the United States. Each new patent was a minor shift away from the original, but each essentially replayed the original claims narrowed first this way, then that. And their ability to describe old art in new terms was a common thread. Our consternation grew with each new issue. The patent holder was a huge multinational company; we were still upstarts trying to make it in fast company. In all, some thirty patents issued worldwide on our process and technology. I began reading patents and patent law furiously, becoming somewhat of an expert by necessity. I didn't know whether we were flying or dying. I discovered the patent office issued invalid patent after invalid patent to our nemesis for several years. Then Goliath asked David to license David's own "invention" at rapacious terms—twenty times the typical royalty. We were sure of our ground in the United States, but the rest of the world was another matter, Japan in particular. We were forced to settle. It was more than a decade and way too many dollars later that this story was closed. The details of it all may never be disclosed, but the above is public record. We were not smart, but we were lucky to escape without material damage to the business.

Meanwhile, Alta was developing and patenting new processes. The first patent was applied for in 1990 and a second followed two years later. Both dealt with dielectric films on titanium for computer chips. At the same time, Alta was developing its in-house resources, relying less on outside contractors, improving both lead times and quality. For example, in 1991, it began to use an electron beam (EB) melting furnace in a high vacuum to melt titanium crystal into ingot. An electron beam helps preserve the purity of the crystal, particularly for oxygen. Proficient in all aspects of metallurgy, from the purely theoretical to the practical, Harry designed, built, and qualified the EB furnace himself. Later on, after Alta was bought by Johnson Matthey, a British company, a second EB furnace was purchased. "That second machine is something of an albatross. It suffers from poor design. The one I designed and built is a gem by comparison. They are both still operating, but mine, though nothing to look at, is the better one."

Harry's ability to do anything that was needed and his willingness to teach was highly valued by everyone. "If you looked under *scientist* in an encyclopedia, you would see Harry's photo beside the definition," said Joe Green. "Harry was my vision of what a scientist was. He hired me, but he wasn't my boss or my supervisor but rather my teacher. I had never really worked with such a person before, not even in college. In the early days, we worked in the same room. I sat about ten feet from him. I'd ask him a question. He'd stop what he was doing, turn his chair around, answer my question, and then turn right back and continue to work without missing a thought. He could zoom in and zoom out at any time. But he was always generous with his time. I always got the impression that he loved to teach. If someone wanted to know something, he would take the time to explain."

In 1991, Bill Boyd announced that he was ready to retire, which meant that the company would have to be sold because he was the major shareholder. Mark Kelly had left the company and moved on to other endeavors in 1988 leaving Mike Popper and Harry to carry on, with Bill still doing the books. They began to look at potential suitors, of which there were several, all of whom were attracted by the fact that Alta's annual sales had grown at a rate of 76 percent per year for six years straight. On October 1, 1992, at the stroke of midnight, Johnson Matthey, PLC, London, acquired the Alta Group for over $14 million. It was a good match because Johnson Matthey is a global specialty chemicals company with a solid science and technology foundation, stretching back to its beginning in 1817 as a precious metals assayer. Among its developments in the 1970s were catalytic systems. On purchasing Alta, Johnson Matthey maintained Alta's corporate policies and expanded the facilities, pumping $50 million into the business. Employment rose to 180 employees, and capacity doubled.

Joe Green remembered that the takeover was good for Harry. "It allowed him to expand into areas of development in which he really thrived. He tried a lot of new things during that time—new processes to refine different metals and metal-working techniques. He loved that kind of thing. At that point, there was not the heavy burden of direct operations on him as there was when the company was in the entrepreneurship stage. He didn't have to manage the day-to-day stuff."[151]

Under Johnson Matthey, one of the most important expansions was the building of a titanium sponge plant that used sodium instead of magnesium—a process that was more expensive but produced the controlled quality feedstock needed for Alta's high-purity operation. The plant's construction was made necessary when RTI and Deeside, the companies from which Alta had been buying sponge, stopped using the Hunter process (a.k.a. the sodium process). RTI and Deeside had made the change for economic reasons, because after the Soviet Union came to an end in 1991, Russia had sold titanium (used in vast quantities in its submarines) at rock-bottom prices on the world market, making the high-cost Hunter process uncompetitive. As a result, Johnson Matthey and Alta were faced with a potentially game-ending problem. Because the remaining high-quality sponge manufacturers were competitors that would prefer Alta to fail, Johnson Matthey and Alta had no choice but to buy as much product as RTI had left, storing it in an abandoned limestone mine that they jokingly called the mushroom mine because of its ideal growing conditions for mushrooms. Then they immediately set to work building their own plant, choosing Salt Lake City, Utah, as the site because Johnson Matthey already had a primary gold refinery there. Its completion eleven months later in March 1996 just so happened to coincide with a visit to Utah of former British Prime Minister Margaret Thatcher. On a goodwill tour supporting the free enterprise system, she graciously agreed on short notice to attend the opening festivities and cut the ribbon. It fell to Harry to take her through the plant and to explain the sponge process in a rudimentary way. He had hardly started when she began to ask him highly technical questions. What he did not realize was that she was a graduate of Oxford University with a degree in chemistry and had worked as a research chemist before entering politics. "Her questions had to do with the salt makeup, the resulting colors in the salt, and how we extracted it. She also asked me about the drying process. I was quite surprised and pleased." Nor did Lady Thatcher go away empty-handed: at the ceremony, she was presented with a high-purity titanium crystal as well as a platinum dragon. Celebration was indeed in order because the plant's completion meant that Alta was no longer standing on the brink. It had gained control of the supply and quality of feedstock.

In June 1999, Johnson Matthey sold their electronics division, which included the Alta Group, to AlliedSignal for $655 million. The following December, AlliedSignal was bought by Honeywell, so Alta is now part of Honeywell Electronic Materials. Shortly thereafter in 2000, Harry retired at the age of seventy-two. His importance to the Alta Group was far more than technical. He brought to the company a sense of cohesiveness and care. Joe Green recalls, "Harry was liked and well-respected among the employees. He had a daily routine. In the morning, he would start his day in the refining area. Then he'd come back to the office and work for a while. Then about 2:00 in the afternoon, he'd go back down to refining. Everybody looked forward to his coming around. They expected him to be there. He could be asked questions at that time. He made himself available. The Alta Group years were really super years. To this day, those of us who are around still reflect on what was accomplished."

CHAPTER 13:
THOSE WHO KEEP RUNNING

If anyone expected Harry to retire quietly from Alta and take up gardening, they obviously didn't know Harry. He is a man who must stay busy all the time, expanding the domain of his mind. Rewording Ecclesiastes 9:11, he likes to tell people that "the race is not always to the swift but to those who keep running." In actuality, the verse reads: "The race is not to the swift, nor the battle to the strong, neither bread to the wise, nor riches to the intelligent, nor favor to those with knowledge, but time and chance happen to them all." Combining the two versions creates one truth: Harry would keep running, but time and chance would overtake him in profound ways.

Pursuing his interest in start-up companies, Harry had formed the Amargosa Group before he retired to encourage would-be entrepreneurs by providing online information on market forecasting, product development, intellectual property, and other topics. He chose the name in homage to his childhood, using the idea of a hidden river running beneath the desert sands as a metaphor for the great risks and rewards of venturing. "Only the rare cloudburst waters its barren stretches to allow seedlings to come forth in bloom for posterity." He wrote on the Amargosa website that venturing carries great rewards, but the "downside is that one must provide the creativity, energy, money, and drive to make a new business happen. Those who enjoy such a challenge would call these the upside. So this column is not for the faint of heart, it is dedicated to the tigers among us who would change the world—hopefully we will leave it better than we found it."[152]

After he retired, he followed his own advice and ventured a few companies, the most successful being Pioneer Materials Inc., based in Torrance, California, with manufacturing operations in Chengdu, China, and Taiwan. The company produces materials for optical recording media, thin-film photovoltaics, and thermoelectric applications.[153] But venturing is nothing if not risky, especially across international borders, and some of Harry's start-ups failed, although he sees them less as failures than as learning experiences that helped him understand how entrepreneurship operates in Asia. Traveling repeatedly to Taiwan and China, he gained a great respect for the Chinese people as he made a concerted effort to comprehend the twisted ins and outs of doing business there.

> *The most significant long-term economic trend of our times begin with the demise of Mao. Having been there, seeing the vibrancy of the people, their focus on entrepreneurship, and the numerous massive construction projects, it is not hard to see why Deng loosed the chains with his statement, "I don't care if it is black or gray. It is a good cat if it catches mice." Business in or with China ultimately makes good sense. This trend will not end soon, and it opens nearly limitless opportunities for entrepreneurship.*

Harry and Kris also began an unusual and long-lasting project together. Kris had become a recognized expert on personal communications with the publication in 1993 of her book *Talk to Me: A Therapist's Guide to Breaking through Male Silence*.[154] She had also been featured in the PBS television series *Seasons of Life* broadcast in 1990 in which she spoke of the difficulties of being a woman in midlife, including what it had meant to her to have separated from Harry for four years and then to have reunited with him in a way that allowed both of them a greater degree of individuality and self-awareness. Drawing on her own painful experiences, she had dedicated her life to understanding and reducing interpersonal conflict. In the process, she had introduced Harry to the seminal work of psychologists, philosophers, and sociologists beginning with Sigmund and Anna Freud and continuing through Hannah Arendt, B. F. Skinner, Albert Bandura, and many others. This passion for understanding human nature took on even greater significance the day after the destruction of the World Trade Center on September 11, 2001, when Harry asked Kris, "How do people do such ghastly things?" After a short pause, she replied, "Look up Adorno," referring to Theodor Adorno, who in his ground-breaking study of Germans after World War II defined the authoritarian personality type and its relationship to hierarchical and obedient behavior. Kris's reading list for Harry also included the works of Stanley Milgram, who showed that the prevalence of authoritarianism and obedience described by Adorno existed not just in Germany but also in America. Then there was Robert Altemeyer, who in his research made strong connections between authoritarianism and political systems around the world, as well as Philip Zimbardo, whose important but controversial Stanford prison experiment pointed to a situational basis for violent behavior and unquestioned obedience. "Zimbardo's experiment especially astonished me. With no more than role assignments and a 'prison policy' modeled after the one at San Quentin, within twenty-four hours, Zimbardo turned twenty otherwise normal college kids into creatures behaving like abusive tyrants or compliant but resentful and rebellious convicts, all by the luck of the draw."[155]

In the back of his mind, Harry's own family history goaded him on. He realized that there was a parallel to the Mountain Meadows massacre that had occurred when his great-great-grandmother Ann Willden was a child in Utah. In that 1857 event, authoritarianism had combined with perceived threat and dangerous rumors to turn Ann's brothers into killers, their motivation for taking part being the survival of their own group. "Zimbardo proved so ably and convincingly that what triggers violence is circumstance. Each of us is at once a troublemaker or a peace lover according to the situation we are facing. It takes very little to tip the scale one way or the other. Therefore, one cannot indict any one ethnic group, religion, or economic system as the troublemaker. The problem is within each of us."

Because it seemed that people are born with a paper-thin barrier separating opposing genetic tendencies toward violence or peace, Harry turned to studying psychopathic and sociopathic behavior and was dismayed to discover that from 1 to 4 percent of all humanity has no conscience to rein in their universal animal impulses.

When they have charisma, as Hitler did, big trouble lies ahead. Our most basic of needs—to live a little longer and better by whatever means—in the end amount to a crack in human personality that gives the charismatic sociopath a ready-made wedge to exploit on a narrow or broad scale. A charismatic sociopath is a singular danger because he or she can highjack corporations, religions, political parties, even nations. But there is hope, first in recognizing the sociopathic behavior soon enough to treat it and second to provide the tools for effective treatment. This is not just a job for psychologists, such as Kris, but for everyone, including parents, teachers, colleagues, even employers. Universal education is needed. Hope also comes from a second source— the fact that certain cultures have become quite peaceful in spite of their violent past, internalizing within their citizens, as well as externalizing in the political and social ties between their citizens, the values of parenting, altruism, and cooperation to balance the instincts of obedience and dominance.[156]

All this intensive study found an effective outlet when Harry and Kris launched a website titled Road to Peace that went online seven months after 9/11.[157] Its mission "is to search out the fundamental reasons for terrorism, violence, and war and work toward fixing them with equal opportunities for peace among all people regardless of ethnicity, belief system, gender, national origin, or station in life." To that end, they posted articles and editorials on a wide range of topics, such as women in the Islamic world, corporate responsibility, and the media and democracy. They posted numerous book and film reviews, for instance, on the book *The Anatomy of Fascism* by Robert O. Paxton (2004). Maintaining the website required a substantial amount of work, but to Harry, "the issues were, and are, so complex, and we did not want to simplify them. We wanted to search for the roots of terrorism in various aspects of religion, economics, human and natural history, anthropology, politics, and psychology."

Probing deeply for the most basic origins of violence, Harry came to the conclusion that genetics is the lowest common denominator for human behavior. Nature enables, and nurture modifies, for better or worse. Adding to his already daunting reading list, Harry began with Charles Darwin and his theory of evolution and then continued on to Gregor Mendel and his many scientific descendants, including James Watson and Francis Crick. He became interested in the evolutionary biologist Richard Dawkins, the primatologist Frans de Waal, and the entomologist Edward Wilson, whose idea of consilience as a unity of all knowledge Harry found particularly powerful.[158] Much of Harry's research made its way onto the Road to Peace website. "The website has been in existence for over ten years now. After

Kris's death in 2004, I kept it going partially in her memory because it was very important to her. For me, it became like an online laboratory notebook of the most fascinating research project I have ever undertaken. It is still very much a work in progress."

For Harry, who has always loved the powerful predictive ability of statistics, the chance of Kris dying from astrocytoma—the same rare tumor that had killed his son Neil twenty years earlier—seemed beyond the realm of reasonable probability. But so it was to be. The first sign that something was very wrong occurred in the spring of 2003 when Kris began to sleep later and later in the morning, waking up groggy. She had long struggled with scoliosis and muscle weakness from having had polio as a young woman, so she thought that the unusual symptom might be related to postpolio syndrome, which can afflict survivors years after the onset of the disease. She sought out an expert on postpolio syndrome who agreed. But then in August, she and Harry traveled to Santa Rosa, California, to visit their daughter Bonnie. It was on that trip that it became clear there was something seriously wrong.

> We stayed in a motel the first night. Kris was extra slow waking up but roused herself only to fall asleep again during the drive to Bonnie's home. At that moment, I became concerned, and upon awakening, she did too. By October, things were continuing to get worse, and we decided a complete workup was overdue. The first week of November provided good news: her heart, lungs, and cardiovascular systems were all fine. An MRI of her brain was scheduled for Thanksgiving eve. The scan was uneventful, and by normal procedure, the receptionist released us. As we were pulling out of the parking lot, however, the receptionist came rushing out: "Please call your family doctor when you get home," she said, leaving no mistake that we might not. We did not know what to expect, but we were still optimistic, having survived so many earlier trials. "You have multiple tumors in the frontal lobe," our doctor said. That news, terse but accurate, was about all we could take. We had scheduled that evening out with some Chinese friends but decided not to cancel since we were without any aces for the evening. Amazingly, we had a fun night out. But surgery in early December brought the

awful confirmation: astrocytoma—metastatic. Our worst
but unspoken fear was realized. The star tumor, against all
odds, had struck again.

Kris's condition continued to decline despite a three-month improvement brought about by focused radiation treatment. Choosing to die at home, she did not want life support, only palliative care. Harry knew he needed to hire nursing help beyond what Hospice could provide, as excellent as that was. A friend recommended a private nurse she had used when her son was dying of a spinal tumor. She had found her to be both professional and deeply compassionate. Her name was Joselyne Mivumbi. A Rwandan, Joselyne had recently earned her RN, was working in a local hospital, and was studying for her bachelor's degree in nursing at LaRoche College in Pittsburgh, the same college where Kris had been on the faculty teaching psychology. Having lost many family members in the genocide in Rwanda in 1994, she had sought a chance to make her own life a refutation of the genocide's obscene inhumanity by pursuing a career in medicine. When Harry contacted her about caring for Kris, she was too busy with work and study to say yes. However, she put him in touch with two Rwandan nursing assistants she knew to be capable. Pauline and Yvonne began caring for Kris when they were available. But all too soon, needing more help, Harry called Joselyne again, and this time, sensing his desperation, she said she would come for a few hours every weekend. Harry appreciated any help he could get. He also hired some practical nurses, cobbling together round-the-clock care for Kris, but he was especially appreciative of the caliber of the women from Rwanda.

That the nurses were black made no difference to Kris. She
was completely color-blind. The good thing is that she had
helped me become color-blind as well. It was another of her
gifts to me over all the years of our marriage. My childhood
playmates, when I had them beyond my brother, were mostly
Mexicans and Indians with assorted Italians, Poles, and a
lone Chinese boy. I don't remember ever seeing a black until
I was in high school in Long Beach. In working closely with
Joselyne, Pauline, and Yvonne, I realized how far I had
come. My notes include an entry on Joselyne's first visit: "She
is a take-charge person in a nice sort of way." Sometime

later, she remarked that I was losing weight. I hadn't even noticed. I could still lift Kris, and that was all that mattered. Kris died peacefully on June 11, 2004.

Kris had always claimed that Harry was a diamond in the rough. He agreed but felt that over their thirty-seven years together, she had done a great deal of polishing. "The polishing agent was her daily questions and analysis of events distant, near at home, and in her family. Her wisdom wore off. It must have, for now I can see a great many people right off for what they are, as she used to. It is like she had become part of me. In a very real way, she prepared me for Josy."

A few weeks after Kris's death, Harry and Jeane, his granddaughter, invited Pauline, Yvonne, and Joselyne out for dinner to thank them for their help in caring for Kris during her final months. Joselyne thought it was a lovely gesture. "When you care for someone during their final days, sometimes you develop an attachment. You really shouldn't, but it is part of human nature. So when a patient dies, the caregiver also suffers loss. That was my experience with both Alex, whom I cared for first, and then with Kris. So it was kind of Harry to acknowledge the emotional tie and to try to say thanks."[159] However, she was surprised and worried by his appearance. "He had lost a lot of weight. I told him so, and he took it to heart. After that, we kept in touch by phone."

Over the next year, their relationship grew slowly and steadily as they learned more about each other's painful pasts. To Harry, it was as if Joselyne tossed him a lifeline when he was drowning. "I was just emerging from a deep funk when Josy and I began talking. The more we talked, the more I liked her and she liked me. Gradually, our friendship and liking for each other grew into mutual love."

For her part, Joselyne also needed the lifeline tossed by Harry. "He is a special man. He has a heart. He is neither complicated nor arrogant. He is smart. He is patient, and we loved each other."

Harry had made a significant effort to comprehend the nature of violence as part of his work on the Road to Peace website, formulating what he calls the five-pillar model of all that is good and bad in humanity: parenting, altruism, cooperation, obedience, and dominance. "Via the five pillars, humanity is perpetually locked in a war with itself because societies reflect nothing less than the five pillars made large." One of the men he had come to admire most was Nelson Mandela, who refrained from vengeance when he toppled apartheid in South Africa, breaking the endless cycles of getting even. However, what Harry learned from Joselyne about Rwanda shook him to the core. He had known violence and death in his own life—the brutal beating by his father when he was a child, the prolonged dying of his mother, the mine collapse that had crushed his partner, his brother's brushes with death—but now in falling in love with Joselyne, he was forced to deal with it in a new way. One of Joselyne's cousins suggested he read Roméo Dallaire's book *Shake Hands with the Devil*. Dallaire was the Canadian general who was head of the United Nations peacekeeping force in Rwanda during the 1994 genocide; he "watched as the devil took control of paradise on earth and fed on the blood of the people we were supposed to protect." In only three months, at least eight hundred thousand people were massacred, many by machete. Bodies piled up along the roads and clogged the rivers—too many to bury, too many to count. Approximately 1.7 million people fled across the borders into surrounding countries. When the bloodbath ended, Dallaire was aghast at his inability to prevent it and at the abject failure of the United Nations and its member countries, including the United States, to respond to his repeated requests for intervention. He returned to Canada a broken man, who out of his own brokenness dedicated himself to finding ways to stop mass atrocities. Dellaire wrote on the last page of *Shake Hands with the Devil*, "The only conclusion I can reach is that we are in desperate need of a transfusion of humanity." On reading his book, Harry found Dallaire to be daunting in his truthfulness, leading "to a watershed in my thinking."[160]

The third of seven children, Joselyne had experienced a happy childhood growing up in Cyangugu, a small city on the western border with Zaire (now the Democratic Republic of Congo). Her parents were middle-class, had jobs in the local hospital, and worked hard to make sure their children got a good education. All that changed in April 1994 when the genocide began. A high-school student at the time, Joselyne cannot forget what happened:

> *The morning of Thursday April 7, 1994, was marked by empty roads with soldiers patrolling them. Those attempting to use the roads to escape were often killed. What happened after that day is hard for me to express in words—the total cruelty and sadism. I wondered what got into people. People I knew very well, either neighbors or from church, turned*

into vicious and cruel killers. It was genocide. Controlled and organized by some members of the government, killers wanted to erase one ethnic group as well as political opponents. In other words, it was against humanity. And yet most people who died knew nothing of politics. A part of my family perished during that awful time, especially those who lived in Butare, my mother's hometown. Grandparents, uncles, aunts, nieces, and nephews—age or gender did not matter. Some were thrown into toilets and buried alive. Others were chopped down by machetes. The devil was all over the place. There was no place to hide, no safe shelter. It has been hard to put closure to all these deaths. I could not comprehend how a human being could do such ghastly things to another human. What amazes me now is how people recovered so quickly without therapy. Is this just a veneer? I'm not sure.

After the genocide ended in July, Joselyne had nowhere to go to school, her high school having been destroyed. A whole year of education was lost. In 1995, she was assigned by the government to attend a boarding school run by Catholic nuns in Nyundo in the northwest part of the country, but it was in a war zone, so her parents refused to let her go. "Things were not good," Joselyne recalls. "The country was destroyed. It was a very dangerous place. There was no trust among people or peace in anyone's heart. There was a lot of anger and revenge. Souls were hurt. Yet people were smiling. Our Rwandan culture teaches us not to show agony to others. It is like wearing a mask."

Fortunately, Joselyne's parents found another school for her to attend called École des Sciences Byimana run by the Marist Brothers, a Catholic order known for its commitment to education worldwide. There she met Brother Rene David Roy, who was to become one of the most important people in her life because he helped her and thirty-eight other students get scholarships to LaRoche College. Br. Rene vividly remembers meeting Joselyne for the first time. "When she came into my classroom, I saw her determination and ability to meet challenges and overcome odds, but never did either one of us imagine the scenario that has since unfolded. Her faith, her dogged determination, and the unexpected and blessed presence of Harry in her life are making her dreams come true. Both are remarkable people whose stories will inspire others as together we work in harmony along the road to peace."[161]

Br. Rene was preparing to return to the United States himself, accompanying the students who had been selected to attend LaRoche College under the auspices of the Pacem in Terris Institute. Named after Pope John's XXIII's 1963 encyclical, the institute was founded in 1993 to bring students from conflict, postconflict, and developing regions of the world to study at the college. They came mainly from Eastern Europe, the Middle East, and Africa. However, the process did not go smoothly for the Rwandans because roadblocks were thrown up by their own government, which insisted on controlling who was allowed to leave the country to study abroad. At the last moment, the bewildered students had the exit door slammed in their faces. Fortunately, donors associated with the Pacem in Terris Institute stepped up to help, and after a year's delay, they were able to come.

In September 2000, with the fall semester already in full swing, the Rwandan students finally arrived on campus. For Joselyne, it was a time of utter loneliness and confusion. "At the beginning, it was hard. We landed at the airport, got picked up and taken to an apartment. The man who was carrying my suitcase set it down by the door very nicely, wished me good luck, and left. I opened the door and looked inside my apartment. It was almost empty, no chairs, just a bed and desk, just enough for a student. The world came crashing down. Then it hit me—I was on my own. What was I going to do? I couldn't speak English. It was the farthest I had been from my parents and friends, and I knew nothing about the American college educational system. I was nervous but remained optimistic about facing a new life and its challenges."

For the first two months, Joselyne suffered from severe culture shock and homesickness, and she seriously considered giving up and returning to Rwanda, but gradually life began to improve. One thing that ameliorated her discouragement was that the college found host families for foreign students. Joselyne's family, Joan and Bob Mitsch, treated her and two other students as if they were their own, helping them to learn about the culture and the language. "Sometimes Joan would call in the evening to encourage me or just to chat in English so I would improve. She and Bob invited me and some of the other students to spend the holidays and vacations with them. I still cherish their dedication, and I am thankful to have had their friendship at a very critical time of my life."

Br. Rene was another one of the rocks of faith on which Joselyne could depend. He had become the principal of Bishop Donahue High School in McMechen, West Virginia, near Wheeling, but at least once a month, he returned to the LaRoche campus. "I witnessed the progress in English that my former students were making as well as in their fields. Josy was interested in nursing and eventually received her diploma from Sewickly School of Nursing. I was present at her pinning. In 2005, Josy insisted that I meet Harry. Kris had died, and Harry was having a very hard time with his loss. He confided to me that had it not been for Josy's loving care of both Kris and himself, he would not have made it through this painful ordeal." A year or so after, Br. Rene heard from a friend that Joselyne was getting married, but he didn't know to whom. "At some point, she told me it was Harry, and though there was quite an age difference, it seemed like a match made in heaven, as it surely is."

Attempting to set what Joselyne had gone through into the vast context of the nature of good and evil, which he had been studying, Harry read several more books and articles about the genocide written from various points of view and discussed them in depth with her. But measured against her experiences and resolute compassion, his book-learning fell short.

> *Josy had on-the-ground information and insights the book writers did not, and they had information she did not, such as what was happening within the United Nations and among its member nations. I had learned the ABCs of conflict resolution, but it took Josy, with her insights, to show me how it works out in practice. How could anyone not love such a person? Josy and I were married in August 2006. The last seven years have been the happiest, most peaceful, and stress-free period of my life.*

In November 2008, Harry and Joselyne traveled to Rwanda to meet her family. She was afraid he might have difficulties adjusting to the culture because the amenities are not what they are in the United States, but he had no trouble whatsoever. "Harry is accepting and versatile," said Joselyne. "He is much like a Rwandan; perhaps it is because he too was born into a difficult and tough life. The Rwandan culture is warm and friendly to people. Family is very important. For example, it is the custom that when you visit people, they offer you something to eat or drink. It is disrespectful to refuse. Harry knew the right thing to do. Everybody loved him."

The highlight of the trip was a visit to the mountain gorillas. Appropriately, Rwanda is called the country of ten thousand hills. Nowhere is that more true than in Virunga National Park in the northwest where the gorillas live. "It is an especially tough place to reach. The gorillas live high in the volcanoes where it is dense and damp," explained Joselyne. "You can't go in for just one day. It is a long way from my town of Cyangugu, sometimes on rough roads; you need four-wheel drive for the final leg." On arrival, visitors are formed into groups led by rifle-carrying park rangers who are trained in tracking the gorillas in the jungle and interpreting their verbal and physical sounds and signs. The family of gorillas that Harry and Joselyne had the opportunity to observe was feeding close to civilization. In fact, as they arrived, two older females and six juveniles were climbing over a stone wall to eat eucalyptus bark from young trees the farmers in the area had planted. However, the silverback male had remained within the park and was providing warning by sounds that he would not tolerate humans approaching. From long experience, the ranger understood the silverback's intentions. It wasn't until after the females and juveniles finished feeding and returned to the jungle that the silverback stopped making warning sounds, at which point the ranger gave the all-clear. He helped the people over the wall and led them up the muddy path that was hedged in by impenetrable foliage, telling everyone to remain quiet; if approached by a gorilla, they were to sit down in the trail in a nonthreatening way. As they got closer to the silverback who was feeding, the ranger signaled with his hand that everyone should sit down. In no rush, the silverback emerged from his lair, turned abruptly on a path through the undergrowth, and approached Harry.

> All was quiet as he came to within a meter of where I was
> sitting. I felt no fear at all although he had the jaws and teeth
> that could bite off an arm. After many years of being around
> animals, both tame and wild, I could sense that silverback's
> frame of mind. In my work on violence and peace, I knew
> of the behavioral commonalities with our hominid brethren,
> including the ability of gorillas, chimpanzees, and bonobos to
> reflect a wide range of humanlike emotion. That silverback
> was at peace with our presence. He had communicated with
> the rangers, finally giving his permission for us to enter, which
> is a clear indication of his intelligence as well as his ability

to command. We were only the latest of many hundreds of
gawky tourists he had allowed in to visit. Having visitors
was old-hat to him. Although I was not afraid, it was, to say
the least, very, very exciting—the moment of a lifetime. Then
the moment passed, and the silverback veered away into the
jungle, and we went back down the mountain.[162]

Since then, Harry and Joselyne have become supporters of the Children of Hope Association in Cyangugu, Rwanda, Joselyne's hometown, an institute that cares for more than a 150 HIV-positive orphans. They have also helped Rwandan students come to the United States for further education, and Harry has continued his study of the nature of violence.

In 2011, Harry was presented with the Titanium Achievement Award from the International Titanium Association (ITA) in recognition of his life work. It was presented by Michael Metz, president of the ITA, who mentioned Harry's eighteen titanium- and tantalum-related patents and forty-four publications on titanium, and his work on the alloy Ti-10V-2Fe-3Al that was used as a landing gear forging on Boeing's 777. However, Harry does not view the ITA award as the closing of his research career. In fact, he is still pushing ahead with theoretical research on the dislocation dynamics that underlie the Larson-Miller parameter—the thorn in his side since his days at Stanford University. "A few years ago, a colleague and I submitted a paper for publication that was rejected, as it should have been, but for the wrong reasons. In retrospect, we claimed both too much and too little, so I am still working on it."

Harry is also involved in preserving the history of the Mojave Desert, the region that shaped him profoundly in the years he lived in the red caboose on the T & T Railroad and then in his grandparents' gas station. When he was a boy, he always wanted to know how things worked, whether it was the noisy water pump at a sandy railroad siding, the nature of fire ants that stung his bare feet, or why there were vast dolomite deposits underlying Death Valley. "I've always asked questions. As a child I drove the adults in my life crazy. It was not until college that I found the tools that enabled me to seek answers on my own with any certainty. Since then, I have done so in the most rigorous way."

Harry looks forward to taking Joselyne and their son, Roy Lloyd Hirwa, to visit the Mojave Desert and Rwanda when he gets older. He also looks forward to sharing with him some of the tools and life skills it took him such a long time to find, value, and master. Born June 23, 2013, Roy is named for two beloved people in Harry's and Joselyne's lives: Br. Rene Roy and Lloyd Rosenberg, Harry's brother. The name *Hirwa* means blessed, fortunate, or lucky one in the Kinyarwandan language. "We chose the name to remind him he is rooted in two cultures and families," said Harry, who, finding himself a father for the fourth time at age eighty-five, is both incredulous and profoundly grateful. "The African culture is remarkable in its energy, cohesiveness, tolerance, responsibility, and togetherness. Our son will also benefit from the best we can arrange from American culture: its can-do ethic is great preparation for the many opportunities life has to offer, also its many challenges." Among those challenges, Harry lists the nature of violence, nuclear weapons, and threats to the biosphere. Harry and Joselyne know that terrible experiences, such as genocide, can result in parents being so fearful for their children's safety that they constrict their world. Instead, they intend to do the opposite: allowing their hard times to shape their parenting style in positive and expanding ways. That means supporting Roy's innate curiosity—curiosity being the inner force that has powered every aspect of Harry's life—and encouraging open-minded dialogue with mutual respect during every phase of his growing-up years, from his first cry through his search-for-self as a teenager. In naming him Hirwa, Joselyne and Harry hope that his life is blessed, fortunate, and lucky—as they themselves have been by his presence.

One of Harry's favorite quotes is from Thomas Alva Edison, who said that genius is 1 percent inspiration and 99 percent perspiration. Harry values all the *aha* moments in his life (the 1 percent inspiration), but he also values the hard work (the 99 percent perspiration) that both precedes and follows the moment of awareness. To those percentages must be added the contribution of his mentors who pointed out the way at critical times. Harry sums up the stages of his life as follows: a lost little boy in the desert who becomes a miner out of necessity, who gives birth to a mechanic-blacksmith, who launches a metallurgist, who begets an entrepreneur-manager, who evolves into a concerned citizen with a broad worldview, culminating in a human being who can nurture. Just as he likes to quote Ecclesiastes 9:11 about the race not being to the swift, so the tenth verse in the same chapter is even more apt: "Whatever your hand finds to do, do it with all your might."

THE END

APPENDIX I: PATENTS

(CHRONOLOGICAL)

H. W. Rosenberg, et al. Eighteen patents issued, two others allowed but not taken up.

TIMET ERA:

1. Lenning, G. A., and H. W. Rosenberg. Corrosion resistant alloy. US Patent 3,161,503, December 15, 1964.

2. Rosenberg, H. W. Titanium base alloy. US Patent 3,268,329, August 29, 1966.

3. Rosenberg, H. W., and E. F. Erbin. Processing titanium alloy sheet products. US Patent 3,333,995, August 1, 1967.

4. Cox, H. D., and H. W. Rosenberg. Titanium base alloys. US Patent 3,457,068, July 22, 1969.

5. ————. Titanium base alloy. US Patent 3,510,295, May 5, 1970.

6. Hunter, D. B., and H. W. Rosenberg. Heat treatable beta titanium base alloy and processing thereof. US Patent 3,595,645, July 27, 1971.

7. Parris, W. M., and H. W. Rosenberg. High strength titanium alloys. US Patent 3,802,877, April 9, 1974.

ALTA ERA:

8. Rosenberg, H. W., and B. Melody. Anodized titanium thin-films. US Patent 5,185,075, February 9, 1993.

9. Cooper, Matthew, and H. W. Rosenberg. Process for producing electrically impervious anodized films on valve metals and product thereof. US Patent 5,211,832, May 18, 1993.

10. Rosenberg, H. W., Nigel Winters, and Yun Xu. Apparatus for producing titanium crystal and titanium. US Patent 6,024,847, February 15, 2000.

11. ———. Method for producing titanium crystal and titanium. US Patent 6,063,254, May 16, 2000.

12. ———. Titanium crystal and titanium. US Patent 6,309,595, October 30, 2001.

13. Rosenberg, H. W., Bahri Ozturk, Guangxin Wang, and Wesley LaRue. Tantalum sputtering target and method of manufacture. US Patent 6,323,055, November 27, 2001.

14. ———. Tantalum sputtering target and method of manufacture. US Patent 6,566,161, May 20, 2003.

15. Rosenberg, H. W., Nigel Winters, and Yun Xu. Titanium materials. US Patent 6,596,228, July 22, 2003.

16. Rosenberg, H. W., Bahri Ozturk, Guangxin Wang, and Wesley LaRue. Tantalum sputtering target and method of manufacture. US Patent 6,955,938, October 18, 2005.

17. ———. Tantalum sputtering target and method of manufacture. US Patent 6,958,257, October 25, 2005.

18. ———. Capacitor containing high purity tantalum. US Patent 7,102,229, September 5, 2006.

APPENDIX II: PUBLICATIONS

(CHRONOLOGICAL ORDER BEGINNING WITH MOST RECENT)

Rosenberg, H. W., M. Cooper, and K. Bloss. "Anodizing Mechanisms in High Purity Titanium." *Proceedings of the Seventh International Conference on Titanium*, San Diego, CA, June 1992.

Rosenberg, H. W., and J. E. Green. "Analyzing High Purity Titanium." *Proceedings of the Seventh International Conference on Titanium*, San Diego, CA, June 1992.

———. "Process Capabilities in Producing High Purity Titanium." *Proceedings of the Seventh International Conference on Titanium*, San Diego, CA, June 1992.

Rosenberg, H. W. "Spectral Interferences in High Purity Titanium." *Sixth International Conference on Titanium*, Cannes, June 1988.

———. "On the Analysis of Plastic Flow in Titanium." *Sixth International Conference on Titanium*, Cannes, June 1988.

———. "Titanium Production." In *Encyclopedia of Materials Science*, vol. 7. New York: Pergamon Press, 1986.

———. "Zirconium Production." In *Encyclopedia of Materials Science*, vol. 7. New York: Pergamon Press, 1986.

————. "Hafnium Production." In *Encyclopedia of Materials Science*, vol. 3. New York: Pergamon Press, 1986.

Carey, Robert S., R. R. Boyer, and H. W. Rosenberg. "Fatigue Properties of Ti-10V-2Fe-3Al." *Titanium Science and Technology*, vol. 2, Fifth International Conference on Titanium, Munich, Germany, 1984, Deutsche Gesellschaft Fur Metallkunde E. V.

Rosenberg, H. W., and R. R. Boyer, eds. *Beta Titanium Alloys in the 1980s*. Warrendale, PA: TMS-AIME, 1984.

Rosenberg, H. W. "Beta Titanium Alloys for Structural Efficiency." *Materials and Processes—Continuing Innovations*. Azusa, CA, 1983.

————. "Ti-15-3: A New Cold-Formable Sheet Titanium Alloy." *Journal of Metals* 35, no. 11 (November 1983).

————. Chapter 10 committee, *Welding Handbook*, vol. 4. Miami: American Welding Society, 1982.

Rosenberg, H. W., J. C. Chesnutt, and H. Margolin. "Fracture Properties of Titanium Alloys." *Application of Fracture Mechanics for Selection of Metallic Materials*. Metals Park, OH: ASM, 1982.

Rosenberg, H. W. "Titanium in the Marine Environment." *Oceans* (September 1982).

Adams, R. E., and H. W. Rosenberg. "A Review of Titanium Ingot Solidification." *Titanium and Titanium Alloys*, Third International Conference on Titanium, vol. 1. New York: Plenum Press, 1982.

Rosenberg, H. W. "Room Temperature Flow Stress and Strain in Ti - (0-15) At% Al Alloys." *Titanium and Titanium Alloys*, Third International Conference on Titanium, vol. 1. New York: Plenum Press, 1982.

————. "Titanium for Energy Sensitive Applications—Introduction." *Titanium for Energy and Industrial Applications*. Warrendale, PA: TMS-AIME, 1981.

————. "On the Nature of the 'Material Constants' in the Sherby-Dorn and Larson-Miller Parameters for Creep in Titanium." *Titanium '80 Science and Technology*, Fourth International Conference on Titanium. Warrendale, PA: TMS-AIME, 1980.

Reinsch, Wayne, and H. W. Rosenberg. "Three Recent Developments in Titanium Alloys." *Metal Progress* (March 1980).

Rosenberg, H. W. "Ti-10V-2Fe-3Al: A Forging Alloy Development." *Forging and Properties of Aerospace Materials*. London: The Metals Society, 1978.

————. "Heat Treatment of Titanium Alloys." SME Technical Paper EM 77–162, 1977.

————. "Stress-Strain Curves in Alpha Ti Alloys—Some Problems and Results." *Metallurgical Transactions* vol. 8A (March 1977). (See also Vol. 9A, March 1978, page 464.)

Rosenberg, H. W., and W. M. Parris. "Alloy, Texture, and Micro-structural Effects on the Yield Stress and Mixed Mode Fracture Toughness of Titanium." ASTM-STP 556, 1974.

Rosenberg, H. W., and Karl Snow. "Microsegregation in Titanium Alloys." TMS Paper No. A73-31, *Light Metals*. New York: EMD-AIME, 1973.

Rosenberg, H. W. "Critical Review-High Temperature Alloys." *Titanium Science and Technology*, Second International Conference on Titanium. New York: Plenum, 1973.

Rosenberg, H. W., and W. D. Nix. "Solid Solution Strengthening in Ti-Al Alloys." *Metallurgical Transactions* (May 1973).

Rosenberg, H. W. "Deformation Mechanics in Alpha Titanium Alloys." PhD dissertation, Stanford University, 1971. Dissertation Abstracts International, vol. 32, Number 8, 1972.

Rosenberg, H. W., and W. D. Nix. "Observation of Coplanar Dislocations in Cross Slip in Ti-15.5 At% Al." *Metallurgical Transactions*, vol. 1 (October 1970).

Rosenberg, H. W. "Alloying Titanium." *The Science, Technology, and Applications of Titanium*, First International Conference on Titanium. London: Pergamon Press, 1970.

————. "Titanium Alloying in Theory and Practice." *The Science, Technology, and Applications of Titanium*, First International Conference on Titanium. London: Pergamon Press, 1970.

Hatch, A. J., H. W. Rosenberg, and E. F. Erbin. "Effects of Environment on Cracking in Titanium Alloys." ASTM-STP 397, 1966.

Rosenberg, H. W. "The Effect of Substitutional Alpha Stabilizers on the Properties of Alpha Titanium." Paper No. 5, *Titanium Metallurgy Course*, New York University School of Engineering, September 1965.

Rosenberg, H. W., H. D. Cox, and E. F. Erbin. "Stress Corrosion and Titanium Alloy Design for High Temperature Applications." AIAA Paper No. 65-764, 1965.

Rosenberg, H. W., and D. B. Hunter. "The Titanium Rich Portion of the Ti-Pd Phase Diagram." *Transactions* AIME, vol. 233, April, 1965.

SELECTED BIBLIOGRAPHY

BOOKS

Austin, Mary. *The Land of Little Rain*. New York: Houghton Mifflin, 1903.

Call, Frank Wendall. *Gandydancer's Children: A Railroad Memoir*. Reno and Las Vegas: University of Nevada Press, 2000.

Calzia, J. P., ed. *Fifty Years of Death Valley Research*. Special Edition. Earth Science Review. Published by Elsevier, 2006.

Caruthers, William. *Loafing along Death Valley Trails*. Pomona, CA: P-B Press, 1951.

Casebier, Dennis G. *Guide to the East Mojave Heritage Trail: Rocky Ridge to Fenner*. Norco, CA: Tales of the Mojave Road Publishing Company, 1989.

Darlington, David. *The Mojave: A Portrait of the Definitive American Desert*. New York: Henry Holt and Company, 1996.

Hayden, H. W., William G. Moffatt, and John Wulff. *The Structure and Properties of Materials, Vol. III, Mechanical Behavior*. New York: John Wiley & Sons, 1965.

Heppenheimer, T. A. *The Space Shuttle Decision: NASA's Search for a Reusable Space Vehicle*. Washington, DC: National Aeronautics and Space Administration, NASA History Office, 1999.

Housley, Kathleen L. *Black Sand: The History of Titanium*. Hartford, CT: Metal Management Aerospace, 2007.

Huff, Mary. *Grandma Ann*. Xlibris, 2001.

Kotre, John N., and Elizabeth Hall. *Seasons of Life*. Ann Arbor: University of Michigan Press, 1997.

Lengner, Ken, and George Ross. *Tecopa Mines: Operating during 82 Years of the Death Valley Region Mining Boom*. Published by authors, 2006.

———. *Remembering the Early Shoshone and Tecopa Area (Southeastern Death Valley Region)*. Published by authors, 2004.

Lingenfelter, Richard E. *Death Valley and the Amargosa: A Land of Illusion*. Berkeley: University of California Press, 1986.

MacDonald, Lenora Johnson. *Our Pioneer Mother*. Self-published by author, 1931. Online at www.handfamily.org.

Miller, Marli B., and Lauren Wright. *Geology of Death Valley National Park*. 2nd ed. Iowa: Kendall/Hunt Publishing Company, 2007.

Myrick, David F. *Railroads of Nevada and Eastern California, Vol. II: The Southern Railroads*. Reno, Las Vegas, London: University of Nevada Press, 1991.

Perkins, Edna Brush. *The White Heart of the Mojave: An Adventure with the Outdoors of the Desert*. New York: Boni and Liveright, 1922.

Reynolds, Robert E., ed. *Land of Lost Lakes*. Abstracts from the 2003 Desert Symposium. California State University, Desert Studies Consortium and LSA Associates, April 2003.

———. *Old Ores: Mining History in the Eastern Mojave Desert*. Abstracts from the 2005 Desert Symposium. California State University, Desert Studies Consortium and LSA Associates, April 2005.

Rosenberg, Kris. *Talk to Me.* New York: G. P. Putnam's Sons, 1993.

Shumway, Gary L., Larry Vredenburgh, and Russell Hartill. *Desert Fever: An Overview of Mining in the California Desert Conservation Area.* Contract No. CA-010-CT6-2776. Prepared for: Desert Planning Staff Bureau of Land Management, US Department of the Interior. Riverside, CA: February 1980.

Walbergh, Mary Lou. *Tales of Tecopa: A Memoir of a Frontier Mining Town.* Santa Ynez, CA: Pacific Slope Press [n.d.].

Watercott, Ray. *Titanium: Part Product, Part Cause, a Casual History Lightly Salted.* Published anonymously for the Titanium Founders Meeting, July 18–19, 1960.

ARTICLES AND PAPERS

California Water Plan Update 2009, vol. 3 Regional Reports, Appendix 10A, page 1. "Flood Descriptions January and February 1969."

Crossley, Frank A. *AIAA-81-0893 Aircraft Applications of Titanium: A Review of the Past and Potential for the Future.* AIAA 1981 Annual Meeting and Technical Display Long Beach CA, May 12–14, 1981.

"Five Deep Manmade Nevada Pits Yield Thousands of Tons of Copper Ore Each Day." *Nevada Highways and Parks.* January–April 1955. (No author.) Online at www.nevadamagazine.com/issues/read/kennecott_copper_corporation.

Flinchum, Robin. "Nona Proctor Rosenberg and Her Life on the T & T Railroad," presented at the Desert Symposium, April 19, 2002.

Hilton, John. "Hunting Gem Stones in Menagerie Canyon." *The Desert Magazine*, December 1939.

Langston, Lee S. "Mounting Troubles." *Mechanical Engineering Magazine*, March 2011, published by the American Society of Mechanical Engineers (ASME), New York, NY.

Leap, Norris. "A Woman Mine Boss Triumphs in 25-Year War with Desert." *Los Angeles Times*, March 4, 1951.

Nix, William D., John C. Bravman, Richard H. Bube, and Roger N. Shepard. *Memorial Resolution: O. Culter Shepard (1902–1997)*, 1997.

Palmer, Judy. "Jack Madison Bootlegging in Shoshone." *Panamint Breeze.* September 2007.

Rosenberg, Harry. "Prospects for Cost Reduction of Titanium via Electrolysis." *High Performance Metallic Materials for Cost Sensitive Applications, TMS (The Minerals, Metals & Materials Society)*, 2002.

Rosenberg, H. W., and J. E. Green. "Electrorefining Titanium: The Process Capability." *Titanium '92 Science and Technology, The Minerals, Metals and Materials Society*, 1993.

Russell, Asa M. "We Lost a Ledge of Gold." *Desert Magazine*, September 1955.

Sarkes, Constantine P. "Titanium Fuselage Environmental Conditions in Post-Crash Fires." National Aviation Facilities Experimental Center, prepared for Federal Aviation Administration, March 1971.

Sprau, David T. "Tonopah and Tidewater (T & T) Railroad Post-Mortem," presented at the Death Valley Conference on History and Prehistory, November 2011.

Supersonic Transport Program Phase 11C Monthly Technical Progress Letter Report, Contract FA-SS-66-5, July 1965. The Boeing Company. n.a.

Welles, Chris. "The $50 Billion Battle to Build the Giant SST." *Life Magazine*, October 28, 1966, 75.

Wright, Lauren A. *Acknowledgement of a Professional Lifetime*. Earth Science Review. Published by Elsevier, 2005.

Wright, Lauren A., and Bennie W. Troxel. *Levi Noble: Geologist: His Life and Contributions to Understanding the Geology of Death Valley, the Grand Canyon, and the San Andreas Fault*. Open-File Report 02-422. US Department of the Interior, US Geological Survey, 2002.

COURT CASE

661 F.2d 279, 1981–2 Trade Cases 64,327. United States of America, Appellant, v. RMI Company; Crucible Inc.; Lawrence Aviation Industries Inc.; Martin Marietta Aluminum Inc.; and Titanium Metals Corporation of America, Appellees. No 80-2757, United States Court of Appeals, Third Circuit.

DOCTORAL THESIS

Rosenberg, Harry Weldon. "Deformation Mechanics of Alpha Titanium Alloys." A dissertation submitted to the Department of Materials Science and the Committee on the Graduate Division of Stanford University in partial fulfillment of the requirements for the degree of Doctor of Philosophy, May 1971. Reprinted from Dissertation Abstracts International, Vol. XXXII, Number 8, 1972.

GOVERNMENT PUBLICATIONS

A History of Significant Weather Events in Southern California Organized by Weather Type. Updated February 2010, NOAA. (Available online at www.wrh.noaa.gov/sgx/document/weatherhistory.pdf).

Paulson, R. W., E. B. Chase, R. S. Robert, and D. W. Moody, compilers. *National Water Summary, 1988–89: Hydrologic Events and Floods and Droughts*. US Geological Survey, Water Supply Paper 2375.

US Geological Survey, Fact Sheet 036-01. Flooding in the Amargosa River Drainage Basin, February 23–24, 1998, Southern Nevada and Eastern California, Including the Nevada Test Site, in Tanko, D. J., and P. A. Glancy. Accessed at http://pubs.usgs.gov/fs/fs-036-01/text/fs03601.htm.

US Geological Survey (2010) Boron Statistics, in Buckingham, D. A., P. A. Lyday, D. S. Kostick, D. E. Polyak, and M. A. Angulo. Historical Statistics for Mineral and Material Commodities in the United States: US Geological Survey Data Series 140. Accessed 2011 at http://pubs .usgs.gov/ds/2005/140/boron.pdf.

US Geological Survey (2010) Lead Statistics, in DiFrancesco, C.A., G. R. Smith, P. N. Gabby, and D. E. Guberman. Historical Statistics for Mineral and Material Commodities in the United States: US Geological Survey Data Series 140. Accessed 2011 at http://pubs.usgs.gov/ds/2005/140/lead.pdf.

US Geological Survey (2010) Talc and Pyrophyllite Statistics, in Porter, K. E., and R. L. Virta. Historical Statistics for Mineral and Material Commodities in the United States: US Geological Survey Data Series 140. Accessed 2011 at http://pubs.usgs.gov/ds/2005/140/talc.pdf.

ORAL HISTORY

Stella Proctor Rook, interviewed by David T. Sprau. Shoshone Museum, October 1995.

George Andrews Ross, interviewed by Harry Ford. Pahrump Valley Museum and Historical Society, April 2004.

WEBSITE REFERENCES

A website for the history of the T & T is maintained by the T & T Railroad Organization. The website is owned and copyrighted by John A. McCulloch, www.ttrr.org. The following material is on the site: Jennings, Bill, and Ralph Wyant. *The Tonopah & Tidewater Railroad*, Pacific News #55 (believed to be January 1976 issue). David T. Sprau, "A Day in the Life of the T & T." Presented at the Fifth Death Valley Conference on History and Prehistory; Inyo Newspaper Clippings Related to the T & T and Its Area, Early January 1907. Primary researcher David A. Wright. *Death Valley Chuck-Walla*. T & T Accident Report—ICC #760 Interstate Commerce Commission (March 11, 1921). T & T Accident Report #1549, Interstate Commerce Commission (November 23, 1929), Statistics of the T & T (extracted from *Encyclopedia of Western Railroad History* courtesy of Bruce Strange).

Bennett, Tom, and George Edmonston Jr. *Oregon Staters and the Pacific Theater*. OSU Alumni Association. Online.

Cronese Homesteaders v. the Mojave River. See www.dustyway.com/2007/ 08/cronese-homesteaders-vs-mojave-river.html.

Goebel, Greg. *The Rise & Fall of the SST* (public domain), www.faqs.org/ docs/air/avsst.html.

"Hyfil or Titanium?" published in *Flight International*. April 30, 1970, n.a. Online at: www.flightglobal.com/pdfarchives/new/1970.

Palmer, Judy. "She Mines Talc in Death Valley: The Story of Louise Grantham," n.p., www.dannyraythomas.com/bookVII/she_mines_ talc_in_death-valley/she-mines-talc_in_death_valley.html.

Putnam, George P. Obituary. http//www.cagenweb/inyo.obittranscriptions/ george-palmer-putnam.txt.

Tecopa Hot Springs Resort: The Dream. www.tecopahotsprings.org/dream .html. Interview with Harry Rosenberg by Amy Noel, copyright 2006.

TELEPHONE AND E-MAIL INTERVIEWS

Boyer, Rodney, February 2012.
Broadwell, Roger, March 2012.
Cawley, Edward, March 2012.

Cooper, Donald, January 2012.

Green, Joseph, March 2012.

Kessler, Harold, January and February 2012.

Nix, William, November 2011, March 2012.

Rosenberg, Joselyne Mivumbi, April 2012.

Roy, Brother Rene David, April 2012.

Talbot, Ethel Proctor, October 2011.

Wright, Lauren, July 2011.

PHOTO CREDITS

All historical photos except those listed below are in Harry Rosenberg's archives. The photos of Cat Mountain, the Amargosa River, the talc and lead mines, and Silver Lake were taken by Kathleen Housley.

Map of the Tonopah and Tidewater Railroad: UNLV Libraries Special Collections.

Map of Death Valley printed by Pacific Coast Borax: UNLV Libraries Special Collections.

McGill, Nevada, Kennecott Copper: Nevada Department of Transportation, 1953.

Elmo Proctor with wagon, the Proctor family in Crucero, Hyten, Hilton: Mary Proctor Huff Collection.

Kroll: Nicolas Lanners Foundation, Luxembourg.

SR-71 *Blackbird*: NASA.

ENDNOTES

CHAPTER 1: THE MIDDLE OF NOWHERE

[1] From June to August 1907, one of the twenty-mule teams was put back in service to haul borax from a mine to the T & T at Zabriskie. The *Goldfield News* quote is from David F. Myrick, *Railroads of Nevada and Eastern California, Vol. II: The Southern Roads* (Reno: University of Nevada Press, 1992), 549.

[2] Richard E. Lingenfelter, *Death Valley and the Amargosa: A Land of Illusion* (Berkeley: University of California Press, 1986), 1.

[3] John Rosenberg, one of Peter's descendants, was born in York in 1820. He became a silversmith, married Mary Sanger, with whom he had ten children, and eventually moved to Iowa. The name Stamy is also spelled Stamey.

[4] The Shoshone and Paiute knew that the playas flooded, but the settlers and railroad men apparently discounted their knowledge. Silver Lake had flooded in the spring of 1910, but the damage to the tracks was less than in 1916. The Mojave River has its source in the San Bernardino Mountains. Unlike most rivers, it flows inland instead of to the sea.

[5] Myrick, 586. According to David Sprau, the Union Pacific and Los Angeles & Salt Lake R & R were forced to detour their transcontinental trains over the T & T rails one time in the 1920s when Afton Canyon was giving them trouble. "Their trains went from Yermo to Ludlow on the ATSF, then to Crucero over T & T where they went back on their own line. T & T to the rescue" (e-mail from Sprau to Housley, July 5, 2012).

[6] To the south of Leeland, the T & T Ranch was established in an effort to grow food for the crews. Leeland no longer exists. There were also two mining towns named Lee, one in California, the other in Nevada, that had come into brief existence during the gold rush, reaching their peak in 1907 when the T & T arrived, declining rapidly thereafter.

[7] Besides the rumors about the killing of Joseph Smith and the plot to kill Brigham Young, Federal troops had entered Utah that year under orders of President James Buchanan, in reaction to which Brigham Young had told local populations to prepare to fight. On September 11, members of Company F, the Mormon militia, killed the men, women, and most of the children after luring them from the security of their circled wagons with a promise of safe passage to Cedar City. It is hard to determine what long-term effect the trials and tribulations of Ann and Neils had on their family, except to say that Ann was revered for her loving steadfastness as made evident by two books written by descendants: *Our Pioneer Mother* by Lenora Johnson MacDonald, and *Grandma Ann* by Mary Huff. Quotes are taken from MacDonald, *Our Pioneer Mother* (1931) 10, 16.

[8] Ella May Wright was the daughter of James Riley Wright and Lydia Ann Allred. James was born in Poland, Indiana, on May 1845. James married Lydia Allred on April 11, 1869, in Uniontown, Kansas. She was the daughter of James G. Allred. They had six children, the youngest being Ella May Wright born October 27, 1880, in Lookingglass, Oregon. She married Elmo Proctor in 1904 in Downey, California.

[9] Dennis G. Casebier, *Guide to the East Mojave Heritage Trail: Rocky Ridge to Fenner* (Norco, CA, 1989), 74–85. See also Mary Huff, *Grandma Ann* (Xlibris, 2001), 218. The Los Angeles and Salt Lake Railroad that went through Crucero was acquired in 1921 by the Union Pacific Railroad.

[10] The birthdates of the other Proctor children were: Mildred, March 30, 1908; James Alfred, August 6, 1910; Stella, January 14, 1913; Alma, September 18, 1916; Mary, April 23, 1920; and Ethel, October 18, 1921.

[11] Mary Proctor Huff's memory of Nona is in a letter written to Harry Rosenberg in 1975.

[12] Nona Proctor kept a diary for 1935 that is in the possession of Harry Rosenberg along with several letters. See also Robin Flinchum, "Nona Proctor Rosenberg and Her Life on the T & T Railroad," presented at the Desert Symposium, April 19, 2002.

[13] Edna Brush Perkins, *The White Heart of the Mojave* (New York: Boni and Liveright, 1922), online www.american-buddha.com.

CHAPTER 2: THE T & T RAILROAD

[14] Ken Lengner and George Ross, *Tecopa Mines* (2006), 39.

[15] The *Death Valley Chuck-Walla* was a magazine published in 1907 in Greenwater. Online Inyo newspaper clippings related to the T & T and its area, Tonopah and Tidewater website.

[16] Lingenfelter, 387, 391. Standard gauge is four feet eight inches.

[17] Consolidated Borax was the parent company of Pacific Coast Borax. It was headquartered in London, England. Pacific Coast Borax owned both the T & T and the Death Valley Railroad, so although the two were separate entities, they were still part of the same company. Quote on clay dust, diary of Nona Proctor Rosenberg.

[18] Perkins, chapter 4, page 5, online.

[19] Myrick, 591.

[20] The following is additional information on some of the less important stops and sidings. Several were named after employees of Pacific Coast Borax, including Rasor, Baker, Val Jean, Sperry, Zabriskie, Gerstley, Evelyn, and Jenifer. Broadwell was a small playa north of Ludlow on top of which the tracks were laid. Harry remembers Soda Lake as desolate with brackish water in which thick reeds and salt grass grew. It is now named Zzyzx. Riggs was named for Frank Riggs, who had a silver mine in the Silurian Hills. Dumont was near the southern opening of Death Valley. The Spanish Trail crossed the T & T near Sperry Wash. Until the mines closed, gypsum was carried by a spur and loaded on the T & T at Acme (a.k.a. Morrison), which was in the Amargosa Canyon. The gypsum mine was closed in 1919 when a cave-in killed the mine owner's two sons. Just north of Tecopa, Zabriskie was also on the banks of the Amargosa. Gerstley was the stop for the Gerstley Borax Mine that shipped ore from 1924 to 1927. Evelyn is near Eagle Mountain on the banks of the Amargosa near a small playa. Scranton and Bradford were near mines for bentonite and other clays. Indian arrowheads and artifacts were plentiful in Scranton. The T & T Ranch, near Leeland, grew crops for the employees of the railroad. In the 1930s, it supplied produce to Furnace Creek Inn and the Amargosa Hotel in Death Valley Junction. The name Ashton refers to ash trees that grew nearby. Marble was mined at Carrara, named after the famous site in Italy, but the stone turned out to be of inferior quality. The spur was dismantled in 1932.

[21] There is a mile-post sign at the Shoshone Museum, Shoshone, California.

[22] David T. Sprau, "A Day in the Life of the T & T," presented at the Fifth Death Valley Conference on History and Prehistory, online.

[23] Nona Proctor Rosenberg letters; Flinchum, 4.

[24] Interview with Stella Proctor Rock by David Sprau, 1995, Shoshone Museum, Shoshone, California.

[25] According to Harry, "the bucket contained an early form of a battery that in appearance and electrode design looked like a gravity cell. But that could not literally be so, as a white powder was used in recharging instead of copper sulfate crystals and water. Moreover, gravity cells degrade rapidly in intermittent use as was the case for pumping water. Tripping the cam on the rod into the cylinder parted a pair of current-carrying points creating a spark that ignited the gas in

the cylinder." Harry recalls that the engine was "a true fuel saver. It could run for hours on one gallon of gasoline."

[26] "Wreck on the T & T," *Tonopah Daily Bonanza*, August 11, 1908, online TTRR website. After the wreck, the T & T built berms and improved drainage. It is not known when the ballast was used. Harry Rosenberg explains desert pavements and desert varnish as follows: "Desert varnish coats the rocks. Many are ventifacts, which are pebbles shaped a bit like an arrowhead on their exposed sides by eons of sandstorms following prevailing wind patterns. The varnish is very thin and is formed by colonies of microscopic bacteria living on the rock surface for thousands of years. Desert varnish is prevalent on the alluvial fans that slope away from the mountains. Bacteria absorb manganese and iron from the environment and deposit it as black layers of manganese oxide or reddish iron oxide—thin layers of occluded clay particles act as a shield for the bacteria against desiccation and extreme heat as well as solar and background radiation. In a photo taken at Riggs, desert pavement had been disturbed local to the siding when the T & T was built. But it was and is prevalent nearby."

[27] Sprau, "Day in the Life."

[28] The *Death Valley Chuck-Walla*, online TTRR website.

[29] T & T Accident Report #1549, Interstate Commerce Commission (November 23, 1929).

CHAPTER 3: GREEK TRAGEDY, MOJAVE BACKDROP

[30] Mary Austin, *The Land of Little Rain* (New York: Houghton Mifflin, 1903), 35.

[31] Perkins, "White Heart of Mojave," chapter 3, online.

[32] William Caruthers, *Loafing along Death Valley Trails* (Pomona, CA: P. B. Press, 1951), 64. See also Charles "Seldom Seen Slim" Ferge, www.findagrave.com; the description of Ma Preston is in Casebier, 106.

[33] Judy Palmer has written a book on Louise Grantham.

[34] Caruthers, 69; Harry still has "a purple bottle of McGiveney's white lightning, a.k.a., poison! It has a few drops in it. It really was terrible stuff. Absolutely undrinkable."

[35] Lengner and Ross, *Tecopa Mines*, 60; Judy Palmer, "Jack Madison Bootlegging in Shoshone," *Panamint Breeze* (September 2007), 14.

[36] Lingenfelter, 440.

[37] Ibid.

[38] Mary Lou Walbergh, *Tales of Tecopa: A Memoir of a Frontier Mining Town* (Santa Ynez, CA: Pacific Slope Press, n.d.), 26.

[39] Caruthers, 66–67. For further information on Smith and Fairbanks, see Ken Lengner and George Ross, *Remembering the Early Shoshone and Tecopa Area* (2004).

[40] Two baskets made by Julia Weed Ross were found in the home of Stella Proctor Rook in Shoshone when she was packing to move. In 2005, her sisters Mary Proctor Huff and Ethel Proctor Talbot, her nephew Harry Rosenberg, and other members of the family gave the baskets back to George Ross in a ceremony at China Ranch. However, Ross told them the baskets should stay in the Rosenberg family. There are plans for the baskets eventually to go to a museum (Robin Flinchum, "Baskets Weave Families Together Forever," *Pahrump Valley Times*, September 21, 2005; see also *George Andrews Ross Oral History* [Pahrump Valley Museum and Historical Society, Interviewed by Harry Ford, April 2004], 4).

[41] Lengner and Ross, 44.

[42] Letter from Mary Proctor Huff to Harry Rosenberg 1975; she also tells a story about a visit of the Rosenbergs to Cronese when they accidentally left Lloyd, then a baby, behind. They were preparing to drive back to Rasor when by accident the car door slammed on Harry's hand. To take care of Harry, Nona first went and put Lloyd down in the bedroom. Once Harry had begun to settle down and his hand was bandaged, they climbed into the car and left. "About half an hour later, we heard Lloyd's cry. My mother rushed to him. Nonie had forgotten her baby!" About thirty minutes later, "the car tore into the drive and created a dust cloud sliding to a stop." They had gotten to Rasor and were about to carry both children into the caboose when they realized their mistake. At the reunion, both Nona and her mother were laughing and crying at the same time, a reaction that Mary, being very young, could not understand. What she could understand was the look of love on Harry Sr.'s face as he held little Harry in his arms and watched the women work through their feelings of fear and relief.

[43] J. J. Floyd was the nineteen-year-old engineer, and the fireman was Charles Taylor. They were blown from the locomotive. Taylor died instantly. Floyd died in a hospital in Los Angeles (David Sprau, "T & T Wrecks, Gold Field Times," March 18, 1927, online TTRR website).

[44] Nona Rosenberg diary (Flinchum, 5).

CHAPTER 4: GROWING UP IN THE DESERT

[45] Joe Nelson was the first person to apply for a homestead on public land in East Cronese Valley in 1907. Between 1907 and 1932, thirty-four homestead applications were filed with the Public Land Office. All but four were canceled (see www.dustyway.com/2007/08/cronese-homesteaders-vs-mojave-river.html).

[46] According to Harry, "After my teeth became noticeably mottled, a doctor we knew realized why. He put both of us on a lime solution that counteracted further mottling for Lloyd. But for me, it was too late. Along about my twenty-first birthday, I finally saved enough money—$140—to have my four upper front teeth capped." Ethel disagrees with Harry about the amount of fluoride in the water at Cronese, maintaining that it was Crucero that had the higher amount. However, Crucero and Cronese share the same aquifer. According to Harry, "It all depends on where in its journey the aquifer contacts a natural deposit of fluorite and so becomes mineralized."

[47] Unfortunately, Harry's family lost track of the geode. It was described by John Hilton in the article "Hunting Gem Stones in Menagerie Canyon," *The Desert Magazine*, December 1939. Hilton described it as a perfect specimen that was absolutely unique.

[48] Casebier, 81.

[49] Hilton, "Hunting Gem Stones."

[50] *The Desert Magazine*, 36.

[51] Casebier, 83, 42.

[52] Ethel Proctor Talbot is Harry's only surviving aunt. The quotes are from e-mails to the author.

CHAPTER 5: THE END OF THE LINE

[53] Subsequent to the flood, the overburden was removed and the tunnel became a cut through Afton Canyon.

[54] Harry met Hilton about thirty years later. "I ran into him at an art show in Death Valley. When I finally was able to get close, I introduced myself and mentioned the above incident. No laugh this time. He honestly had no memory of me or the incident. Or did he remember all too well?"

[55] Myrick, 591.

[56] For information on the end of the T & T, see David T. Sprau, "Tonopah and Tidewater (T & T) Railroad Post-Mortem," presented November 2011 Death Valley Conference on History and Prehistory. Once when Harry was on a business trip to England, he visited with David Peacock, a railroad buff. Harry told him about the rails being sent to Egypt, and Peacock replied that he had been told by an Egyptian friend about a rail line appearing very rapidly in the desert during the war. In his memoirs of the borax industry, Gerstley states the rails were sent to the Persian Gulf.

57 Charlie Brown had traded land set aside for a school by the State of California for land contiguous to the hot springs, which he then sold to Harry Sr. Around the same time, Jim Francis lost his lease on the springs and the county eventually took it over and operated it.

58 Lengner and Ross, *Early Shoshone and Tecopa Area* (2004), 70.

59 Tom Bennett and George Edmonston Jr., "Oregon Staters and the Pacific Theater," OSU Alumni Association, online.

60 In 1953, Ted Ogston came out of retirement to serve as acting superintendent of Death Valley National Monument. Harry kept in touch with the Ogstons and saw Helen four or five times after graduation. "My last contact came via telephone in 1968. Her husband Ted was in his nineties, and she was caring for him at home in Sun City, Arizona. They also had a summer home in Cody, Wyoming. By then, I had found my life mate, and Helen pleaded with me to bring her by. Kris was in school full-time, had four children to manage, with a part-time job and me on top of it all. We kept putting off the promised visit until it was too late."

61 Putnam: http//www.cagenweb/inyo.obittranscriptions/george-palmr-putnam .txt.

CHAPTER 6: WORKING IN THE HOLE

62 US Geological Survey (2010), Boron Statistics, in D. A. Buckingham, P. A. Lyday, D. S. Kostick, D. E. Polyak, and M. A. Angulo, Historical Statistics for Mineral and Material Commodities in the United States: US Geological Survey Data Series 140.

63 Lengner and Ross, *Tecopa Mines*, 27.

64 Lingenfelter, 395.

65 Lingenfelter, 407–408. Today, almost all the talc produced in the United States is open pit.

66 In 1940, the nationwide production of talc was 255,000 metric tons with a unit value of $12.20 per metric ton. In 1947, these figures rose to 469,000 metric tons with a unit value of $16.40 per metric ton and then soared to 559,000 metric tons and a unit value of $19.00 in 1950 (US Geological Survey [2010] Talc and Pyrophyllite Statistics, in K. E. Porter and R. L. Virta, Historical Statistics for Mineral and Material Commodities in the United States: US Geological Survey Data Series 140).

67 A good description of mining equipment during different eras, including carbide lamps, is found in *Tecopa Mines* by Ken Lengner and George Ross (see Section 11.0 "The Miner and His Tools," 93–101).

[68] Because of the danger of explosion caused by an open flame, carbide lights are no longer used in mines.

[69] Amargosa chaos—"A structural term for a mosaic of fault-bounded, typically gigantic blocks, derived from a stratigraphic succession and arranged in proper stratigraphic order, but occupying only a small fraction of the thickness of the original succession. In the Death Valley region, where LF Noble coined the term, chaos is normally viewed as a product of extreme coastal extension" (Miller, Wright, 36).

[70] Lauren A. Wright, *Acknowledgements of a Professional Lifetime* (Elsevier 2005), 8.

[71] It would be half a century before Harry would see Wright again. By then, Wright had retired from teaching geology at Penn State University. Harry had retired from the Alta Group. Their friendship picked up where it had left off in the desert, based on respect and mutual interest.

CHAPTER 7: THE NOONDAY MINES

[72] California State Division of Mines, 1951, *Tecopa Mines*, Lengner and Ross, 81; Lingenfelter, 359.

[73] US Geological Survey (2010) Lead Statistics, in C. A. DiFrancesco, G. R. Smith, P. N. Gabby, and D. E. Guberman, Historical Statistics for Mineral and Material Commodities in the United States: US Geological Survey Data Series 140.

[74] Davis had coauthored with S. H. Lorain a paper for the US Bureau of Mines titled "Mining and Milling Methods and Costs of the Golden Anchor Mining Co., Burgdorf, Idaho," 1938. In her book *Tales of Tecopa*, Mary Lou Walbergh, the daughter of Jim Francis, claims that Bill Rogers, a miner, discovered the vein of lead.

[75] Lengner and Ross, *Tecopa Mines*, 76–77.

[76] Caruthers, 158.

[77] Newspaper articles on the crash focusing on the death of Carole Lombard are online. The quote is from an article datelined Los Angeles, January 17, 1942.

[78] Lengner and Ross, *Early Shoshone*, 73.

[79] US Geological Survey, Lead Statistics (2010).

[80] Lengner and Ross in *Tecopa Mines* include a flow chart for the mill, 140–142.

[81] Lengner and Ross, *Tecopa Mines*, 110–111.

[82] Interview with Chick Joy by Susan Sorrells, September 2011, Shoshone Museum.

CHAPTER 8: LEAVING THE AMARGOSA

[83] Rosenberg, "Origins of an Ethos," presented to the Alta Group, n.d.

[84] The term *consilience* was coined by William Whewell in the nineteenth century and made popular by E. O. Wilson in his book by that title published in 1998.

[85] At that time, the degree of engineering required a year of study beyond the master's level. Information is from the *Memorial Resolution: O. Culter Shepard (1902–1997)* by William D. Nix, John C. Bravman, Richard H. Bube, and Roger N. Shepard. Harry wrote: "He turned ninety in '92, and I went to the reception the department held for him. I only flew three thousand miles; others came from around the globe. He had shrunk five inches and was frail and weak. But his inner zest was still there as he caught up on his ex-students' lives and times. Colleagues came too. Craig Barrett, now chairman of Intel (and a member of my graduate committee), came. Many of his students are famous and others merely successful like me. When asked what he thought about so many students surpassing him, he replied, 'Why now that I think it, I would not want it any other way.' Being simple, straight, and direct can have profound results. In these ways, he was like Helen, Norman, and Kris. As part of the Stanford festivities, pictures of his early life were screened. I, like many others in the audience, asked who that odd guy with a huge mop of black hair was in one picture. He and others close to the family roared with laughter. That odd guy was Cutler before he had turned prematurely gray. He was the grandest of men. When I arrived, he greeted me as a long-lost son. I nearly cried. We had just sold Alta, and my proceeds were still in the trunk of my car."

[86] Kennecott purchased the adjacent properties of Consolidated Coppermines in 1958. Kennecott closed its Nevada mines in 1978. It was acquired by Standard Oil of Ohio in 1981. It is now part of Rio Tinto.

[87] "Five Deep Manmade Nevada Pits Yield Thousands of Tons of Copper Ore Each Day," *Nevada Highways and Parks* (January–April 1955, n.a.).

[88] There were two reverbatory furnaces, although only one was used at a time. According to the article in *Nevada Highways and Parks*, it took about twenty hours to convert a charge of eighteen pots of matte to blister copper in the converter.

[89] Harry recalls about Michael Speer that in spite of his idiosyncrasies, he liked him. "I was shocked to hear years later that he was murdered by a hitchhiker he picked up north of Fresno on Highway 99."

[90] Harry explained the research for Kennecott as follows: "Ores usually consist of particles of metal as cations combined with one or more anions to form a chemical compound. To separate the values from waste (gangue), ores must be crushed to

gravel and ground to fine particles roughly the size of the naturally occurring metal compounds, such as copper sulfide or copper-iron sulfide. The ores being processed by the mill at McGill were on the fine side, and the grinding operation was already near optimum before we began our research. In retrospect, we should have been looking at the regrind line used to further reduce the screen size of the flotation product before a final flotation treatment. Maybe it too was optimized, but our work came to naught, as so often happens in applied research. I always wondered if that step were even necessary. A null research result would have saved Kennecott tons of money and made the operation more competitive."

CHAPTER 9: THE WONDER METAL TITANIUM

[91] The conventional term is strength-to-weight ratio; however, the term strength-to-density ratio is more accurate. Strength as used in metallurgy is an intensive property. Weight is extensive in that it has no boundary or limit. Density is intensive being bounded by the unit volume as strength is bounded by unit area.

[92] Today, approximately 90 percent of all titanium ore is used for paint additives.

[93] According to Stanley Seagle, heated titanium does not always explode. "Usually the first explosion in a contained area is the expansion of water to steam and then the possibility of hydrogen recombining with oxygen in a very exothermic reaction" (e-mail to author, August 2012). The danger of putting water on a titanium fire is seen in the example of the melting through of a crucible in a vacuum-arc melting furnace. At least two such explosions occurred in the United States and one in the United Kingdom in the 1950s and '60s. An explosion at TIMET resulted in one death. However, small local and limited fires confined to small volumes can be safely doused with copious water. The ratio of metal to water is critical.

[94] The information on William Kroll is from Kathleen L. Housley, *Black Sand: The History of Titanium* (Hartford, CT: Metal Management Aerospace, 2007).

[95] Ibid., xii.

[96] Ibid., 48. Titanium's density was also the reason the US Army was assiduously carrying out research at its arsenal in Watertown, Massachusetts, although the cost-benefit ratio was not as favorable in ordnance as it was for aircraft. The development of more powerful ammunition meant that ordnance had to be made stronger, but if steel plating were made any thicker, the ordnance would be too heavy to transport to the battlefield. The Soviet blockade of Berlin in 1948 underscored the value of lighter vehicles that could be airlifted. Weight also made a difference in the manpower needed to operate ordnance. Research by the US Army's Watertown Arsenal had shown that when titanium was used in the base of the 81-mm mortar instead of steel, crew size could be reduced from four soldiers to three. From the perspective of the US Navy, titanium's excellent corrosion

resistance in seawater made its use for ship and submarine hulls an attractive possibility but only if enormous amounts of titanium could be made economically.

[97] Other new companies were partnerships between P. R. Mallory (now Duracell) and Sharon Steel, named Mallory-Sharon, and between Remington Arms (in which DuPont had a majority interest) and Crucible Steel, named Rem-Cru (eventually changed to Crucible). Wah Chang Corp. got into the business when it acquired the Bureau of Mines' zirconium plant in Albany, Oregon. When the bureau closed down its metallurgical research facilities in the 1950s, several of its staff members and scientists formed the Oregon Metallurgical Corporation (Oremet).

[98] There is also a very brittle omega phrase with a crystal structure similar to an alpha or a distorted alpha that is not stable at room temperature.

[99] Housley, 70.

[100] Eventually, Harry became proficient at 6 Sigma, which was developed by Motorola in 1986. It is a statistically based method of eliminating defects and errors thereby reducing variability particularly in manufacturing. About his use of statistics at TIMET on the manufacture of sponge, Harry wrote: "Several technical issues in data analysis arose. I remember two in particular. Metal purity was always something we watched. In calculating control limits by the handbook method, I often got negative lower control limits. When I inquired of my cohorts and others, their pat answer always amounted to 'do it like the book.' It would be years before I figured that one out—from a book! The book was of a different kind. It dealt with the kinds of data being analyzed and how that affected the method of calculation. Our early rulebook dealt only with the bell curve, as it is by far the most important in all of statistics. But it doesn't fit all situations and ours was a perfect example. Bell curves are symmetrical on both sides of the mean or average value. Our negative control limits arose under conditions where our chemical analyses were limited on the lower side by zero. When the mean value approaches zero, the analytical errors tend to be most often on the high side, skewing the data to the high side. *Aha,* I thought to myself, *logarithms of analyses must be used, not the raw numbers.* Taking logs *normalizes* the distribution of possible numbers. And they can be controlled by textbook means" (e-mail to author).

[101] Interview with Cooper by author.

[102] Kennedy speech online at: University of Virginia Miller Center.

[103] Watercott, 41.

[104] Greg Goebel, *The Rise & Fall of the SST,* August 3, www.faqs.org/docs/air/avsst.html.

[105] Interview with Kessler by author. TIMET had two laboratories. Henderson was for the development of alloys. Toronto was for the development of effective production techniques, such as sheet-rolling.

[106] Chris Welles, "The $50 Billion Battle to Build the Giant SST," *Life Magazine*, October 28, 1966, 75; Constantine P. Sarkes, "Titanium Fuselage Environmental Conditions in Post-Crash Fires," National Aviation Facilities Experimental Center, prepared for Federal Aviation Administration, March 1971, 2.

[107] Interview with Boyer by author. Boyer earned his bachelor's and master's degrees in metallurgical engineering from the University of Washington. He retired from Boeing in 2012 after a forty-seven-year career with the Boeing Commercial Airplane Group as a titanium specialist. He is a fellow of ASM and was presented the International Titanium Association Achievement Award in 2002. In "Supersonic Transport Program Phase 11C Monthly Technical Progress Letter Report, Contract FA-SS-66-5, July 1965, The Boeing Company," it was reported that: "New results from titanium alloy high temperature exposure tests have shown that the high temperature stress corrosion problem in titanium alloys is not as serious as previously believed. Previous testing has been based on laboratory conditions much more severe than those of typical SST service life. The principal difference between the two conditions relates to time at temperature. The laboratory conditions held high temperatures for protracted periods, several hundred hours in many cases. However, typical SST operating conditions involve hot periods of 2.5 hours or less on a typical flight followed by a cool period at low speed or on the ground" (n.a., 2). According to Don Cooper, who was manager of TIMET's Toronto laboratory at the time, Ti-6Al-4V was not suited for skin any more than 8-1-1, the problem being the development of microscopic sheer cracks that developed during cold rolling. "We identified that problem not long before the SST was cancelled" (interview with Cooper by author).

[108] Kessler, interview. Harry continued research on 8-1-1 and received a patent on a heat-treatment.

[109] A beta alloy developed by Stanley Seagle at RTI at around the same time contained 6 percent Cr. It is currently used in many aerospace and commercial applications.

[110] Housley, 78.

[111] Ibid., 79.

[112] Ibid., 92.

[113] Harry's sharpened listening skills paid off with a supplier who came to see him with ideas about using more of their product in one of the new alloys. Harry listened attentively before patiently explaining why the product they supplied would not alloy as they envisioned. Subsequently, the supplier established their

own research and development laboratory to prove their point. Harry stayed in touch with them and even visited their lab. "Although they never qualified an alloy, they remained loyal and good suppliers, partly, they later said, because of my respect for, patience with, and understanding of them. But I had gained these attributes the hard way."

[114] See appendix for patent list. During this period, Harry developed an alloy 2-4-4 for the US Navy that had potential. It was relatively immune to hot salt cracking. The alloy 6-2-4-6 was developed because industry wanted a similar alloy to 6-2-4-2 to be used in the disks and low compressor stages; however, a patent was not granted. Harry also worked on Ti-15V-3Cr-3Al-3Sn (known as 15-3), although it was not his invention. Instead, it was a standard he used for comparison in a US Air Force contract. "Against perhaps a dozen alloys, each better in some regard, it usually occupied second place in this property or that. From that point on, we and our customers took 15-3 seriously."

[115] Cooper, interview.

CHAPTER 10: IN SEARCH OF DEEPER UNDERSTANDING

[116] For her analysis, Kris was not provided the names of employees, only numbers.

[117] E-mail from William Nix to author, November 2011. In 2003, Nix became professor emeritus after a long and successful career at Stanford University. He joined the faculty at Stanford in 1963, serving as director of the Center for Materials Research from 1968 to 1970. He was appointed professor in 1972. In 1989, he was named the Lee Otterson Professor of Engineering at Stanford University. He served as chairman of the Department of Materials Science and Engineering from 1991 to 1996. He is the recipient of two honorary doctorates and many awards, the most recent being in 2007 when he received the Von Hippel Award from the Materials Research Society.

[118] Ibid; also, interview with Nix by author.

[119] Harry Weldon Rosenberg, "Deformation Mechanics of Alpha Titanium Alloys," a dissertation submitted to the Department of Materials Science and the Committee on the Graduate Division of Stanford University in partial fulfillment of the requirements for the degree of doctor of philosophy, May 1971, reprinted from Dissertation Abstracts International, Vol. XXXII, Number 8, 1972, Appendix I, 245. From the abstract: "Although a large quantity of engineering data on the effects of aluminum alloying additions to binary and higher titanium alloys is available, the detailed strengthening mechanisms are largely unexplored. Because Al is the most important alloy addition to Ti commercially, there is need to better understand the Ti-Al system. Toward this end, a broad experimental program of research was undertaken wherein the effects of binary Al additions

up to 15 atomic percent on crystallographic texture, plastic strain ratios, strain hardening, dislocation substructures, and apparent activation parameters of alpha Ti were studied. The results are synthesized in a self-consistent fashion in this dissertation."

[120] Cooper, interview.

[121] According to Harry: "The constant C embodies a total derivative that includes three factors that lead to the total number of kinks in motion. There can be only so many edge kinks in a screw dislocation before it is no longer a screw, but screw dislocations are all one sees at the higher aluminum alloy contents. C is in fact a structure partial (total differential with respect to temperature) of the mechanical factors that lead to the total number of edge kinks in motion that contribute to plastic strain. Fortunately, each alloy system behaves in a relatively unique way, which is why each alloy system has its own unique constant C. That constant can be determined readily and accurately by statistical means. Research begets research. For example, given the above, one must still ask: Why do titanium alloys deform as they evidently do? In other metals, deformation produces very different dislocation structures. Examples of full dislocation loops abound where edges and screws combine to enclose a full half plane. Not so for Ti-Al alloys. In a sense, we metallurgists are still blacksmiths, with plenty to learn" (see H. W. Rosenberg, "On the Analysis of Plastic Flow in Titanium," The Sixth World Conference on Titanium, Societe Francaise de Metallurgie, 1988, part one, 111). In 1980, he published "On the Nature of 'Material Constants' in the Sherby-Dorn and Larson-Miller Parameters for Creep in Titanium" in *Titanium '80 Science and Technology*, TMS. He considers these papers to be steps in the right direction. As of 2013, Harry is in the process of preparing another paper for publication.

[122] Cooper, interview.

[123] Data on the 1969 flood come from *A History of Significant Weather Events in Southern California Organized by Weather Type*, updated February 2010, NOAA, online.

[124] Bobby's death hit his younger sister Jan Christian very hard. Making it her lifelong mission to understand what had happened to him, she wrote a book *Leave No Brother Behind: A Sister's War Memoir*.

CHAPTER 11: A TURBULENT TIME

[125] Cooper, interview.

[126] Goehler e-mail to Boyer and author.

[127] After going into receivership, Rolls-Royce was not privatized by the British government until 1987. In the article "Hyfil or Titanium?" published in *Flight*

International, April 30, 1970, the author wrote: "It now seems possible that Rolls-Royce may have to use a titanium fan on the first of the RB.211-22 turbofans to be fitted to the Lockheed TriStar. But no decision on this matter has yet been taken by the company. There have been bird-and-grit ingestion problems with the unique Hyfil fan blades of the RB.211, which use laminated carbon-fibre construction. The titanium unit was developed in case such problems should arise and nearly half of all the development hours of the RB.211 test programme so far have been completed using the titanium fan. The flights of the engine in the VC10 test bed have been made with such a fan fitted." www.flightglobal.com/pdfarchives/new/1970.

[128] Lee S. Langston, "Mounting Troubles," *Mechanical Engineering Magazine* (March 2011, American Society of Mechanical Engineers, New York, NY), online.

[129] Ibid.

[130] T. A. Heppenheimer, *The Space Shuttle Decision: NASA's Search for a Reusable Space Vehicle,* Washington, DC: NASA History Office, 1999, chapter 7, online.

[131] Kessler, interview.

[132] The civil complaint was filed by the government on September 28, 1978. 661 F.2d 279, 1981-2 Trade Cases 64,327. United States of America, Appellant, v. RMI Company; Crucible, Inc.; Lawrence Aviation Industries, Inc.; Martin Marietta Aluminum, Inc.; and Titanium Metals Corporation of America, Appellees, No 80-2757, United States Court of Appeals, Third Circuit, argued July 13, 1981, decided October 13, 1981, online.

[133] Patent # 3,802,877: W. M. Parris, and H. W. Rosenberg: High Strength Titanium Alloys: US Patent, April 9, 1974.

[134] According to Roger Broadwell, who worked at TIMET, Rockwell gave up on using 10-2-3 for plate after a year. Broadwell helped to solve the remaining forging problems with 10-2-3 after Harry left TIMET. He eventually joined Wyman-Gordon (e-mail from Broadwell to author, March 19, 2012).

[135] After the use of 10-2-3 on the 777, Boeing shifted to Ti-5Al-5Mo-5V-3Cr for the 787 Dreamliner, developed from the Russian alloy VT22. Airbus continues to use 10-2-3.

[136] "A temperature as derived from the Tiller equation governing solidification is equivalent to a missability gap in a phase diagram in which two phases, alpha and beta in titanium, don't mix; instead, they coexist. To avoid solidification of separate phases, the temperature gradient in the molten pool must be high," explained Harry. "A similar problem presented itself with the alloy Ti-17, a deep hardenable alloy for engine fan disks. It was fixed by slowing the melting rate. But with 10-2-3, additional measures were needed to extract heat as the ingots solidified."

[137] Boyer, interview; e-mail from Broadwell to author.

[138] John N. Kotre and Elizabeth Hall, *Seasons of Life* (Ann Arbor: University of Michigan Press, 1997), 315.

[139] According to Cooper, Joe Byrne was partially justified in his displeasure with 10-2-3 because it slowed down TIMET's melt shop and it demanded hard alpha-beta work. "For the forgers, it was a dog because they had to do an elongated forging. They had to figure out how to get the minimum of 25 percent work into it. One way was to put a steel cylinder around it so as to contain it so the cylinder could be upset. It was Roger Broadwell, who was TIMET's manager of quality control at Toronto, who figured out how to reach the 25 percent alpha-beta requirement." Triple melting, with the third melt being "low and slow" at 11 KA for steady state, inverting the electrode after each melt and homogenization of the ingot at 2,100 degrees Fahrenheit for twenty-four hours were all part of the solution. Cooper, interview. E-mail from Broadwell to author.

[140] Interview with Cawley by author.

[141] In 1985, Allegheny International Inc. and NL Industries sold the majority of their titanium unit to Kelso & Co and a group of TIMET managers.

[142] Keith Rosenberg's children are Christopher, Mary Beth, and Patrick. Neil's children are Charles, Marie, and Jeane. Marie has a son named Daniel—Harry's first great-grandchild.

[143] Astrocytoma is a highly variable disease that originates in a type of glial cell called an astrocyte. It occurs more commonly in males. It is classified into four grades by WHO, the first being a tumor that rarely metastasizes and the fourth, known as glioblastoma, being a tumor that metastasizes rapidly. Both Neil and Kris had glioblastomas, grade 4.

CHAPTER 12: HIGH-PURITY TITANIUM AND THE ALTA GROUP

[144] Government agencies provided the price and volume data for many years on almost any commercial item. According to Harry, he "discovered that the power-law inherent in price elasticity of structural metals produced exponents and coefficients that hardly changed one year to the next. And I also was amazed that nonstructural metals as well as nonmetal structural materials produced very similar exponents in each group over time frames of decades. Of the three sectors I studied, only their power-law coefficients distinguished one sector from another. Error bars extending the trend lines produced order-of-magnitude projections that were consistent from year to year."

[145] Cawley, interview.

[146] Harry states that Grumman's interest in nitinol arose because "it looked like the perfect coupling for hydraulic lines that actuated the control surfaces on airfoils. The story goes that they loved the fact that it was easy to expand a nitinol coupling at liquid-nitrogen temperatures, install it while cold, and by the time it warmed to ambient temperature, it shrank back to size, squeezing two lengths of hydraulic tubing together in a death grip so tight, the hydraulic tubing would burst before the coupling would." Raychem produced nitinol in commercial volumes.

[147] The process that A. E. Van Arkel, J. H. de Boer, and J. D. Fast developed was also used for zirconium. Simplified, the iodide refining process involves the heating of high-quality titanium sponge to 500 to 800 degrees Celsius in a closed container called a retort. A vacuum is then created into which iodine is admitted. The resulting chemical reaction creates volatilized titanium iodide (TiI_2). At this point, a filament in the retort (that reaches from the top almost to the bottom) is heated via electric current to 1,000 to 1,200 degrees Celsius. The titanium iodide then decomposes to metal on the filament as crystals while the liberated atoms of iodine return via diffusion to the sponge where they react to make more titanium iodide that diffuses back to the filament.

[148] Interview with Green by author.

[149] In addition to those people already mentioned, Harry's list of excellent employees is long, among them being: Diana Bender, Judy Bingle, Matthew Cooper and his uncle Jack Cooper, Ed Crease, Wei Guo, Richard Hawk and his daughter Stacey Hawk, Werner Hort, David Lehn and his wife, Gene Metts, Shannon Morris (who became a patent agent while at Alta, working with the legal department of Johnson Matthey on patent matters), Benoit Pouliquen, Raselee Prete, Mary Semier, Norma Stoops, Karen Sylvester, Steve Turner, Gary Wang, Jeff Boots, Carl Washington, Joe White, and Yun Xu. "There are probably several others whose names escape me now, but each was important."

[150] Harry states that there was never any proof that the man had done the shooting. Nor does he feel the man's time with Alta was a complete waste because it led to a patent. There were a few other employees and managers who caused problems on a lesser scale, often by dwelling too much on profitability without paying close enough attention to quality or who did not have the capacity to resolve discord in an acceptable way.

[151] Some of Harry's research after the takeover led to new patents. His last titanium patent at Alta was *Apparatus for producing titanium crystal and titanium, Patent number: 86024847*. Nigel Winters and Yun Xu are listed with him as inventors. The patent was filed on February 2, 1998, and issued on February 15, 2000. It was followed by patents on high-purity iodide tantalum.

CHAPTER 13: THOSE WHO KEEP RUNNING

[152] www.Amargosa.net.

[153] In 2010, Pioneer Materials entered into a global distribution agreement with Matheson Tri-Gas, Inc., Basking Ridge, New Jersey.

[154] Kris Rosenberg, *Talk to Me: A Therapist's Guide to Breaking through Male Silence* (New York: G. P. Putnam's Sons), 1993. The PBS documentary series *Seasons of Life* was broadcast in 1990. The book to accompany the series was published in hardcover by Little, Brown and Company in 1990 and in paperback by University of Michigan Press in 1997. The broadcast (Midlife episode) is available online at Annenberg Learning.

[155] Harry states: "There is controversy over the Zimbardo study because none of us is proud of such a heritage. Many, maybe most, of us find it easy to just live on in denial. And people in high places see Zimbardo's work as a threat to the system that blames the victim, and if that fails, hang the lowest-ranking person. Further, there are those who believe experimenting with human subjects is unethical or even immoral, never mind that there is no other way to understand human behavior under controlled conditions. And finally, any new reality is hard for some to accept simply because dogma dies hard. In fact, Zimbardo's Stanford prison experiment recounted in his book *The Lucifer Effect* foretold with uncanny accuracy the abuses of both Abu Ghraib and Guantanamo. And even more disturbingly, the experiment confirms the fact that our prisons do not rehabilitate; more often than not, they seem to make people worse. Like evolution, the experimental evidence continues to pile up that our genome is a dichotomy, useful for survival in the jungle but not that well-suited for peaceful civilized living."

[156] In regard to sociopaths and psychopaths, Harry read the works of Martha Stout, author of the book *The Sociopath Next Door*; Paul Babiak and Robert Hare, the authors of *Snakes in Suits*; and Justin Frank, author of *Bush on the Couch*, among others.

[157] www.RoadtoPeace.org.

[158] Harry's study of violence and evolutionary biology culminated in 2009 when he joined a group retracing Darwin's voyage of the *Beagle*. The trip included the Galapagos, Uruguay, Patagonia, Easter Island, Cook Island, New Zealand, Australia, Mauritius, South Africa, and Cape Verde, finally ending at London's Museum of Natural History and the Darwin exhibition. The trip was under the auspices of Stanford University.

[159] Interview with Joselyne Mivumbi Rosenberg by author.

160 Roméo Dallaire, *Shake Hands with the Devil: The Failure of Humanity in Rwanda* (New York: Carroll & Graf Publishers, 2004).

161 Quotes from Br. Rene David Roy are from e-mails to the author.

162 Upon leaving, each member of the party was given a certificate verifying that he or she had tracked and met the Rwandan mountain gorillas. Harry was impressed with the knowledge of the park rangers at Virunga National Park as well as at a southern park they visited to observe monkeys in the wild.

INDEX

CPSIA information can be obtained at www.ICGtesting.com
Printed in the USA
BVOW07s0719081113

335782BV00001B/4/P

9 781491 707906